Daniel Pinkham

Daniel Pinkham, 1982. Photo by Stephen Trefonides

Daniel Pinkham

A Bio-Bibliography

Kee DeBoer and *John B. Ahouse*

Donald L. Hixon, Series Adviser

Bio-Bibliographies in Music, Number 12

Greenwood Press
New York • Westport, Connecticut • London

University of Texas
at San Antonio

Library of Congress Cataloging-in-Publication Data

DeBoer, Kee.
  Daniel Pinkham, a bio-bibliography.

  (Bio-bibliographies in music, ISSN 0742-6968 ; no. 12)
  Includes index.
  1. Pinkham, Daniel—Bibliography. 2. Pinkham, Daniel—
Discography. 3. Music—Bio-bibliography. I. Ahouse,
John B. II. Title. III. Series.
ML134.P667D4 1988   016.78'092'4   88-157
ISBN 0-313-25503-2 (lib. bdg. : alk. paper)

British Library Cataloguing in Publication Data is available.

Library of Congress Catalog Card Number: 88-157
ISBN: 0-313-25503-2
ISSN: 0742-6968

First published in 1988

Greenwood Press, Inc.
88 Post Road West, Westport, Connecticut 06881

Printed in the United States of America

10 9 8 7 6 5 4 3 2 1

Contents

Contents

Preface

Ever since the mid-1940s when he was a recent graduate from Harvard, Daniel Pinkham has composed music at a remarkably consistent rate. His more than 300 musical compositions cover his entire career as performer and teacher, and are in part a measure of his success at securing commissions from a variety of organizations and individuals. From this it follows that Pinkham is performed widely and often, so that a bibliography of his music becomes inseparable from an accounting of the many concerts at which his works have held a featured place.

This bio-bibliography follows the pattern of other publications in the series and is divided into the following sections:

1) A biography

2) A complete catalogue of works and a selected list of performances, classified by performing requirements and arranged alphabetically. All works are provided with a "W" number to facilitate cross-referencing; and each principal entry contains information on vocal/instrumental layout, duration, text source if appropriate, and publisher.

3) A discography listing commercially-produced sound recordings, provided with "D" numbers to correspond with the "W" numbers in the **Works and Performances** section.

4) A bibliography divided into two parts: the first includes references to general reviews of the composer's music or to reviews of two or more works grouped together (coded "BG"), while the second part is a compilation of reviews of specific works (with the prefix "B"). Once again, the "B" numbers in the bibliography correspond to the "W" numbers in the **Works and Performances** section.

Preface

5) Appendices

    I.   Chronological listing of works by date of composition

    II.   Alphabetical listing of works

    III. Poems used as texts, listed by author

    IV.   Biblical sources used as texts

    A composer as active as Daniel Pinkham scarcely holds still for a publication such as this Bio-Bibliography. Since completion of the text in July 1987, four more compositions have come forth from his pen:

Angels Are Everywhere (1987; Ione; 12 min.)
    For three-part treble chorus and piano

In Wintry Fields (1987; Ione; 5 min.)
    For solo guitar

Petitions (1987; Ione; 15 min.)
    For organ

Reeds (1987; Peters; 10 min.)
    For solo oboe

Acknowledgments

A number of individuals and institutions contributed to the completion of this volume. In particular, the excellent resources at the New England Conservatory of Music Library, the Boston Public Library, and Broadcast Music Incorporated proved invaluable to our research. Librarians at dozens of other institutions provided prompt and essential information in answer to our many requests.

Special thanks are due to John Holtz, Howard Holtzman, and Edward Low for their very supportive interest in the project and for lending their personal knowledge of Daniel Pinkham's music. Members of our own library have been helpful in every way: our particular thanks to Catherine Lewis-Ida, Sharlene LaForge, and Pat Young Matzke for sharing our concerns and our deadlines.

And above all we thank Daniel Pinkham for his gracious hospitality, for his patience with our questions, and for his industry in turning his own files inside out for elusive facts and dates.

Publishers Directory

ACA: American Composers' Alliance, 170 West 74th
                Street, New York, N. Y. 10019

AMP: American Music Publishers, Inc., 866 Third
                Avenue, New York, N. Y. 10022

C. Fischer: Carl Fischer, Inc. 62 Cooper Square, New York,
                N. Y. 10003

Highgate: Highgate Press, 131 West 86th Street, New
                York, N. Y. 10024

Ione: Ione Press, distributed by E. C. Schirmer,
                138 Ipswich Street, Boston, Mass. 02215

King: Robert King Music Co., 7 Canton Street, North
                Easton, Mass. 12356

Peters: C. F. Peters Corp., 373 Park Avenue South,
                New York, N. Y. 10011

Row: R. D. Row, distributed by Carl Fischer Inc.,
                62 Cooper Square, New York, N. Y. 10003

G. Schirmer: G. Schirmer, Inc. 866 Third Avenue, New York
                N. Y. 10022

Zimmermann: Zimmermann Musikverlag, D-6000 Frankfurt 90,
                Gaugrafenstrasse 19-23

Daniel Pinkham

Biography

Disclaiming any unusual precocity in music, Daniel Pinkham nevertheless recalls the routine of childhood piano lessons and his innocent first attempts to peddle to parents and friends the melodies he had copied from his keyboard exercises. When it was duly pointed out to the six-year-old that salable music needed to be original, he quickly adapted, and the composer Pinkham was born.

I.

The oldest of three boys, Daniel Rogers Pinkham had come into the world on June 5, 1923, in Lynn, Massachusetts, bearing a surname that was nationally as well as locally famous. Three generations earlier the Vegetable Compound and other patent remedies of Lydia E. Pinkham had become household standbys, and though the founder of the firm realized only limited wealth, her children and grandchildren had made "Lydia Pinkham" into an eminently profitable industry. Daniel's father, who was to rise to presidency of the company in the 1960s, was in a position to provide his sons with a private education, which for Daniel meant continuing a family tradition by attending Phillips Academy in Andover. Pinkham recalls his father's view that wrestling and exposure to Old Testament narratives were the most meaningful parts of an Andover education; for Daniel however, it was to be music, though not without a similar exposure to the cadences of Scripture.

Music at Phillips Academy was the domain of Carl Pfatteicher (1882-1957), the school organist and director of the glee club. An ordained Lutheran minister of Pennsylvania Dutch origin, Pfatteicher was a musicologist as well, with an interest in Heinrich Schuetz that was "ahead of its time"[1] as

Pinkham recalls it.   Under his mentor Pinkham studied organ, became student carillonneur, and was one of six boys chosen to live in Park House, where music was emphasized.   In embarking on a musical education, Pinkham may also have been influenced somewhat from the maternal side.   His mother, Olive Collins White Pinkham, was active as an educator in Massachusetts; her mother in turn had been an early graduate of the New England Conservatory.

At age sixteen the young musician experienced a musical revelation, a kind of musical epiphany as Pinkham describes it. This occurred at a concert in Andover by the Trapp family, one of the very first appearances in America by the Austrian emigré ensemble that was to go on to such celebrity in the 1950s. With their unfamiliar instruments -- viola da gamba, virginal, and a quartet of recorders, together with the timbre of children's voices--the Trapps produced a spare, clean sound that spoke to the young Pinkham as no music had before, becoming "a part of my way of looking at things."

As a first result of this encounter, Pinkham began to read everything the Academy library owned on 17th and 18th century music ("The Dolmetsch book on interpretation I simply memorized; it was my Bible at that time,") and soon acquired a Neupert tabletop clavichord from Germany to compete for his practice time.   When opportunities arose at the Academy, Pinkham composed his first choral music, even then "strictly for performance," so the pragmatic young musician could hear and judge the result for himself. Finishing at Andover a year early as the result of an accelerated program of studies, Pinkham was able to enter Harvard College in 1940 as a music major.

At Harvard Pinkham came under the guidance of Arthur Tillman Merritt (b. 1902), from whom he says he "learned more about composition than from any other teacher." Merritt's strength as professor of counterpoint lay in teaching the "manipulation of notes and lines without reliance on rote or formula" and in requiring students to set Latin texts for their exercises at all times. Pinkham pursued choral composition with Archibald "Doc" Davison (1883-1961), a man he remembers as an inspired organist and conductor. Beginning in his second year he studied composition with Walter Piston, who emphasized consistency of style and filled the younger musician with practical ideas on "what works and what won't" in actual performance.

A medical deferment enabled Pinkham to remain at Harvard to complete his B.A. in 1943, with his Masters following a year later.   His M.A. thesis, with Davison as advisor, embraced Pinkham's research into notes inégales, evidence of his continued preoccupation with baroque performance practice. Staying on in Cambridge, he continued compositional studies in seminars with Piston and with Aaron Copland; the next logical step for the young composer was to approach

Nadia Boulanger in 1945. He had met the eminent French musician and teacher as early as 1941 when he loaned his budding "voix du compositeur" to a weekly madrigal group she conducted at the Longy School. Now, however, he enrolled for private lessons, working intensely for the next two years, after which he had become so self-critical, "so concerned for where each note goes," that for the space of a solid year he "could not compose at all."

In the summer of 1947, he had the opportunity of studying with Arthur Honegger at Tanglewood. The Swiss composer-in-residence spoke little English, so Pinkham became his translator and chauffeur, remaining at his side for days at a time while learning and absorbing the older man's ideas on the teaching of orchestration. This ideal situation was cut short by Honegger's heart attack and subsequent return to Switzerland at midsummer. His replacement, Samuel Barber, was a much less effective teacher in Pinkham's view; but if he did not learn a great deal from their formal sessions, he found Barber all the more inspiring in his afterhours devotion to songwriting and "the music of English," an interest Pinkham was cultivating alongside two other students of Barber's, Ned Rorem and William Flanagan.

II.

Throughout his Harvard years Pinkham was continuing to prepare himself as a performer on the harpsichord and organ. He studied the former with Wanda Landowska and her pupil Putnam Aldrich (1904-1975). His organ teacher was E. Power Biggs, with whom he learned repertory and developed a working collaboration, replacing Biggs on occasional broadcast concerts from the Germanic (now Busch-Reisinger) Museum at Harvard. It was Biggs who gave the first professional performance of a Pinkham work, presenting his **Sonata No. 1** for organ and strings (with Arthur Fiedler) in 1944.

As the only professional harpsichordist in the Boston area in the days before what he whimsically calls the "earlier than thou" movement took hold, Pinkham was soon called on to provide the keyboard continuo in performances of the Bach Passions and other works with the Boston Symphony under Munch and Markevitch. In 1948 came the chance to pursue the performing side of his musicianship on a regular basis as half of a violin-harpsichord duo. Joining with Robert Brink (b. 1924), "a fine player with unlimited technical ability and an elegant, beautiful tone," Pinkham began a 10-year performing career which took the duo through parts of the United States and Canada and on two State Department-sponsored tours to postwar Europe. Their choice of repertory reflected a mutual interest in early music, in chamber music sonorities, and in experimentation: the two performed all the Corelli sonatas, as well as works of Marini, J.S. Bach, and Mozart "up to the limits of the harpsichordist's ability" as Pinkham acknowledges. He recalls, with understatement, that Brink possessed "a sensitivity to ensemble style which would make the delivery of 18th century pieces really quite reasonable." Among their contemporaries they commissioned and played music by Henry Cowell, Alan Hovhaness, and Walter Piston; and it was for Robert Brink that Pinkham composed his violin concerto (1958).

Pinkham also concertized alone during this time, transporting his harpsichord thousands of miles by station wagon to keep engagements in remote parts of the U. S. and Canada. Award of a Fulbright grant in 1950 offered a tempting alternative, but Pinkham turned it down because he feared losing the momentum of his performing career.

For the performance of larger ensemble works, Brink and Pinkham founded the Cambridge Festival Players in the mid-1950s, a somewhat ad hoc organization made up of freelance and retired musicians from Boston's various orchestras. Brink served as concertmaster and Pinkham conducted the group, formed initially to produce a recording of Purcell's Fairy Queen. About this time, however, Pinkham was experiencing a gradual shift in his interests in the direction of Renaissance music, and the Brink-Pinkham duo finally curtailed its activities after Brink developed a hand affliction ("trigger finger") which necessitated refingering of the violinist's music, with a corresponding loss of tone and intonation. Brink moved over to a second career as professor of violin at the New England Conservatory where the two have remained close friends. For Pinkham, a similar caesura intervened in 1961 in the form of a broken finger, followed the next year by a life-threatening attack of hepatitis. After a slow recovery, the composer was strongly advised to abandon travel and concertizing in favor of his teaching career at the Conservatory and his two-year-old position at King's Chapel.

Teaching, indeed, had been a concomitant of much of the previous fifteen years, beginning with his appointment at age 23 to the Boston Conservatory of Music. Subsequently Pinkham was named special lecturer in music history at Simmons College in Boston in 1953. He was lecturer-recitalist in Devon, England, in the summer of 1954, before being appointed teaching associate for the harpsichord at Boston University later that year. He returned to Harvard as visiting lecturer in 1957-58, joining the faculty at the New England Conservatory of Music the next year to teach undergraduate music history, theory, and composition, as well as harpsichord.

The guest professorship at the New England Conservatory became a permanent appointment a year later and from that point forward has been his mainstay, absorbing nearly all his teaching activity since then. With the arrival of Gunther Schuller as director in 1967, Pinkham petitioned for a restructuring of the curriculum to enable him to create and chair his own Department of Early Music Performance, a highly congenial arrangement that has gone unchanged to the present.

Under Pinkham the department now gives degrees in "Harpsichord as a Studio Instrument" and in "Early Music Performance." Although he does not take private pupils, he has, through the Conservatory, taught and influenced hundreds of students in the areas of his greatest historical interest. In a typical semester Pinkham's teaching schedule includes: an undergraduate survey course in baroque music; a graduate survey of Renaissance or baroque sacred music; a seminar in baroque instrumental music--primarily Bach; and a repertoire class in baroque music, in which student instrumentalists are "seduced" into performing pre-classical music, and liking it.

In the fall of 1958, Pinkham had also been alerted to an imminent opening to succeed Elwood Gaskill as organist and choir director at King's Chapel, Boston's most venerable musical institution. The decision to seek this position was to be decisive for shaping the balance of his career. Founded in 1686 (the present building was erected in 1753-58), King's Chapel had housed the first pipe organ in an American church (1713), and was the scene of the first known music festival (1786) in the new United States. Today the diminutive Chapel remains a landmark in downtown Boston, where a slender iron fence still protects it from the high-rise rescaling of the city center. Prominent among earlier organists and conductors at the historic site were William Selby in the 18th, B. J. Lang in the late 19th, and, for a brief period, Virgil Thomson in the present century.

Under its most recent music directors, King's Chapel had employed a sixteen-voice male choir exclusively. When asked, as part of the interview process, what operational changes he might make at the Chapel, Pinkham proposed several things: greater involvement of the Chapel's Music Committee in handling non-musical matters and providing liaison with the parishioners, and replacement of the all-male choir with a smaller, mixed choir, to be augmented by volunteers and conservatory students, thus saving costs while permitting greater versatility in programming. Pinkham's ideas convinced the Committee, who chose him over others he feels might have been superior organists.

In 1962 Pinkham received a Ford Foundation grant in connection with his position as choral conductor. This enabled him to commission four new works for mixed chorus and strings (the commissions went to William Flanagan, Ulysses Kay, Ned Rorem, and Charles Wuorinen), all of which were subsequently performed by the Chapel Choir and commercially recorded. Two years later he had the satisfaction of inaugurating a new three-manual organ, the first of a number of tracker-action organs to be built in the United States by Charles B. Fisk. This was the result of a gift from Amelia

7

Peabody, whose father had donated the Chapel's previous organ in 1912.

The weekly schedule at the Chapel focuses on the Sunday service at 11:00 a.m. Pinkham arrives early to practice his own organ solos; from 9:30-10:30 he rehearses the choir. The large-scale Christmas Eve concert with chamber orchestra is an annual tradition, and he also programs three concerts per year in a subscription series, including both contemporary and ancient music. Space considerations in the Chapel limit the performing forces to a maximum of twenty singers and a few instrumentalists, but Pinkham has presented a wide range of music including many of his own works in recent years. Occasional late night concerts of avant-garde music ("at 11:00 p.m. when decent people are in bed") have been another Pinkham innovation at the Chapel.

III.

Early retirement for Pinkham the harpsichordist meant substantially more time available for Pinkham the composer. Seemingly to underscore this turn of events, a lengthy article appeared in 1961 hailing Daniel Pinkham as a young composer of great promise and significant achievement.[2] The author, Boston music critic Warren Storey Smith, made a point of Pinkham's New England origins, as if to secure his place in a dynasty of regional musician/composers. Asked whether he sees himself in any way sprung from the likes of Parker, Foote or Chadwick, Pinkham dismisses the idea: "Warren at the time was very interested in the 19th century, and wanted to be able to say, 'Here comes another Boston composer . . .'." The article, nonetheless, was a significant "Hat's Off!"; and the appended list of works would have done any composer proud for the fifteen-year period they represented. Indeed, by 1961 he had already written some ninety compositions, including several of his "greatest hits," viz. the **Wedding Cantata** and the **Christmas Cantata**, which were making his name known to choral societies in many other parts of the country.

Twenty-five years after Warren Storey Smith's perceptive appreciation, Pinkham the composer can be assessed as one whose musical principles were formed very early in life and who has remained remarkably true to most of them in spite of his penchant for experimentation and musical problem-solving. "Lean," "lucid," "lyrical," "dissonant," "neo-classical," "eclectic," "essentially tonal," "practical" -- are words that have come to the minds of reviewers for over three decades. His music, while not programmatic, is often what he calls "affective," using titles or narratives to provide an extra-musical continuum to which the music can respond. He is known for his meticulous setting of language to render it as comprehensible as possible in performance. His instrumentation is spare and translucent, showing a prefer-

8

ence for winds over strings, a delight in percussion effects, and a positive predilection for high, bell-like sonorities that still recall his fascination with the sounds of the Trapp choir. A further quality is defined by his friend, music critic Richard Dyer: "Pinkham . . . takes the trouble to explore the basic vocality of whatever instrument -- or machine -- he is writing for. That's why no matter how advanced the idiom or how unconventional the sound source, a certain basic, slightly diffuse, very humane sweetness sings through."[3]

Pinkham tends to write concise, madrigal-sized compositions or sectionalized longer works ("mosaics of a lot of small things") that grow by the accretion of segments of five or six minutes' duration. If a broad development in his oeuvre can be adduced, it is that larger commissions in recent years have enabled him to pursue his cherished desire to compose extended theatrical works, e.g.: **Jonah, Daniel in the Lions' Den, Descent Into Hell, The Garden Party**. Of the satisfaction of having created his **Passion of Judas** (1975), he remarked, "After hearing that piece, I can say I don't envy anyone's career."

The influences on Pinkham's style are diverse, befitting a scholar-composer who acknowledges no particular school of composition. When Pinkham took up composition, the neo-classic Stravinsky was at his zenith; his is the overriding influence as it was for so many in the early post-war era. From Nadia Boulanger Pinkham gained an appreciation of Fauré, whose harmonic language preoccupied him in his formative years. Hindemith's Gebrauchsmusik is an acknowledged model for some of his work, and he feels a special sense of identification with Purcell, Britten, and Ned Rorem for their scrupulous attention to the musical values of the English language. The organ music of Messiaen, the sonorities of Hovhaness, and the "pseudo-folk" qualities of Aaron Copland are admired as well; but behind all his creative work stands his devotion to the baroque and pre-baroque composers, whose aesthetics, procedures, and sonorities are an ever-present influence on his music. As for his fascination with tinkling bells, he tells of his astonishment over a passage in Wilfred Mellers' Composers in a New Found Land: "[We can] consider Pinkham's music a sequel to [Charles Tomlinson] Griffes's Sonata."[4] Pinkham avers, "I had never even thought of it until that reference came out--about Griffes--[but] hearing some of those pieces, particularly one called "Clouds," the first minute or so I thought, you know, that's a piece I could have written -- from the choice of sonorities. Then the clouds get blown away in a different direction."

A belated and unexpected influence on Pinkham's work arrived in 1970 when he undertook to rehearse a score by Richard Felciano (b. 1930), a composer he calls "a very grave and serious thinker about music and sound." Felciano's Pentecost Sunday is written for organ, electronic tape, and

male voices; and Pinkham found himself immediately intrigued
by the way the tape element took over the role of providing
cues and pitches for the chorus, at the same time filling
King's Chapel with new and more resonant sounds than were
possible with a conventional ensemble. He recalls:

>   It occurred to me, spinning off from what he had
> started, that it might be a useful experiment, particu-
> larly in churches which did not have the budget to hire
> musicians in addition to the organist, to give some
> kind of extra color possibility. Consequently I did a
> lot of pieces for choir with tape, organ with tape, and
> with other instruments.

Pinkham sought out technical training and acquired the latest
equipment to be able to pursue these new possibilities; and
for roughly the next ten years, tape tracks became a regular
part of his musical language. The fascination with electronics ended, however, as decisively as it began, when the
composer realized that it had all "become too easy":

>   When you find that shopgirls are able to compose
> symphonies on their lunch break, then there's nothing
> that's really very distinguishing or personal about it.
> Although I have to admit the industry is still in its
> infancy, I've never been attracted to most of the
> [electronic] sounds. They are perhaps too perfect, too
> regular; they don't have that random quality you find
> in the sound of a good violin. [The tape experience]
> certainly colored my concerns with sonority, but I've
> gone right back to writing more vocal music, solo vocal
> music, than I have for a long time.

Texted music -- vocal music -- is clearly the norm for
Pinkham. So many of his texts are religious that he often
finds himself stereotyped, to which he replies, "I have never
been a church composer. I am a <u>composer</u>. I am perfectly
willing and able to provide music for weddings, funerals, Bar
Mitzvahs, and anything else." Nevertheless, he acknowledges
being "enormously attracted" to church rhetoric and liturgy,
and to religious stories. This is not necessarily a matter
of personal piety or conviction, so much as the wish to work
with texts and ideas which are known to his audiences and
which -- not incidentally -- are in the public domain.

Similarly, Pinkham reads modern poetry "for the wrong
reasons: I look at it from a cannibal's point of view," which
is to say he is on the lookout for verses that might gain
rather than lose by being stretched onto a musical frame. A
friend of forty years standing, now retired from law practice
in Los Angeles, Howard Holtzman sends Pinkham whatever he
writes and has been the source of various texts set by the
composer. Pinkham has also turned frequently to the works of
Robert Hillyer (1895-1961), the quietist poet and Harvard
professor, whose <u>Collected</u> <u>Verse</u> gained a Pulitzer Prize in

1934, and to the stories and poems of Norma Farber (1909-1984), a trained singer whose writings for children won various awards in her later years. The composer's account of the genesis of his **Passion of Judas** shows how this process led him to a finished musical work:

I had a poem by the late James Wright, called "Saint Judas," which was a very powerful poem about Judas on the way out to hang himself, when he sees a man beaten up. He goes to save him -- a sort of redemptive quality in Judas. And then there was a poem by Norma Farber called "Tell Me about the Mother of Judas." You see an ordinary Jewish boy growing up, going through the Seder, but filled with avarice and greed.

Then I was given a television playlet, about eleven minutes long, by R. C. Norris, who is a teacher in Texas. It was called "The Rescue of the Innocents," a tiny play about a Jewish couple who at the time of Herod's decree have sent somebody out to turn all their goods into money, so they can bribe a soldier to take them and their baby out [of danger]. The plan miscarries, and the Roman soldier comes in. You hear the baby cry and this gives it all away. But finally he lets himself be bribed, and he says, "you've spent a lot of affection on this child. What's the child's name?" "His name is Judas."

Now that was something where I said, "Boy, that's powerful!" The image is wondrous. But that was not a piece in itself. You can't end an opera with a shock. It doesn't work that way. So I just had all those things hanging around for no particular reason, when the National Presbyterian Church in Washington commissioned me to write a biggish piece. So I thought, "I'll glue those Judas pieces together." There was an opening psalm, and there's a psalm in the middle, and a concluding psalm, and then some readings from about four references to Judas in the Gospels. So it's a curious kind of mosaic. It was tricky, but it so happened that these things together worked like martinis -- it's stronger than the individual ingredients, and it simply worked wonderfully.

Pinkham does not see himself as an inspirational composer who writes out of inner necessity; he finds his frequent commissions are more than enough to absorb his creative energies. Though he may on occasion have trouble starting a piece, once an idea reaches paper, the composition "will begin to write itself." Details of the work-in-progress are often tried out with his "guinea pigs," the musicians at King's Chapel, and he allows nothing of his to be published without hearing it first in a satisfactory performance. Frequently Pinkham has written with specific artists in mind,

11

such as mezzo Pamela Gore, soprano Barbara Wallace, tenor Kim
Scown, or organist Leonard Raver, all of whom have shared in
the premieres of numerous works of his. As director of the
New England Conservatory chorus over many years, Lorna Cooke
deVaron has been a loyal interpreter of his music; many other
works have found a hearing in Southern California through the
efforts of a friend and sometime Bostonian colleague, Edward
Low, who presently directs the Neighborhood Choir in Pasadena.

Writing takes place in the small frame house he shares
with organist Andrew Holman on a side street in Cambridge.
The work space itself is shared with the chamber organ
Pinkham acquired in the days when he performed with the
Boston Symphony. His preferred time for composing is in the
forenoon when he finds that ideas come more easily; other
parts of the day are given over to the meticulous copying of
scores and parts in an elegant hand on fine, Swiss-made
paper.   Players attest to his care in providing cues and
interpretive directions in his published music. With his
pragmatic view of musical execution, the composer often
suggests alternatives in scoring to facilitate performance.

With each new work Pinkham likes to set himself certain
musical or technical problems, which, once solved, no longer
intrigue him in planning future compositions. He has not
written for string quartet, in part because he feels the
medium has been so thoroughly mined by others; his
comparative neglect of symphonic music is due to "the
realities of the market place," which effectively preclude
proper rehearsal time for new music. He observes: "Unless
you write for a good civic or community orchestra, which I
did for my **Symphony No. 3**, for the Plymouth, Massachusetts,
Philharmonic, it is lucky if you get more than a reading
before performance time."[5]

The composer has received numerous honors for his achieve-
ment, including honorary doctorates from Nebraska Wesleyan
University (Litt.D. 1976), Adrian College (Mus.D. 1977), and
Westminster Choir College (Mus.D. 1979); and he has been
presented with the Bohemian Club Prize and the St. Botolph
Club Award.   He is Past Dean of the Boston chapter of the
American Guild of Organists, and a Fellow of the American
Academy of Arts and Sciences. He holds honorary memberships
in the Phi Mu Sinfonia and the Signet Society of Harvard
University. He was appointed by then-Governor Endicott
Peabody as the first music advisor to the Massachusetts
Council on the Arts.

In twenty-five years of ignoring his doctor's advice to
"slow down," Pinkham has criss-crossed the country for
countless premieres and honors, and for appearances at
increasingly frequent "Pinkham Festivals." By virtue of
putting down his professional roots early in his career,
however, and leaving them undisturbed, he has remained

closely identified with the region where his musical life began. Boston, in the meantime, has become the early music capital of the country, not least through the efforts of Pinkham himself; and no place could be a more suitable home for the musician and his music. Approaching his 65th birthday, Daniel Pinkham has achieved the near-impossible: without deserting the musical language of his time, he has successfully returned to the ethos and the rewards of his beloved mid-baroque, when a composer in his lifetime could expect to be heard, to be paid, and to participate in the performance of his own music.

1 Unless otherwise indicated, quotations derive from interviews with Daniel Pinkham conducted by the authors in July 1986 and March 1987.

2 Smith, Warren Storey. "Daniel Pinkham." American Composers Alliance Bulletin 10:9-14 (#1, 1961)

3 Dyer, Richard. "Landmark Concerts." Boston Globe, September 9, 1975.

4 Mellers, Wilfrid. Music in a New Found Land: Themes and Developments in the History of American Music. New York: Oxford University Press, 1987, p.156.

5 Pinkham, Daniel. Letter to Gilbert Chase, 2 June 1986.

Works and Performances

"See" references are guides to citations in the **Bibliography** or **Discography** sections of this volume.

MUSIC FOR STAGE

W1.   **Beggar's Opera** (1956; unpublished; 2 hrs. 30 min.)

For vocal soli, chorus, orchestra 1-1-0-0, 1-1-0-0, timpani, harpsichord and strings
Adaptation of John Gay libretto
Commissioned by Cambridge Drama Festival

Premiere

W1a.   1956 (July 25): Cambridge, Mass.; Sanders Theatre, Harvard University; Shirley Jones; Jack Cassidy
See: B1a, B1b, B1c

Other selected performance

W1b.   1957 (March 13): New York, N. Y.; New York City Center; City Center Light Opera Company; Shirley Jones; Jack Cassidy

Daniel in the Lions' Den See: W117

For tenor, baritone and bass baritone soli, mixed chorus, narrator, 2 pianos, percussion and electronic tape

The Descent Into Hell See: W118

For mixed chorus, soprano, tenor and baritone soli,

brass ensemble, percussion, organ and electronic
tape

W2. **The Dreadful Dining Car** (1982; Ione; 60 min.)

A melodrama in one act
For mezzo-soprano, other vocal soli, mixed chorus,
guitar, flute, clarinet, trumpet, double bass, percussion and piano
Text based on "Cannibalism in the Cars", a short
story by Mark Twain, and "Sing for Baby" and "Moon
Carol", poems by Norma Farber
Commissioned by the University of North Dakota Department of Music

Premiere

W2a. 1983 (May 1): Grand Forks, N. D.; University of
North Dakota
See: B2a

Other selected performances

W2b. 1983 (November 17): Boston, Mass.; Jordan Hall, New
England Conservatory of Music

W2c. 1984 (March 23): Pasadena, Calif.; Neighborhood
Church; Neighborhood Chorus and Orchestra; Daniel
Pinkham, conductor

W3. **The Garden of Artemis or Apollo's Revels** (1948; ACA,
released to Ione; 28 min.)

A Tableau Chantant in the Antique Manner
For soprano, contralto and baritone soli, women's
chorus, flute, clarinet and strings
Text: Robert Hillyer
Dedicated to the memory of Fanny Peabody Mason
See: D3a

Premiere

W3a. 1948 (October 17): Cambridge, Mass.; Sanders Theatre,
Harvard University; Nancy Trickey, soprano; Eunice
Alberts, contralto; Paul Tibbetts, baritone; Daniel
Pinkham, conductor
See: B3a

W4. **Garden Party** (1976; Ione; 45 min.)

For mixed chorus, soprano and baritone soli, two
actors, clarinet, viola, double bass, percussion,

16

piano and electronic tape
Text based on Bible, Genesis 2 and 3, poems by Norma
Farber, "How Like a Man", "While Eve", and "Tree of
Blame" and poems by Daniel Pinkham
See: B4c

Premiere

W4a.   1977 (March 25): Boston, Mass.; Jordan Hall, New
        England Conservatory of Music; Handel and Haydn
        Society; David Evitts, Barbara Wallace, Wayne
        Rivera, Keith Kibler, soli; Thomas Dunn, conduc-
        tor
        See: B4a, B4b

Other selected performance

W4b.   1978 (February 24): Pasadena, Calif.; Neighborhood
        Church; Neighborhood Chorus; Cara Clove, Michael
        Monroney, Thomas H. Hubbard, Walter Wood, soli;
        Daniel Pinkham, conductor

W5.   **The Left-Behind Beasts** (1985; Ione; 25 min.)

        A play with music for children to perform
        For actors, unison chorus of treble voices, chamber
        orchestra and children's percussion ensemble
        Text by Daniel Pinkham suggested by title of story
        by Norma Farber, "How the Left-Behind Beasts Built
        Ararat"
        Commissioned by James Otis Elementary School in
        collaboration with WBZ-TV's Fund for the Arts
        Dedicated to Clifford J. Brooks

        Premiere

W5a.   1985 (June 14): East Boston, Mass.; Church of the
        Most Holy Redeemer; children from the James Otis
        Elementary School and the Children's Program of
        the Opera Company of Boston; James Grimes, con-
        ductor
        See: B5a

        Other selected performance

W5b.   1986 (June 13): Martha's Vineyard, Mass.; Tisbury
        School; students of the school; chamber orchestra;
        Jerome Shannon, conductor
        See: B5b

W6.   **A Mast for the Unicorn** (1986; Ione; 20 min.)

        A play with music for children to perform

17

For SSSBBB soli, actors, unison chorus of treble
voices, chamber orchestra, children's percussion
ensemble
Text by Daniel Pinkham, based on a story by Norma
Farber
Commissioned by Tisbury School and supported by a
grant from the Massachusetts Council on the Arts
and Humanities

Premiere

W6a. 1986 (June 13): Martha's Vineyard, Mass.; Tisbury
      School; children from the school; Michael Hume,
      conductor
      See: B6a

W7. **Narragansett Bay** (1946; unpublished; 30 min.)

     A ballet with book by Jan Veen
     For orchestra 2(pic)-1(Ehn)-2-1, 2-2-3-0, timpani,
     percussion, piano and strings

     Premiere

W7a. 1946: Boston, Mass.; Jordan Hall, New England Con-
      servatory of Music; Daniel Pinkham, conductor

     The Passion of Judas See: W130

     For SMzTBarB soli, narrator, mixed chorus and in-
     strumental ensemble

MUSIC FOR ORCHESTRA

W8. **Catacoustical Measures** (1962, c1962; Peters; 4 min.
     30 sec.)

     For 3(pic)-2(Ehn)-3(bcl)-3(cbsn), 4-4-4-1, timpani,
     percussion, harp, celesta, piano and strings
     Commissioned by Bolt, Beranek & Newman, Cambridge,
     Mass., to test the acoustics of Philharmonic Hall,
     Lincoln Center, New York

     Premiere

W8a. 1962 (May 28): New York, N. Y.; Lincoln Center; New
      York Philharmonic Society; Leonard Bernstein,
      conductor
      See: B8a, B8b

Other selected performances

W8b.   1962 (September 30): New York, N.Y.; Young People's
        Concert; Lincoln Center; New York Philharmonic So-
        ciety; Leonard Bernstein, conductor

W8c.   1973 (April 6): Houghton, N.Y.; Houghton College;
        Houghton College Symphony Orchestra; Daniel Pink-
        ham, conductor

W8d.   1979 (April 7): Ft. Collins, Colo.; Rocky Mountain
        Contemporary Music Festival; Lincoln Community
        Center; Colorado State University Chamber Orches-
        tra; Dave Harman, conductor

Centennial Elegy   See: **Symphony No. 1** W20

W9.   **Concertante No. 1**   (1954, c1955; ACA, released to
        Ione; 9 min.)

        For violin and harpsichord soli, string orchestra
        and celesta
        Dedicated to Donald Outerbridge
        Movements: Introduzione; Cantilena; Burlesca
        See: B9a, B9b, B9f, B9g, B9h, B9i, D9a

        Premiere

W9a.   1954 (December 16): Boston, Mass.; Jordan Hall, New
        England Conservatory of Music; Robert Brink, vio-
        lin; Claude Jean Chiasson, harpsichord; Edward
        Low, celesta; Cambridge Festival Orchestra; Daniel
        Pinkham, conductor
        See: B9c, B9j

        Other selected performances

W9b.   1955 (November 19): New York, N. Y.; McMillan Thea-
        ter, Columbia University; Robert Brink, violin;
        Claude Jean Chiasson, harpsichord; Edward Low,
        celesta; members of the Symphony of the Air;
        Daniel Pinkham, conductor

W9c.   1956 (January 25): New York, N.Y.; Metropolitan
        Museum of Art; Robert Brink, violin; Jean Claude
        Chiasson, harpsichord; MGM String Ensemble; Izler
        Solomon, conductor

W9d.   1957 (May 21): Schenectady, N. Y.; Union College
        Memorial Chapel; Tri-City Symphony Orchestra;
        Robert Brink, violin; Daniel Pinkham, harpsichord
        See: B9d

W9e. 1958 (February 12): New York, N. Y.; American Music
      Festival; Town Hall; Robert Brink, violin; Edward
      Low, harpsichord; Knickerbocker Chamber Players;
      Daniel Pinkham, conductor
      See: B9e

W10. **Concertante No. 2** (1958; ACA, released to Ione; 16
      min.)

      For solo violin and string orchestra
      See: BG11

      Premiere

W10a. 1958 (May 8): Boston, Mass.; Jordan Hall, New Eng-
      land Conservatory of Music; Robert Brink, violin;
      Cambridge Festival Orchestra; Daniel Pinkham,
      conductor
      See: B10b

      Other selected performance

W10b. 1959 (April 5): Lexington, Mass.; Cary Memorial
      Hall; Robert Brink, violin; Lexington Philharmonic
      Chamber Orchestra; Eleftherios Eleftherakis, con-
      ductor
      See: B10a

      Concertino See: W60

      For organ and string orchestra

W11. **Concertino in A for Small Orchestra and Obbligato
      Pianoforte** (1950, c1952; ACA, released to Ione; 18
      min.)

      For piano and chamber orchestra 1-1(Ehn)-0-0,
      0-2-0-0 and strings
      Dedicated to Paul Doguereau

      Premiere

W11a. 1950 (May 3): Cambridge, Mass.; Sanders Theatre,
      Harvard University; Paul Doguereau, piano; Cam-
      bridge Festival Orchestra; Daniel Pinkham, conduc-
      tor
      See: B11a, B11b

W12. **Divertimento** (1954, c1969; ACA, released to Ione;
      7 min.)

For soprano recorder or oboe, harp or harpsichord
and string orchestra
Also scored without orchestra See: **Duet** W31
Movements: Prelude; Aria; Dithyramb; Recessional

Premiere

W12a. 1958 (May 8): Boston, Mass.; Jordan Hall, New Eng-
       land Conservatory of Music; Richard Summers, oboe;
       Cambridge Festival Orchestra; Daniel Pinkham, con-
       ductor

Other selected performance

W12b. 1983 (May 26): Boston, Mass.; Jordan Hall, New Eng-
       land Conservatory of Music; John Tyson, recorder;
       Conover Fitch, harpsichord; Conservatory String
       Ensemble; Daniel Pinkham, conductor
       See: B12a

W13. **Five Short Pieces** (1952; ACA; 9 min. 30 sec.)

       For string orchestra, optional oboe, English horn,
       and 2 horns

       Selected performance

W13a. 1954 (December 16): Boston, Mass.; Jordan Hall, New
       England Conservatory of Music; Cambridge Festival
       Orchestra; Daniel Pinkham, conductor
       See: B13a, B13b, B13c

W14. **In Grato Jubilo** (1949; unpublished, registered with
       ACA)

       An occasional cantata composed and performed by for-
       mer students of Serge Koussevitzky's Berkshire Music
       Center on the occasion of Mr. Koussevitzky's retire-
       ment
       For soprano, wind orchestra 1-1-1-1, 1-3-2-0 and
       double bass
       Text by David McCord, based on Bible, Revelations 5:
       9, 10
       Six movements composed by Irving Fine, Daniel Pink-
       ham, Gardner Read, Allen Sapp, Herbert Fromm, Lukas
       Foss

       Premiere

W14a. 1949 (May 2): Boston, Mass.; Retirement banquet for
       Serge Koussevitsky; Phyllis Curtin, soprano; mem-
       bers of the Boston Symphony Orchestra; Lukas Foss,
       conductor

W15.   **Masks**   (1978; Ione; 14 min.)

For harpsichord, flute, oboe/English horn, clarinet, percussion and strings
Commissioned by Phillips Academy, Andover, Mass. in observance of its Bicentennial
Contents: The Mask of Comedy; The Mask of Tragedy; The Mask of Reminiscence; The Mask of Deceit

Premiere

W15a.   1978 (January 22): Andover, Mass.; Addison Gallery, Phillips Academy; Carolyn Skelton, harpsichord; Daniel Pinkham, conductor

Other selected performances

W15b.   1979 (February 27): Boston, Mass.; Jordan Hall, New England Conservatory of Music; Maryse Carlin, harpsichord; John Heiss, flute; Frederic Cohen, oboe; Robert Annis, clarinet; Adrienne Hartzell, violoncello; Robert Brink, violin; Daniel Pinkham, conductor

W15c.   1981 (October 13): Boston, Mass.; Jordan Hall, New England Conservatory of Music; Wendy Young, harpsichord; instrumental ensemble; Daniel Pinkham, conductor
        See: B15a

W16.   **Now the Trumpet Summons Us Again**   (1964, c1965; Peters; 5 min.)

For high voice amd orchestra or chamber orchestra or instrumental ensemble or piano
Text: John F. Kennedy's inaugural address, January 20, 1960

Premiere

W16a.   1964 (December 14): Boston, Mass.; Jordan Hall, New England Conservatory of Music; Anna Marie Obressa, soprano
        See: B16a

Other selected performances

W16b.   1966 (July 17): Boston, Mass.; Isabella Stewart Gardner Museum; Barbara Wallace, soprano; Daniel Pinkham, piano

W16c.   1975 (May 8): Boston, Mass.; Jordan Hall, New Eng-

land Conservatory of Music; Lynn Hoffman, soprano; students in the Eleanor Steber Seminar

W16d. 1983 (August 31): Boston, Mass.; Church of the
Immaculate Conception; Boston Academy of Music;
Barbara Wallace, soprano

W17. **Organ Concerto** (1970, c1970; Peters; 22 min.)

For organ and orchestra 0-0-0-0, 2-2-2-1, timpani,
percussion (2) and strings

Premiere

W17a. 1970 (July 1): Buffalo, N. Y.; Kleinhans Music Hall;
Leonard Raver, organ; members of the Buffalo Phil-
harmonic Orchestra
See: B17a

W18. **Seven Deadly Sins** (1974, c1974; Ione)

For orchestra, organ and electronic tape
Commissioned by Eastern Illinois University on the
occasion of its 50th anniversary

Premiere

W18a. 1974 (March 6): Charleston, Ill.; Fine Arts Theater,
Eastern Illinois University; Gary Zwicky, organ;
University Mixed Chorus; University Symphony Or-
chestra; Daniel Pinkham, conductor
See: B18a

W19. **Signs of the Zodiac** (1964, c1964; Peters; 21 min.)

For orchestra 2(pic)-2(Ehn)-2(bcl)-2, 4-3-2(btrb)-1,
timpani, percussion (2), harp, piano/celesta,
strings and optional speaker
Text: poems by David McCord
Commissioned by Arthur Bennett Lipkin for the Portland Symphony Orchestra
Contents: Aries, the Ram; Taurus, the Bull; Gemini,
the Twins; Cancer, the Crab; Leo, the Lion; Virgo,
the Virgin; Libra, the Balance; Scorpio, the Scor-
pion; Sagittarius, the Archer; Capricornus, the
Goat; Aquarius, the Waterbearer; Pisces, the Fishes
See: BG35, B19c, B19d, B19e, B19f, D19a

Premiere

W19a. 1964 (November 10): Portland, Me.; Portland Symphony
Orchestra; Arthur Bennett Lipkin, conductor; David

McCord, narrator
See: B19a, B19b

Other selected performance

W19b. 1979 (April 7): Ft. Collins, Colo.; Rocky Mountain
Contemporary Music Festival; Lincoln Community
Center; Colorado State University Symphony Orches-
tra; Wilfred Schwartz, conductor

Sonata No. 1 See: W77

For organ, 2 violins, violoncello, optional viola
and double bass, or with string orchestra

Sonata No. 2 See: W78

For organ, string quartet, optional double bass, or
with string orchestra

Sonata No. 3 See: W79

For organ, 2 violins, violoncello, double bass, optional viola or string orchesta

W20. **Symphony No. 1** (1961, c1961; Peters; 17 min.)

Original title: **Centennial Elegy**
For orchestra 3(pic)-2(Ehn)-2(bcl)-2(cbsn), 4-3-3-1,
timpani, percussion, harp, celesta, piano, strings
Commissioned by Broadcast Music, Inc., on the occa-
sion of its 20th anniversary
Dedicated to Carl Haverlin
Movements: Maestoso; Sciolto; Adagietto
See: B20a

Premiere

W20a. 1961 (April 29): Washington, D. C.; Cramton Audito-
rium, Howard University; Inter-American Music
Festival under the auspices of the Pan-American
Union; Orquestra Sinfonica Nacional de Mexico;
Luis de la Fuenta, conductor

W21. **Symphony No. 2** (1962, c1964; Peters; 16 min.)

For orchestra 2(pic)-2(Ehn)-2(bcl)-2, 4-3-3-1,
timpani, percussion (3), harp, piano and strings
Dedicated to Michigan Civic Orchestra Association
Movements: Aria; Three Epigrams (Energico, Con Nos-

24

talgia, Lento); Ballade; Envoy
See: B21a, B21b, B21c, B21d, B21e, B21f, D21a

Premiere

W21a. 1963 (November 23): Lansing, Mich.; Sexton Auditorium; Lansing Symphony Orchestra; Gregory Millar,
conductor
See: B21g

Other selected performance

W21b. 1964 (November 17): Louisville, Ky.; Louisville
Symphony Orchestra; Robert Whitney, conductor

W22. **Symphony No. 3** (1985, rev. 1986, c1986; Peters; 17
min.)

For orchestra 2(pic)-2(Ehn)-2-2, 4-3-3-1, timpani,
percussion, celesta, harp and strings
Commissioned by Plymouth Philharmonic Orchestra on
the occasion of its seventieth season

Premiere

W22a. 1986 (February 8): Plymouth, Mass.; Memorial Hall;
Plymouth Philharmonic Orchestra; Rudolf Schlegel,
conductor
See: B22a, B22b

W23. **Violin Concerto** (1956; ACA, released to Ione; 19
min.)

For solo violin and orchestra 0-2-0-0, 2-0-0-0,
harp, celesta and strings
See: BG34

Premiere

W23a. 1956 (September 8): Falmouth, Mass.; Coonamessett
Music Festival; Robert Brink, violin; Daniel Pink-
ham, conductor
See: B23a

MUSIC FOR BAND

W24. **A Crimson Flourish** (1986; Ione; 4 min.)

For large concert band

Premiere

W24a. 1986 (September 5): Cambridge, Mass.; Harvard Uni-
       versity; Harvard University Band

Nebulae <u>See</u>: W68

For organ, band and electronic tape

W25. **Orbits** (1974; Ione; 7 min.)

For band and electronic tape

Premiere

W25a. 1974 (April 5): Holland, N. Y.; Holland Center High
       School

W26. **Prelude, Epigram and Elegy** (1967; Ione; 7 min.)

For small band
Commissioned by Northeastern University

Premiere

W26a. 1967 (May 6): Boston, Mass.; Northeastern Univer-
       sity; M.I.T. Band

Other selected performance

W26b. 1971 (February 19): DePere, Wisc.; Pennings Hall,
       St. Norbert College; Concert Band
       <u>See</u>: B26a

Serenades <u>See</u>: W50

For solo trumpet and band or wind ensemble, timpani,
percussion, optional saxaphones, baritone and tuba

MUSIC FOR INSTRUMENTAL SOLOS AND ENSEMBLES

W27. **Brass Quintet** (1983, c1983; Ione; 22 min.)

For 2 trumpets, horn, trombone and tuba
Commissioned by the Boston University School of
Music in consortium with its resident ensembles
Alea III and the Empire Brass Quintet. Commission
was made possible by an award from the New Works

Program of the Massachusetts Council on the Arts and Humanities

Premiere

W27a. 1983 (December 9): Boston, Mass.; Morse Auditorium, Boston University; Empire Brass

W28. **Brass Trio** (1970, c1970; Peters; 5 min.)

For trumpet, horn and trombone
Dedicated to the memory of Walter Hinrichsen
American Music Awards Series

Premiere

W28a. 1970 (April 8): Boston, Mass.; Jordan Hall, New England Conservatory of Music

Other selected performances

W28b. 1978 (May 9): Bemidji, Minn.; Thompson Recital Hall, Bemidji State University; Charles Decker, trumpet; Bonnie Swanson, horn; Thomas Swanson, trombone

W28c. 1980 (January 21): Boston, Mass.; Jordan Hall, New England Conservatory of Music; Robert Earl Nagel, Jr., trumpet; Paul Ingraham, horn; John Swallow, trombone

W28d. 1980 (February 13): Norman, Okla.; Oklahoma Festival of Contemporary Music; Holmberg Hall, University of Oklahoma; Dorothy McClaren, trumpet; Julie Scharnberg, horn; Marta Hofacre, trombone

W29. **Cantilena and Capriccio** (1954, c1957; rev. 1970, c1972; Ione; 7 min.)

For violin and harpsichord
See: B29a, B29c, D29a

Premiere

W29a. 1954 (June 7): Frankfurt, Germany (Cantilena only)

Other selected performances

W29b. 1958 (May 8): Boston, Mass.; Jordan Hall, New England Conservatory of Music; Robert Brink, violin; Daniel Pinkham, harpsichord

W29c. 1960 (March 30): New York, N. Y.; Contemporary Music Festival; Caspary Hall, Rockefeller Institute;

27

Robert Brink, violin; Daniel Pinkham, harpsichord

W29d. 1960 (May 11): Boston, Mass.; Jordan Hall, New Eng-
land Conservatory of Music; Robert Brink, violin;
Daniel Pinkham, harpsichord
See: B29b

W29e. 1962 (August 1): Boulder, Colo.; University of Colorado; Abraham Chavez, violin; Daniel Pinkham,
harpsichord

W29f. 1963 (January 9): Nashville, Tenn.; Peabody College;
Jerri Cadek Lucktenberg, violin; George Lucktenberg, harpsichord

W29g. 1972 (January 25): Boston, Mass.; Jordan Hall, New
England Conservatory of Music; Eric Rosenblith,
violin; Blanche Winogron, harpsichord

W30. **Concertante** (1966; Peters; 14 min.)

Original title: **A Feast of Lights**
For harpsichord and guitar soli, percussion and
strings or organ
Commissioned by Helen Keaney

Premiere

W30a. 1967 (December 27); Boston, Mass.; King's Chapel;
Helen Keaney, harpsichord; David Harris, guitar;
Leonard Raver, organ; Stom Yomashita and Richard
Kashanski, percussion; Daniel Pinkham, conductor

Other selected performance

W30b. 1968 (May 23): Boston, Mass.; New England Conservatory of Music; Helen Keaney, harpsichord; David
Harris, guitar; Daniel Pinkham, conductor

W31. **Duet** (1954, c1969; ACA, released to Ione; 7 min.)

For soprano recorder or oboe and harpsichord or harp
Also scored for orchestra See: **Divertimento** W12
Commissioned by American Recorder Society, Boston
Chapter, Arthur Loeb, president
Movements: Prelude; Aria; Dithyramb; Recessional

Selected performances

W31a. 1957 (March 11): Boston, Mass.; Young Women's Christian Association; Arthur Loeb, recorder; Edward
Low, harpsichord

W31b. 1981 (April 12): Waterville, Maine; Lorimer Chapel,
       Colby College; Mary Colbath, recorder; Adel Hein-
       rich, harpsichord

W32. **Duo** (1945, c1954; ACA; 10 min.)

      For violin and violoncello
      Dedicated to Aaron Copland
      Movements: Preamble; Variations

W33. **Eclogue** (1965, c1971; Ione; 3 min.)

      For flute, harpsichord, handbells (two players)
      Dedicated to Eric Herz and Leonard Raver

      Selected performances

W33a. 1975 (June 11): Farmington, Conn.; Hartt College of
       Music Fifth Annual International Contemporary
       Organ Music Festival; First Church of Christ,
       Congregational; Edward Clark, harpsichord; John
       Lagerquist, flute; Mary Bon and Neil Keen, hand-
       bells

W33b. 1981 (April 12): Waterville, Maine; Lorimer Chapel,
       Colby College; Christy Gauss, flute; Adel Hein-
       rich, harpsichord

W34. **Envoi** (1959; ACA; 4 min.)

      For English horn, 2 French horns and strings

W35. **Etude** (1964, c1969; Ione; 3 min.)

      For clarinet
      Dedicated to Harry Schmidt

      A Feast of Lights See: **Concertante** W30

W36. **Fanfare, Aria and Echo** (1962, c1963; Peters; 6 min.)

      For two horns and timpani
      Dedicated to Philip Nesbit and Joseph Rinello

      Premiere

W36a. 1962 (April 20): Boston, Mass.; New England Conser-
       vatory of Music; Philip Nesbit and Joseph Rinello,
       horns; Joseph Laspisa, timpani

Other selected performance

W36b. 1982 (March 28): Pasadena, Calif.; Neighborhood
       Church; Jim Atkinson and Bill Alsup, horns; Timm
       Boatman, timpani

W37.   "Four Interludes" from **The Dreadful Dining Car** W2
       (1982; Ione; 8 min.)

       For solo guitar

       The Gate of Heaven See: W167

       For mixed chorus and/or brass choir and organ

W38.   **He Scatters the Snow** (1972, c1974; Ione; 7 min.)

       For clarinet and electronic tape
       Related text: Bible, Apocrypha, Ecclestiasticus 43:
       17, 18
       Dedicated to Philip Fields

       Selected performances

W38a. 1975 (January 24): Boston, Mass.; New England Con-
       servatory of Music; Bruce Creditor, clarinet

W38b. 1978 (May 9): Bemidji, Minn.; Thompson Recital
       Hall, Bemidji State University; Lawrence Mallet,
       clarinet

W39.   **In My Visions of the Night** (1973, c1973; Ione)

       For wind ensemble, organ and electronic tape
       Commissioned by Manatee Junior College, Bradenton,
       Florida

W40.   **Inaugural Marches** (1983, c1983, rev. 1987; Ione; 8
       min.)

       For brass quintet or brass choir
       Marches No. 1 and No. 2 commissioned for the inau-
       guration of Laurence Lesser as President of New
       England Conservatory of Music; March No. 3 commis-
       sioned for the installation of Margaret A. McKenna
       as President of Lesley College
       Movements: Crisp; Festive; Exuberant

       Premiere

W40a.   1983 (October 16): Boston, Mass.; New England Con-
        servatory of Music; Honors Brass Quintet

        Other selected performances

W40b.   1986 (February 21): Durant, Okla.; Montgomery Audi-
        torium, Southeastern Oklahoma State University;
        University Brass Ensemble; Daniel Pinkham, con-
        ductor

W40c.   1987 (September 16): Boston, Mass.; Longy School of
        Music; Lenox Brass Quintet
        See: B40a

W41.   **Introduction, Nocturne and Rondo**   (1984; Zimmermann;
       10 min.)

       For mandolin and guitar
       Commissioned by John Curtis

W42.   **Little Brass Book**   (1979, c1981; Ione; 10 min.)

       For brasses and percussion
       Dedicated to Roger Voisin, Ken and Nancy, Stan Enge-
       bretson, Tom Everett, Harvey Phillips, J. Stanley
       Ballinger
       Contents: A Flourish for a Festive Occasion; Tucket
       I; Tucket II; Tucket III; Tucket IV; Intrada

       Selected performance

W42a.   1981 (October 13): Boston, Mass.; New England Con-
        servatory of Music; David Washburn and Roger Wash-
        burn, trumpets (Tucket I only)

W43.   **Musette**   (1972, c1972; Ione; 5 min.)

       For violin (viola), violoncello and electronic tape
       or for 2 double basses and electronic tape
       Dedicated to Adrienne Hartzell

       O **Wholesome Night**   See: W286

       For flute and guitar or medium voice and guitar

W44.   **Prelude, Adagio and Chorale**   (1968, c1969; Peters; 7
       min.)

       For brass quintet and optional unison chorus

31

Related text: Bible, Psalm 134
Commissioned by Wykeham Rise School, Washington,
Conn.

Premiere

W44a. 1968 (June 7): Washington, Conn.; Wykeham Rise
School; Botolph Brass Ensemble of Boston; the
Wykeham Rise Choir; Daniel Pinkham, conductor

Other selected performance

W44b. 1981 (October 13): Boston, Mass.; Jordan Hall, New
England Conservatory of Music; David Washburn,
Roger Zacks, trumpets; David Lintz, horn; James
Messbauer, trombone; Clifford White, tuba

W45. **Prelude and Scherzo** (1981, rev. 1982, c1982; Ione;
5 min.)

For flute, oboe, clarinet, bassoon and horn
"Scherzo" was commissioned by WGBH Educational Foundation in honor of the 30th anniversary of WGBH-FM.
Revised work commissioned by the New England Conservatory of Music on the occasion of the awarding of
the honorary Doctor of Music degree to Seiji Ozawa

Premieres

W45a. 1981 (October 6): Boston, Mass.; Radio station WGBH;
New England Woodwind Quintet

W45b. 1982 (October 8): Boston, Mass.; New England Conservatory of Music; Scholarship Wind Ensemble
(Revised edition)

Other selected performance

W45c. 1983 (May 2): Boston, Mass.; Jordan Hall, New England Conservatory of Music; Contemporary Music
Ensemble

W46. **Prelude for Flute and String Trio** (1944, c1954; ACA;
5 min.)

For flute and strings
Dedicated to Georges Laurent

Prothalamion See: W95

For oboe, 2 horns and strings or for organ

W47.   **Rondo**   (1959; ACA; 3 min.)

For oboe, 2 horns, celesta and strings

W48.   **Scherzo**   (1959; ACA; 3 min.)

For oboe, 2 horns, celesta and strings

W49.   **Serenade**   (1951, c1951; ACA, released to Row; 16 min.)

For violin and harpsichord or piano and optional small orchestra
Composed for the concerts of the Brink-Pinkham Violin and Harpsichord Duo

Premieres

W49a.   1951 (November 15): St. John, New Brunswick; Robert Brink, violin; Daniel Pinkham, harpsichord

W49b.   1951 (November 20): Frederick, Md.; Hood College (U. S. premiere)

W50.   **Serenades**   (1979, c1981; Ione; 14 min.)

For solo trumpet and band or wind ensemble 2-3-2-2, 4-3-3-1, timpani, percussion (3), optional saxaphones (3), baritone and tuba
Commissioned by Harvard University Wind Ensemble on the occasion of its 60th anniversary
Dedicated to the memory of Walter Piston

Premiere

W50a.   1980 (March 7): Cambridge, Mass.; Sanders Theatre, Harvard University; Rolf Smedvig, trumpet; Harvard Wind Ensemble; Thomas Everett, conductor

Other selected performances

W50b.   1980 (December 11): Boston, Mass., Jordan Hall, New England Conservatory of Music; Conservatory Wind Ensemble; Frank Battisti, conductor
See: B50a

W50c.   1986 (February 21): Durant, Okla.; Montgomery Auditorium, Southeastern Oklahoma State University; University Wind Ensemble; David Tolley, trumpet; Daniel Pinkham, conductor

33

W51.   "Siciliana and Sailor's Dance" from **Narragansett Bay**
        W7 (1944, c1952; ACA; 3 min.)

        For violoncello and piano

W52.   **Sonata da Requiem** (1978, c1978; Ione; 9 min.)

        For violin, viola da gamba, handbell in B
        Dedicated to the memory of H.M.P.
        Movements: Prelude, Variation and Knell

        Premiere

  W52a. 1978 (January 22): Boston, Mass.; New England Con-
         servatory of Music; Daniel Stepner, baroque vio-
         lin; Laura Jeppesen, viola da gamba; Nancy Joyce
         Roth, handbell

         Other selected performance

  W52b. 1981 (October 13): Boston, Mass.; New England Con-
         servatory of Music; Daniel Stepner, baroque vio-
         lin; Laura Jeppesen, viola da gamba; John Grimes,
         handbell
         See: B52a

W53.   **Sonata for Clarinet and Pianoforte** (1946, rev. 1949,
        c1952; ACA; 12 min.)

        For clarinet and piano

W54.   **Sonatina** (1946, c1952; ACA; 15 min.)

        For violin and harpsichord or piano
        Dedicated to Wanda Landowska

W55.   **Trumpet Voluntary** (1955, c1955; ACA; 2 min.)

        For trumpet and organ
        Dedicated to Roger Voisin

        Premiere

  W55a. 1955 (September 24): Cambridge, Mass.; Busch-
         Reisinger Museum; Roger Voisin, trumpet; Daniel
         Pinkham, organ

W56.   **Vigils** (1982, c1982; Ione; 11 min.)

        For solo harp

Dedicated to Carol Baum
Movements: Drammatico, Andante Sereno; Andante
Serioso; Presto Scherzando; Allegro, Drammatico
See: B56d

Premiere

W56a. 1983 (June 1): Methuen, Mass.; Methuen Memorial
       Music Hall; Carol Baum, harp

Other selected performances

W56b. 1984 (February 5): Boston, Mass.; King's Chapel;
       Carol Baum, harp
       See: B56c

W56c. 1984 (July 22): Nantucket, Mass.; Old North Church;
       Sandra Bitterman, harp
       See: B56a

W56d. 1984 (October 29): Cambridge, Mass.; Sanders
       Theatre, Harvard University; Carol Baum, harp
       See: B56b

MUSIC FOR ORGAN WITH OTHER INSTRUMENTS

W57.   **"And the Angel Said. . . "** (1974; Ione; 4 min.)

       For organ and electronic tape
       Dedicated to Yuko Hayashi

W58.   **Concertante No. 3** (1962, c1963; Peters; 12 min.)

       For organ, celesta, percussion and timpani
       Commissioned by American Guild of Organists, Boston
       Chapter
       Movements: Aria; Scherzo, Elegy
       See: B58b

Selected performances

W58a. 1962 (April 8): Boston, Mass.; Church of the Advent;
       Leonard Raver, organ; members of the New England
       Conservatory Orchestra; Daniel Pinkham, conductor

W58b. 1962 (July 29): University Park, Pa.; Schwab Audito-
       rium, Pennsylvania State University; Leonard
       Raver, organ; Edward Gamble, celesta; Harry Owen,
       timpani; Mary Jean Sakowski, percussion

W58c. 1964 (January 26): Boston, Mass.; Symphony Hall;

John Ferris, organ; Martin Hoherman, celesta;
Charles Smith, percussion; Everett Firth, tim-
pani; members of the Boston Symphony Orchestra;
Daniel Pinkham, conductor

W58d. 1964 (May 18): New York, N. Y.; Interchurch Center
Chapel; Samuel Walters, organ; David Lowry, celesta; Wayne Brotherton, percussion; Richard Wilder-
mouth, timpani; Daniel Pinkham, conductor
See: B58a

W58e. 1971 (June 18): Hartford, Conn.; Hartt College of
Music Contemporary Organ Music Workshop; Center
Church; Marilyn Mason, organ; Clinton Adams,
celesta; Alexander Lepak and Richard Lepore, percussion

W59. **Concertante No. 4** (1964, c1966; Peters; 12 min.)

For organ, 2 trumpets in C, tenor trombone, bass
trombone or tenor-bass trombone, and percussion
Commissioned for the dedication of the Peabody
Memorial Organ built by Charles Fisk, King's Chapel,
Boston
Movements: Canzona; Procession; Plaint
See: B59b

Premiere

W59a. 1964 (February 2): Boston, Mass.; King's Chapel;
Leonard Raver, organ; Daniel Pinkham, conductor
See: B59a, B59c

W60. **Concertino** (1947, c1952; ACA; 12 min.)

For organ and string orchestra
Dedicated to E. Power Biggs
Movements: Intrada, Aria, Finale

Premiere

W60a. 1947: New York, N. Y.; Ernest White, organ; Busch
Chamber Players

W61. **Diversions** (1980, c1983; Ione; 10 min.)

For organ and harp
Commissioned by Elizabeth Sollenberger for the 1981
Portland Regional Convention of American Guild of
Organists
Movements: Jovial; Hushed; Dancing
See: B61a, D61a

W61a. 1981 (July 1): Portland, Maine; American Guild of
       Organists Regional Convention; Leonard Raver,
       organ; Carol Baum, harp

Other selected performance

W61b. 1981 (October 4): Boston, Mass.; King's Chapel;
       James David Christie, organ; Carol Baum, harp

W62. **For Evening Draws On** (1973, c1976; Ione; 6 min.)

      For organ, English horn and electronic tape
      Related text: Bible, Luke 24:29
      Dedicated to John Holtz for the 1973 Hartt College
      of Music Contemporary Organ Music Workshop
      See: BG4, D62a

      Premiere

W62a. 1973 (June 14): Hartford, Conn.; Hartt College of
       Music Contemporary Organ Music Workshop; Trinity
       College Chapel; Leonard Raver, organ; Kenneth
       Roth, English horn
       See: B62a

W63. **Gifts and Graces** (1978, rev. 1979, c1979: Ione; 5 min.)

      For organ and trombone or French horn
      Commissioned by Jeffrey Price

      Premiere

W63a. 1978: Wenham, Mass.; Gordon College; Jeffrey Price,
       trombone

      Other selected performances

W63b. 1979: Hartford, Conn.; Hartt College of Music Inter-
       national Contemporary Organ Music Festival; Jeff-
       rey Price, trombone; Leonard Raver, organ

W63c. 1985 (October 25): Newark, Del.; University of Dela-
       ware; Ray Urwin, organ; Jay Hildebrandt, trombone

W64. "Gloria" from **Christmas Cantata** W114 (1957, c1968;
      King; 3 min.)

      For organ, 2 trumpets, horn and trombone

      Selected performances

W64a.   1973 (March 2): Notre Dame, Ind.; O'Laughlin Audi-
        torium, St. Mary's College; University of Notre
        Dame Brass Choir

W64b.   1987 (May 3): Long Beach, Calif.; St. Luke's Epis-
        copal Church; Mark Garrabrant and Kevin Brown,
        trumpets; Bruce Wagner and Rich Bullock, trom-
        bones; David Koehring, organ

W65.   **Liturgies** (1974, c1976; Ione; 8 min.)

        For organ, timpani and electronic tape
        Dedicated to John Grimes
        Movements: Allegro; Con Moto Preciso e Delicato;
        Adagio; Adagio e Espressivo
        See: D65a

        Premiere

W65a.   1974 (June 6): Hartford, Conn.; Hartt College of
        Music Fourth Annual International Contemporary
        Organ Music Festival; Millard Auditorium; Leonard
        Raver, organ; Alexander Lepak, timpani
        See: B65a

W66.   **Miracles** (1978, c1978; Ione; 18 min.)

        For flute and organ
        Related text: adapted from Bible, John 2:1-11;
        Luke 8:22-25; John 5:1-9; Mark 5:1-13; Mark 10:
        46-52
        Dedicated to Liselyn and Barry, Doriot Anthony
        Dwyer and Yuko Hayashi
        Contents: Miracle at Cana; Miracle on the Lake;
        Miracle at Betheseda; Miracle in the Country of
        Gerasenes; Miracle at the Roadside
        See: B66a, D66a

        Premieres

W66a.   1977 (December 30): Boston, Mass.; King's Chapel;
        Liselyn Adams (Turley), flute; Barry Turley, organ
        (Miracle at Cana only)

W66b.   1978 (May 5): Boston, Mass.; Old West Church; Doriot
        Anthony Dwyer, flute; Yuko Hayashi, organ
        (complete work)

        Other selected performances

W66c.   1978 (July 13): New Britain, Conn.; Hartt College
        of Music Eighth Annual International Contemporary

Organ Music Festival; South Congregational/First
Baptist Church; Leonard Raver, organ; Phyllis
Aronson, flute

W66d.   1979 (September 23): Cleveland Heights, Ohio; St.
        Paul's Episcopal Church; Kathryn A. Harris, flute;
        Margaret R. Scharf, organ

W66e.   1980 (January 27): Boston, Mass.; Marsh Chapel,
        Boston University; Doriot Anthony Dwyer, flute;
        Yuko Hayashi, organ
        See: B66b

W67.   **Mourn for The Eclipse of His Light**   (1973, c1980;
       Ione, 7 min.)

       For violin, organ and electronic tape
       Commissioned by American Guild of Organists Midwin-
       ter Conclave, 1973, St. Petersburg, Florida, with
       the support of Mr. and Mrs. J. O. Stephens

       Premiere

W67a.   1973: Clearwater, Florida; Trinity Presbyterian
        Church; V. Earle Copes, organ; Ronald Copes,
        violin
        See: B67a

W68.   **Nebulae**   (1975, c1975; Ione)

       For organ, band and electronic tape
       See: D68a

       Premiere

W68a.   1975 (May 9): Caldwell, N. J.; First Presbyterian
        Church; Caldwell High School Band; Jerry Gardner,
        conductor

       Organ Concerto   See: W17

       For organ and orchestra

W69.   **The Other Voices of the Trumpet**   (1971, c1972; Ione;
       7 min.)

       For trumpet, organ and electronic tape
       Related text: Bible, Revelations 8:13
       Commissioned for the 1971 Hartt College Contempo-
       rary Organ Music Workshop
       See: BG16, B69a, B69c, D69a

Premiere

W69a. 1971 (June 18): Hartford, Conn.; Hartt College of
       Music Contemporary Organ Music Workshop; Center
       Church; Marilyn Mason, organ; Ronald Kutik, trum-
       pet
       See: B69b

Other selected performances

W69b. 1973 (April 6): Houghton, N.Y.; Houghton College;
       Keith Clark, trumpet; Daniel Pinkham, organ

W69c. 1980 (July 25): Hartford, Conn.; Hartt School of
       Music Tenth Anniversary of International Contempo-
       rary Organ Music Festival; Cathedral of St.Jo-
       seph; Marilyn Mason, organ; Michael Galloway,
       trumpet

W69d. 1983 (August 31): Boston, Mass.; Church of the Imma-
       culate Conception; Paul Perfetti, trumpet; Jeffrey
       Brody, organ

W69e. 1986 (April 26): Flagstaff, Arizona; Ardrey Memorial
       Auditorium, Northern Arizona University; Charles
       T. Way, trumpet; Karl Wienand, organ

W70.   **Partita for Guitar and Organ Manuals** (1984; Ione;
       12 min.)

       For guitar and organ

W71.   **Pastorale** (1987; Ione; 4 min.)

       For organ and harp

W72.   **Psalms for Trumpet and Organ** (1983, c1983; Ione; 13
       min.)

       For trumpet and organ
       Commissioned by Vladimir Flowers for Marshelle Coff-
       man and G. Nicholas Bullat on the occasion of the
       inauguration of the organ at First United Church of
       Oak Park, Illinois
       Contents: Let God Arise, Let His Enemies Be Scat-
       tered; He Leads Me Beside the Still Waters; Out of
       the Depths Have I Called to Thee, O Lord; The Lord
       Has Gone Up With a Trumpet Fanfare

       Premiere

W72a.   1983 (October 9): Oak Park, Ill.; First United
         Church of Oak Park; Edgewood Brass Quintet; G.
         Nicholas Bullat, organ

W73.   **See That Ye Love One Another**   (1971, c1971; Ione; 3
        min.)

        For organ or guitar or harpsichord and electronic
        tape
        Related text: Bible, I Peter 1:22

        Selected performances

W73a.   1972 (June 8): Hartford, Conn.; Hartt College of
         Music Contemporary Organ Music Workshop; Millard
         Auditorium; Edward Clark, organ

W73b.   1972 (November 5): Pasadena, Calif.; Neighborhood
         Church; Keith Jones, organ

W74.   **The Shepherd's Symphony** (1973, c1974; Ione; 4 min.)

        For organ, one or more soft melody instruments
        (flute, recorder, oboe, clarinet, tenor or treble
        viol, violin, viola), electronic tape and optional
        percussion

        Selected performances

W74a.   1975 (June 11): Farmington, Conn.; Hartt School of
         Music Fifth Annual International Contemporary Or-
         gan Festival; First Church of Christ, Congrega-
         tional; Edward Clark, organ; Janet Piez, oboe;
         John Lagerquist, flute; Carol Anderson, percussion

W74b.   1985 (October 25): Newark, Del.; University of Dela-
         ware; Larry Peterson, organ; Lloyd Shorter, oboe;
         Victoria Wells, flute; Luciano Leone, clarinet

W75.   **Signs in the Sun**   (1967, c1967; Peters; 7 min.)

        For two organs
        Related text: Bible, Luke 21:25-28
        Commissioned by Riverside Church (New York) for the
        dedication of the rebuilt chancel organ
        See: B75a

        Premiere

W75a.   1967 (May 3): New York, N.Y.; Riverside Church;
         Frederick Swann and Donald MacDonald, organs
         See: B75b

Other selected performance

W75b. 1975 (June 13): Hartford, Conn.; Hartt College of
       Music Fifth Annual International Contemporary
       Organ Music Festival; Trinity Episcopal Church;
       Marian Craighead and David Craighead, organs

W76. **Sonata for Organ and Brasses** (1947, c1953; ACA; 13
      min.)

      For organ, 2 cornets, trombone and baritone
      Dedicated to E. Power Biggs

      Premiere

W76a. 1958 (April 28): New York, N.Y.; St. Thomas Church;
       Leonard Raver, organ; The Chamber Brass Players;
       Maurice Peress, conductor
       See: B76a

      Other selected performance

W76b. 1962 (January 21): University Park, Pa.; Schwab
       Auditorium, Pennsylvania State University; Leonard
       Raver, organ

W77. **Sonata No. 1** (1943, c1952; rev. 1964, c1966; Ione;
      4 min.)

      For organ, 2 violins, violoncello, optional viola
      and double bass, or with string orchestra
      Dedicated to E. Power Biggs

      Premiere

W77a. 1944 (Feb.): Cambridge, Mass.; Germanic Museum, Har-
       vard University; E. Power Biggs, organ; Fiedler
       Sinfonetta; Arthur Fiedler, conductor

W78. **Sonata No. 2** (1954, rev. 1964, c1966; Ione; 7 min.)

      For organ, string quartet, optional double bass, or
      with string orchestra
      Dedicated to Oliver Daniel

      Premiere

W78a. 1954 (May 16): New York, N.Y.; Hunter College; Jul-
       liard String Quartet; Daniel Pinkham, organ

W79.   **Sonata No. 3**   (1986; Ione; 14 min.)

For organ, 2 violins, violoncello, double bass, optional viola, or with string orchestra

Premiere

W79a.   1987 (April 27): Osterville, Mass.; St. Peter's Church; Richard Benefield, organ

W80.   **Toccatas for the Vault of Heaven**   (1971, c1972; Ione; 5 min.)

For organ and electronic tape
See: D80a

Premiere

W80a.   1972 (June 9): Hartford, Conn.; Hartt College of Music Contemporary Organ Music Workshop; Trinity College Chapel; Leonard Raver, organ

W81.   **Variations**   (1969, c1970; Peters; 11 min.)

For oboe and organ
Dedicated to Kenneth Roth
Movements: Prelude; Dithyramb; Scherzo; Fantasia; Nocturne; Finale
See: B81a

Selected performance

W81a.   1975 (February 13): Winchester, Va.; Shenandoah College and Conservatory of Music; Leo Settler, oboe; Stephen Cooksey, organ

W82.   **When the Morning Stars Sang Together**   (1972, c1972; Ione; 7 min.)

For organ and electronic tape
Related text: Bible, Job 38:1-7
Commissioned by Elizabeth Travis Sollenberger for the 1972 Hartt College of Music Contemporary Organ Music Workshop
See: B82a

Premiere

W82a.   1972 (June 5): Hartford, Conn.; Hartt College of Music Contemporary Organ Music Workshop; Organ Studio; Elizabeth Sollenberger, organ

Works and Performances

Other selected performance

W82b. 1985 (October 25): Newark, Del.; University of Delaware; Ray Urwin, organ

MUSIC FOR SOLO ORGAN

W83.   **Blessings** (1977, c1977; Ione; 17 min.)

Related text: Bible, Genesis 32:24-29; Genesis 26:
23; Luke 1:39-42; Revelations 7:11, 12
Commissioned by John Holtz for the 1977 Hartt Col-
lege of Music International Contemporary Organ
Music Festival
Contents: Jacob Wrestles with the Angel and Receives
His Blessing; The Lord Appears to Isaac and Blesses
Him; God's Blessing on Mary and on the Fruit of Her
Womb; The Blessing Before the Throne of God

Premiere

W83a. 1977 (June 6): Hartford, Conn.; Hartt College of
Music Seventh International Contemporary Organ
Music Festival; Trinity College Chapel; John
Holtz, organ

W84.   **Blest Be the Ties** (1986, c1986; Ione)

For organ manuals
Also used as movement in **Versets** W99
Dedicated to Catherine Crozier

W85.   **Canon for Organ** (1955; ACA; 1 min.)

W86.   **Epiphanies** (1978, c1980; Ione; 30 min.)

Related text: Bible, Matthew 2:2-5, 7, 8; Matthew
3:13-17; Matthew 16:13-19; Matthew 17:1-8; Acts 26:
12-18
Commissioned by Sarah-Maud and Robert Sivertsen for
the inauguration of the Charles Fisk organ in the
House of Hope Presbyterian Church, St. Paul, Minn.
Contents: The Star in the East; By the Waters of
the Jordan; You Are Peter, the Rock; The Voice from
the Cloud; On the Road to Damascus
see: B86b, D86a

Premiere

W86a.   1980 (January 27): St. Paul, Minn.; The House of
         Hope Presbyterian Church; Joan Lippincott, organ

         Other selected performance

W86b.   1980 (October 17): Cambridge, Mass.; Memorial
         Church, Harvard University; Joan Lippincott, organ
         See: B86a

W87.   **Five Voluntaries for Organ Manuals** (1965, c1971;
        Ione; 8 min.)

        Composed for the service of rededication of the
        Brattle Organ, St. John's Church, Portsmouth, New
        Hampshire
        Movements: Quick and Cheerful; Plaintive; Nimble;
        Wistful
        See: BG19, BG29, D87a

        Premiere

W87a.   1965 (July 18): Portsmouth, N. H.; St. John's
         Church; Donald Vaughan, organ

W88.   **Four Short Pieces for Manuals** (1962, c1963; Ione; 6
        min.)

        Dedicated to Ted Hallman; Fritz Noack; John Fesper-
        man and Max Miller
        Movements: Prelude; Aria; Interlude; Ostinato
        See: BG19

        Selected performance

W88a.   1981 (April 12): Waterville, Maine; Lorimer Chapel,
         Colby College; Adel Heinrich, organ

W89.   **In the Isles of the Sea** (1986; Ione; 5 min.)

        Related text: Bible, Isaiah 24:15
        Commissioned by the Kamehameha Schools/Bernice
        Pauahi Bishop Estate for the occasion of the dedica-
        tion of the Bernice Pauahi Bishop Memorial Chapel,
        Honolulu, Hawaii

W90.   **Man's Days Are Like the Grass** (1980, c1985; Ione; 6
        min.)

        Related text: Bible, Psalm 103:15, 16
        Commissioned by the families of O. Keith Barnes and
        Richard Shirey for the 30th anniversary of the

dedication of the organ in Westminster United Presbyterian Church, Akron, Ohio
See: D90a

Premiere

W90a. 1981 (January 25): Akron, Ohio; Westminster United Presbyterian Church; Richard Shirey, organ

W91. **Pastorale on the Morning Star** (1962, c1963; Highgate; 3 min.)

Commissioned by the National Council of Churches
Dedicated to Leonard Raver
See: BG19, D91a

Premiere

W91a. 1962 (September 10): New York, N. Y.; Church of the Ascension; Leonard Raver, organ

W92. **Prelude and Chaconne** (1953, c1953; ACA; 5 min. 30 sec.)

Dedicated to Clarence Walters and Carl F. Pfatteicher

Premiere

W92a. 1953 (January 18): Cambridge, Mass.; Busch Reisinger Museum; Daniel Pinkham, organ

W93. **A Proclamation** (1984, c1986; Ione; 4 min. 30 sec.)

Dedicated to the memory of Charles Fisk

Premiere

W93a. 1984 (January 22): Boston, Mass.; King's Chapel; Leonard Raver, organ

Other selected performances

W93b. 1984 (February 3): Sacramento, Calif.; Westminster Presbyterian Church; Leonard Raver, organ

W93c. 1986 (March 23): Pasadena, Calif.; Neighborhood Church; Andrew Paul Holman, organ

W94. **A Prophecy** (1968, c1971; Ione; 4 min.)

Commissioned by Harvard University for the dedica-
tion of Isham Memorial organ, built by Charles Fisk
Dedicated to E. Power Biggs
See: BG19, BG29

Premiere

W94a. 1968 (February 5): Cambridge, Mass.; Memorial
       Church, Harvard University; E. Power Biggs, organ

Other selected performances

W94b. 1972 (June 6): Hartford, Conn.; Hartt College of
       Music Contemporary Organ Music Workshop; Organ
       Studio; Diane Kyrcz, organ

W94c. 1979 (September 23): Cleveland Heights, Ohio; St.
       Paul's Episcopal Church; Margaret R. Scharf, organ

W94d. 1983 (October 9): Oak Park, Ill.; First United
       Church of Oak Park; G. Nicholas Bullat, organ

W94e. 1985 (October 25): Newark, Del.; University of Dela-
       ware; Larry W. Peterson, organ

W95.   **Prothalamion** (1955, c1955; ACA; 3 min.)

       For organ; also scored for oboe, 2 horns, strings
       Dedicated to ALC and JDC

       Premiere

W95a. 1955 (February 20): New York, N. Y.; CBS Radio Net-
       work; Daniel Pinkham, organ

       Other selected performances

W95b. 1958 (May 25): New York, N.Y.; Church of the Incar-
       nation; Leonard Raver, organ

W95c. 1958 (July 31): New York, N.Y.; St. Paul's Chapel,
       Columbia University; Leonard Raver, organ

W96.   **Proverbs** (1979, c1982; Ione; 20 min.)

       Related text: Bible, Proverbs 13:2; 4:7, 9; 16:7;
       18:4
       Commissioned by the Goethe Institute and the Boston
       German Cultural Center for New England
       Dedicated to Werner Jacob
       Movements: Allegro; Con Moto; Andante Lamentoso e
       Flessibile; Vivo (added in 1980)
       See: BG33, B96a, D96a

Premieres

W96a. 1979 (November 19): Nuremberg, Germany; Sebaldus-
       kirche; Werner Jacob, organ

W96b. 1980 (June 19): Wallingsford, Conn.; Rosemary Hall,
       Choate School; James David Christie, organ
       (expanded version)

Other selected performance

W96c. 1982 (October 24): St. Louis, Mo.; Webster College

W97.   **Revelations** (1956, c1965; Ione; 6 min.)

       For organ
       Dedicated to William Self
       Movements: Pastorale; Litany; Toccata
       See: BG19, D97a, D97b

Selected performances

W97a. 1956 (April 8): Boston, Mass.; Emmanuel Church; Jean
       Fleming, organ

W97b. 1973 (June 12): Hartford, Conn.; Hartt College of
       Music Contemporary Organ Workshop; Organ Studio;
       Jeffrey Shaw, organ

W97c. 1979 (July 23): Cleveland Heights, Ohio; St. Paul's
       Episcopal Church; Margaret R. Scharf, organ

W98.   **Suite** (1950; c1952; Ione; 11 min.)

       Dedicated to Homer Wickline, the memory of Janet
       Fairbank, Ernest White, Paul Calloway
       Movements: Introduction; Epitaph (also published
       separately See: W101); Morning Song; Toccata
       See: BG19, B98a, B98b

Selected performances

W98a. 1957 (November 27); New York, N. Y.; St. Paul's
       Chapel; Trinity Parish; Leonard Raver, organ

W98b. 1965 (February 27): Berea, Ohio: Fanny Nast Gamble
       Auditorium, Baldwin Wallace College Conservatory
       of Music; Warren Barryman, organ

W98c. 1981 (April 12): Waterville, Maine; Lorimer Chapel,
       Colby College, Adel Heinrich, organ

W99.   **Versets for Small Organ**   (1985, c1985; Ione; 11 min.)

Seven short pieces for small organ
An additional short work "Blest Be the Ties" was
added in April 1986 as an appendix but not included
in final publication
"Ponder This in Your Hearts" and "And All the Bells
Rang Out the Good News" to be included in an an-
thology published by Oxford University Press on the
occasion of the 100th anniversary of the American
Guild of Organists
Dedicated to Barry Turley
Contents: Let Us Be Patient and Watch; Rise Up Now
and Be Merry; Where You Go, I Will Go; Ponder This
in Your Hearts; My Laments Have Been Turned Into
Dancing; As It Was Foretold; And All the Bells Rang
Out the Good News; Blest Be the Ties

<u>Premiere</u>

W99a.   1985 (September 29): Sandwich, Mass.; First Church
        of Christ

<u>Other</u> <u>selected</u> <u>performance</u>

W99b.   1986 (March 23): Pasadena, Calif.; Neighborhood
        Church; Andrew Paul Holman, organ

MUSIC FOR PIANO, HARPSICHORD, CELESTA

Cantilena and Capriccio <u>See</u>: W29

For violin and harpsichord

Concertante <u>See</u>: W30

For harpsichord and guitar soli, strings and percussion

Concertante No. 1 <u>See</u>: W9

For violin and harpsichord soli, string orchestra
with celesta

Concertante No. 3 <u>See</u>: W58

For organ, celesta, timpani and percussion

Concertino in A for Small Orchestra and Obbligato Piano See: W11

For piano and chamber orchestra

W100. **Concerto for Celesta and Harpsichord Soli** (1955, c1955 & 1971; ACA, released to Ione; 10 min.)

For celesta and harpsichord soli
Dedicated to Henry Cowell
Movements: Prelude; Ricercare; Canzona
See: BG32, B100a, B100b, B100d, B100f, B100g, B100h, D100a

Premiere

W100a. 1955 (November 19): New York, N.Y.; McMillan Theater, Columbia University; Edward Low, celesta; Daniel Pinkham, harpsichord
See: B100c, B100e

Other selected performances

W100b. 1957 (June 19): Boston, Mass.; American Academy of Arts and Sciences; Edward Low, celesta; Daniel Pinkham, harpsichord

W100c. 1958 (May 8): Boston, Mass.; Jordan Hall, New England Conservatory of Music; Edward Low, celesta; Daniel Pinkham, harpsichord

W100d. 1960 (March 30): New York, N.Y.; Contemporary Music Society; Caspary Hall, Rockefeller Institute; Edward Low, celesta; Daniel Pinkham, harpsichord

W100e. 1962 (July 6): Oberlin, Ohio; Allen Art Museum; Walter Aschaffenburg, celesta; Edward Mattos, harpsichord

W100f. 1974 (June 5): Farmington, Conn.; Hartt College of Music Fourth Annual International Contemporary Organ Music Festival; First Church of Christ, Congregational; Edward Clark, celesta; Leonard Raver, harpsichord

W100g. 1984 (October 29): Cambridge, Mass.; Sanders Theatre, Harvard University; James David Christie, celesta; John Finney, harpsichord

W101. **Epitaph for Janet Fairbank** (1948, c1952; ACA; 3 min. 30 sec.)

Also used as movement in **Suite** W98
For harpsichord or piano solo
Dedicated to the memory of Janet Fairbank

W102. **Four Short Pieces** (1947; ACA; 7 min.)

For two pianos
Dedicated to Nadia Boulanger
Movements: Chorale; Interlude; Cantus Firmus; Finale
See: BG19

W103. **Goin' 60** (1985; Ione; 1 min.)

For solo piano
Composed for sixtieth birthday of Gunther Schuller

W104. **Holland Waltzes** (1982, c1982; Ione; 8 min.)

For two pianos
Commissioned by the two-piano team of Conway and
Aschbrenner

Premiere

W104a. 1982 (March 12): Holland, Mich.; Hope College; Joan
Conway and Charles Aschbrenner, pianos

Other selected performance

W104b. 1987 (April 25): Forest City, Iowa; Odvin Hagen
Music Center, Waldorf College; Mary Helen Schmidt
and Timothy Schmidt, pianos

W105. **Homage to Wanda Landowska** (1959; ACA; 30 sec.)

For harpsichord

W106. **Lessons** (1971, c1973; Peters; 10 min.)

For harpsichord
Commissioned by Helen Keaney
Movements: Con Moto Moderato ed Espressivo; Allegro
Energico; Fantasia, Senza Misura e Drammatico;
Sciolto; Con Moto; Adagio Serioso e Molto Flessibile

Selected performances

W106a. 1973 (September 23): Boston, Mass.; Isabella Gardner
Stewart Museum; Helen Keaney, harpsichord

W106b. 1978 (May 9): Bemidji, Minn.; Thompson Recital Hall, Bemidji State University; Sylvia Dyrhaug, harpsichord

W106c. 1982 (March 28): Pasadena, Calif.; Neighborhood Church; Jennifer Paul, harpsichord

W107. **Partita** (1958, c1964; Peters; 29 min.)

For harpsichord
Commissioned by WGBH-TV, Boston
Dedicated to Melville Smith, Silvia Kind, Albert Fuller, Sylvia Marlowe, David Fuller, Claude Jean Chiasson
Movements: Toccata, Andante and Fugue; Three Inventions; Interlude and Rondo; Fantasia; Scherzo and Trio; Envoi
See: B107a, B107b, B107c, D107a

Selected performances

W107a. 1960 (November 20): Plainfield, Vt.; Haybarn Theater, Goddard College; Ray McIntyre, harpsichord (Fantasia only)

W107b. 1964 (January 26): Boston, Mass.; Isabella Gardner Stewart Museum; Helen Keaney, harpsichord

W107c. 1973 (March 2): Notre Dame, Ind.; O'Laughlin Auditorium, St. Mary's College; Arthur Lawrence, harpsichord

W108. **Passacaglia** (1954, c1954; ACA)

For two pianos
Dedicated to Paul Doguereau

W109. **Prelude for Piano** (1946, c1955; ACA; 30 sec.)

For solo piano
Dedicated to Dr. and Mrs. A. LeRoy Johnson

W110. **Scherzo for Harpsichord** (1958; unpublished; 1 min. 30 sec.)

MUSIC FOR CHORUS (EXTENDED WORKS)

W111. **Ascension Cantata** (1970, c1972; Ione; 11 min.)

For mixed chorus, band or symphonic wind ensemble,
percussion and optional organ
Text: Bible, Psalm 47:5 and Mark 16:14-19; Latin
Antiphons
Commissioned by Ohio State University on the occa-
sion of its Centennial
Dedicated to Maurice Casey
See: BG41

Premiere

W111a. 1970 (March 20): Columbus, Ohio; Ohio State University; University Symphonic Choir and Chorale;
School of Music Wind Ensemble; Daniel Pinkham,
conductor
See: B111a

W112. **Before the Cock Crows** (1984; Ione; 12 min.)

For mixed chorus, SMzATB soli, flute, clarinet,
harp and string quartet
Commissioned by Bay Village Church

Premiere

W112a. 1985 (January 27): Bay Village, Ohio; Bay Village
Church; Daniel Pinkham, conductor

W113. **Before the Dust Returns** (1981; Ione; 9 min.)

For mixed chorus, 2 horns, double bass and organ
Commissioned by Bucknell University

Premiere

W113a. 1981 (November 21): Lewisburg, Pa.; Rooke Chapel,
Bucknell University; Chapel Choir; University
Chorale; high school students; Judith Vicks and
Lisa Levitz, horns; Richard Pinkerton, organ;
James Bertrand, double bass; Daniel Pinkham, con-
ductor

W114. **Christmas Cantata; Sinfonia Sacra** (1957, c1958; King;
10 min.)

For mixed chorus with double brass choir or with
brass quartet and organ
Dedicated to the New England Conservatory Chorus,
Lorna Cooke deVaron, conductor
Contents: Quem Vidistis Pastores; O Magnum Mysterium;
Gloria in Excelsis Deo

<u>See</u>: BG42, B114a, B114b, B114e, B114g, B114j, B114k, B114l, D114a, D114b, D114c, D114d, D114e

Premiere

W114a. 1957 (December 1): Worcester, Mass.; Clark University; New England Conservatory Chorus and Double
Brass Choir; Lorna Cooke deVaron, conductor
<u>See</u>: B114f, B114i

Other selected performances

W114b. 1957 (December 10): Boston, Mass.; Jordan Hall, New
England Conservatory of Music; Conservatory Chorus
and Brass Ensemble; Lorna Cooke deVaron, conductor
<u>See</u>: B114d

W114c. 1958 (July 15): Lenox, Mass.; Berkshire Music Center; Tanglewood Choir and Double Brass Choir;
Joseph La Rosa, conductor

W114d. 1959 (April 19): Boston, Mass.; Symphony Hall; New
England Preparatory Schools Chorus; Boston Sym-
phony Orchestra; Edward Gammons, organ; Wilfred
Pelletier, conductor
<u>See</u>: B114h

W114e. 1960 (June 19): Boston, Mass.; Boston Arts Festival;
Public Gardens; Chorus Pro Musica; Festival Brass
Ensemble; Alfred Nash Patterson, conductor
<u>See</u>: B114m

W114f. 1960 (November 10): New York, N. Y.; St. Paul's
Chapel, Columbia University; Juillard Brass Ensemble; University Chorus; Peter Flanders, conductor

W114g. 1960 (December 2): Stanford, Calif.; Dinkelspiel
Auditorium, Stanford University; Stanford Chorale
and Brass Ensemble; Harold Schmidt, conductor

W114h. 1962 (July 4): Boulder, Colo., University of Colorado Summer School Chorus; Warner Imig, conductor

W114i. 1966 (December 18): Washington, D. C.; Washington
Cathedral; Church of the Reformation Choir; Capitol Hill Symphony; Harlan C. Snow, conductor

W114j. 1971 (February 19): DePere, Wisc.; Pennings Hall,
St. Norbert College; College Chamber Singers and
Brass Quartet; Daniel Pinkham, conductor

W114k. 1976 (December 15): Cambridge, Mass.; Sanders Theatre, Harvard University; Cecilia Society; Daniel
Pinkham, conductor
<u>See</u>: BG12, B114c

W114l. 1980 (December 7): Oberlin, Ohio; Oberlin College;
College Musical Union and College Choir; Daniel
Moe, conductor

W114m. 1982 (December 17): Los Angeles, Calif.; Dorothy
Chandler Pavilion; Roger Wagner Chorale; Roger
Wagner, conductor

W114n. 1986 (December 5): Flagstaff, Ariz.; Northern Arizona University; University Singers

W115. **The Conversion of Saul** (1961; Ione; 10 min.)

For mixed chorus, tenor and bass soli, trumpet and
organ

W116. **A Curse, a Lament and a Vision** (1984; Ione; 12 min.)

For mixed chorus unaccompanied or with piano
Text: Bible, Job 5; Isaiah 13:4-6, 9, 10, 13; Isaiah
27:1, 13; Isaiah 25:9; Isaiah 26:19; Isaiah 35:9,
10; Apocrypha, Ecclesiasticus 41:1-4
Commissioned by Cantari Singers of Columbus, Ohio
Contents: Job's Curse; Death, How Bitter; The Day
of the Lord

Premiere

W116a. 1985 (January 27): Columbus, Ohio; First Congregational Church; Cantari Singers; Maurice Casey,
conductor
See: B116a

Other selected performance

W116b. 1987 (March 22): Pasadena, Calif.; Neighborhood
Church; Neighborhood Chorus; Daniel Pinkham, conductor

W117. **Daniel in the Lions' Den** (1972, c1974; Ione; 24 min.)

For tenor, baritone and bass baritone soli, mixed
chorus, narrator, 2 pianos, percussion and elec-
tronic tape
Text based on Bible, Daniel 6; Apocryphal Book of
Bel and the Snake; Psalm 116 and a hymn by John
Newton
Commissioned by Music for Voices Project
See: BG41, BG42, B117b, B117e

Premiere

W117a. 1973 (February 11): Paramus, N.J.: Bergen Community College; Music for Voices Workshop Chorus and Pro Arte Chorale; Brant Ellis, baritone; Jean Shepherd, narrator; Robert Sharon and Neville Dove, pianos; John Nelson, conductor
See: B117f

Other selected performances

W117b. 1973 (April 27): Boston, Mass.; Jordan Hall, New England Conservatory of Music; Handel and Haydn Society; David Evitts, baritone; Peter Johnson, narrator; Thomas Dunn, conductor

W117c. 1974 (February 22): Pasadena, Calif.; Neighborhood Church; Thomas Yeakle, baritone; Reuben Moulton, tenor; Gordon Ramsey, bass; Brandock Lovely, narrator; Daniel Pinkham, conductor

W117d. 1974 (March 6): Charleston, Ill.; Eastern Illinois University; University Mixed Chorus and Concert Choir; Dale Morgan, narrator
See: B117a

W117e. 1979 (April 7): Ft. Collins, Colo.: Rocky Mountain Contemporary Music Festival; Colorado State University; John Lueck, baritone; Brian Leatherman, tenor; Brent Ohman, baritone; University Chamber Singers
See: B117c, B117d

W117f. 1980 (February 15): Oklahoma Festival of Contemporary Music; Holmberg Hall, University of Oklahoma; University Concert Choir; Nat Eck, narrator; Terry Cook, James Hawkins and John Casey, vocal soli; Howard Woodard, conductor

W117g. 1985 (October 25): Newark, Del.; University of Delaware; University Chorale; J. Michael Foster, narrator; Steven Combs, baritone; Andrew Cottle, conductor

W118. **The Descent Into Hell** (1979, c1980; Ione; 20 min.)

For mixed chorus, soprano, tenor and baritone soli, brass ensemble (2 horns, 3 trumpets, 3 trombones), percussion, organ and electronic tape
Text based on a Greek narrative describing the Harrowing of Hell as found in the Apocrypha translated by M. R. James
Commissioned by West Virginia Wesleyan College on the occasion of its 90th anniversary
Contents: Introit; Scene in Hell

Premiere

W118a. 1980 (October 17): Buckhannon, W. Va.; West Virginia
Wesleyan College; University Concert Chorale and
Orchestra; Caroline Dees, soprano; Larry R.
Parsons, tenor; Peter Infanger, bass baritone;
Daniel Pinkham, conductor
See: B118a

W119.   **Easter Cantata**   (1961, c1962; Peters; 12 min.)

For mixed chorus, brass ensemble 0-0-0-0, 2-4-3-1,
timpani, percussion and celesta
Text: Bible, John 20:13; Matthew 28:5-7; Psalm 68:
18, 32-34; Psalm 118:24
Dedicated to Herff Applewhite, Lorna Cooke deVaron,
Warner Imig, Harold Schmidt
Contents: Prelude; O They Have Taken Away My Lord;
And the Angel Said Unto Them; Go Quickly and Tell
That He is Risen From the Dead; This Is the Day
Which the Lord Hath Made
See: BG32, BG35, BG42, B119a, B119c

Selected performances

W119a. 1971 (February 20): DePere, Wisc.; Pennings Hall,
St. Norbert College; College Concert Choir and
Brass Ensemble; Daniel Pinkham, conductor
See: B119d

W119b. 1974 (March 6): Charleston, Ill.; Fine Arts Theater,
Eastern Illinois University; University Mixed
Chorus and Brass Ensemble; Daniel Pinkham, conduc-
tor

W119c. 1987 (April 24): New York, N. Y.; Lincoln Center;
Musica Sacra; Richard Westenburg, conductor
See: B119b

W120.   **An Emily Dickinson Mosaic**   (1962, c1963; Peters; 10
min.)

For chorus of women's voices and piano or small
orchestra 2-0-2-0, 0-0-0-0, percussion, celesta and
strings
Text: poems by Emily Dickinson
Commissioned by Mt. Holyoke College for the 125th
anniversary of its founding
Contents: The Brain Is Wider Than the Sky; The
Heart Is the Capital of the Mind; The Mind Lives on
the Heart; To Be Alive; Exhilaration Is the Breeze;
Each Life Conveys to Some Centre
See: BG44

Premiere

W120a. 1962 (June 1): South Hadley, Mass.; Chapin Auditorium, Mt. Holyoke College; College Glee Club and Orchestra; Ruth Douglass, conductor
See: B120b

Other selected performance

W120b. 1975 (May 30): Detroit, Mich.; Wayne State University; Women's Chorale; Daniel Pinkham, conductor
See: B120a

Fanfare of Praise See: **Fanfares** W121

W121. **Fanfares** (1975, c1975; Ione; 12 min.)

Earlier three-movement version was entitled **Fanfare of Praise**
For tenor solo, mixed chorus, optional unison chorus or congregation, 2 trumpets, 2 trombones, timpani, percussion (2) and organ
Text: Bible, Isaiah 11:1, 2, 6; Isaiah 60:1; Isaiah 62:10,11; Psalm 150
Commissioned by Isabel W. Sondheim in memory of her husband, Dr. Sidney J. Sondheim, for the 100th anniversary of the Reading Choral Society, Dr. Peter LaManna, director
Contents: Prophecy; Proclamation; Alleluia; Psalm
See: BG41, B121d, D121a

Premieres

W121a. 1975 (April 13): Pasadena, Calif.; Neighborhood Church; Neighborhood Chorus; Daniel Pinkham, conductor

W121b. 1975 (April 25): Reading, Pa.; Rajah Theater; Reading Choral Society; Kenneth Reigel, tenor; Peter LaManna, conductor
See: B121b

Other selected performances

W121c. 1976 (June 20): Boston, Mass.; Trinity Church; Worcester Concert Choir and Choir of Archdiocesan Choir School; Gerre Hancock, organ
See: B121e

W121d. 1976 (December 15): Cambridge, Mass.; Sanders Theatre, Harvard University; Cecilia Society; Kim

Scown, tenor
See: BG12

W121e. 1978 (May 11): Bemidji, Minn.; Thompson Recital
Hall, Bemidji State University; Varsity Choir and
Concert Choir; Wayne Ellingsen, tenor; Daniel Zit-
zow, organ; Daniel Pinkham, conductor

W121f. 1982 (December 14): New York, N.Y.; Carnegie Hall;
New York City Gay Men's Chorus; Gary Miller, con-
ductor
See: B121a

W121g. 1987 (March 9): Boston, Mass.; Jordan Hall, New Eng-
land Conservatory of Music; Conservatory Chorus;
Lorna Cooke deVaron, conductor
See: B121c

W122. **Four Elegies** (1975, c1979; Ione; 24 min.)

For mixed chorus, tenor solo, and piano or small
orchestra 0-0(Ehn)-0-1, 1-0-0-0, organ and strings
Text: poems by Robert Herrick, Richard Crashaw,
Henry Vaughan and John Donne
Dedicated to the memory of Ralph A. Hall
Contents: To His Dying Brother, Master William
Herrick (Robert Herrick); Upon the Death of a
Friend (Richard Crashaw); Silence, and Stealth of
Dayes (Henry Vaughan); At the Round Earth's Imagin'd
Corners (John Donne)

Premiere

W122a. 1976 (June 12): Cambridge, Mass.; Sanders Theatre,
Harvard University; Cecilia Society; Richard Con-
rad, tenor; Donald Teeters, conductor
See: B122b

Other selected performances

W122b. 1976 (June 16): Boston, Mass.; Old North Church;
Cecilia Society; Richard Conrad, tenor; Donald
Teeters, conductor
See: B122a

W122c. 1980 (February 15): Norman, Okla.; Oklahoma Festival
of Contemporary Music; Holmberg Hall, University
of Oklahoma; University Concert Choir; James Wain-
ner, tenor; Howard Woodard, conductor

W123. **Getting to Heaven** (1987; Ione; 15 min.)

For soprano solo, mixed chorus, brass quintet and

harp
Text: poems by Emily Dickinson

Premiere

W123a. 1987 (Oct. 24): Boston, Mass.; Faneuil Hall; Daisy
       Newman, soprano; Lenox Brass Quintet; Carol Baum,
       harp; Daniel Pinkham, conductor
       See: B123a

W124. **Hezekiah** (1979, rev. 1986; Ione; 10 min.)

       For mixed chorus, STB soli, trumpet and organ
       string quintet or string orchestra added in revised
       version
       Commissioned in memory of C. Burt McDonald on the
       20th anniversary of John D. Herr as Minister of
       Music at Plymouth Church of Shaker Heights, Ohio

       Premiere

W124a. 1981 (April 8): Shaker Heights, Ohio; Plymouth
       Church

       Other selected performance

W124b. 1983 (August 31): Boston, Mass.; Church of the
       Immaculate Conception; Boston Academy of Music;
       Paul Perfetti, trumpet; Jeffrey Brody, organ

W125. **In Heaven Soaring Up** (1985, c1985, rev. 1986; Peters;
       15 min.)

       For mixed chorus, contralto and tenor soli, oboe,
       and harp
       Text: poems by Edward Taylor
       Commissioned by King's Chapel, Boston for the ob-
       servance of its 300th anniversary
       Contents: The Coach for Glory; Thy Spinning Wheele;
       Ascended Up On High

       Premiere

W125a. 1986 (January 12): Boston, Mass.; King's Chapel;
       Pamela Gore, contralto; Bruce Kolb, tenor; Carol
       Baum, harp; Barbara Knapp, oboe; Choir of King's
       Chapel; Daniel Pinkham, conductor
       See: B125a

       Other selected performance

W125b. 1986 (March 23): Pasadena, Calif.; Neighborhood
       Church; Neighborhood Chorus; Priscilla Phillips,

contralto; Dennis Mills Heath, tenor; Kathi Robin-
son, oboe; JoAnn Turovsky, harp; Daniel Pinkham,
conductor

W126. **Jonah** (1967, c1967; Ione; 26 min.)

A dramatic cantata
For mezzo-soprano, tenor, bass baritone soli, mixed
chorus and orchestra 3(pic)-3(Ehn)-3(bcl)-2(cbsn),
4-3-3(btrb)-1, timpani, percussion (6), harp, celesta and strings
Text based on the Bible, Jonah 1 and 2; Psalm 139:
7-12; Psalm 116:1, 2, 8, 9; Proverbs 25:23; Ezekiel
27:5-7; 13, 16-19, 22
Commissioned by Paderewski Fund for the Encourage-
ment of American Composers, in honor of the 100th
anniversary of the New England Conservatory of Music
See: B126a, B126c, B126h

Premiere

W126a. 1967 (May 17): Boston, Mass.; Jordan Hall, New England Conservatory of Music; Miriam Boyer, contralto; Donald Richardson, tenor; Mark Pearson,
bass; Conservatory Chorus and Orchestra; Lorna
Cooke deVaron, conductor
See: B126b, B126d, B126e, B126f, B126g

W127. **The Lamentations of Jeremiah** (1966, c1966; Peters;
11 min.)

For mixed chorus and instrumental ensemble 0-0-0-0,
2-2-2-0, double bass, timpani and percussion (2)
Text: Bible, Lamentations 1:1-5
Commissioned by the American Choral Directors Asso-
ciation for the Music Educators National Conference,
Kansas City
See: BG42, B127b

Premiere

W127a. 1966 (March 17): Kansas City, Mo.; Music Educators
National Conference; De Pauw University Choir;
Luther College Choir; instrumental ensembles from
University of Missouri at Kansas City
See: B127a

Other selected performance

W127b. 1968 (May 13): Pasadena, Calif.; Neighborhood
Church; American Guild of Organists, Pasadena
Chapter; Neighborhood Chorus

W128. **Lauds** (1983; Ione; 12 min.)

>   For two-part chorus (SA, TB, or ST/AB), 2 horns,
>   oboe, organ and percussion

>   Selected performance

W128a. 1983 (December 12): New York, N. Y.; Carnegie Hall;
       New York Gay Men's Choir

W129. **Magnificat** (1968, c1969; Peters; 8 min.)

>   For soprano solo, chorus of women's voices, 2 oboes,
>   2 bassoons and harp, or with piano
>   Text: Bible, Luke 1:47-55, translated by Jean Lunn
>   Commissioned by Wells College, Aurora, N. Y., on
>   the occasion of its 100th anniversary
>   See: BG44, B129a, D129a

>   Premiere

W129a. 1968 (May 2): Aurora, N. Y.; Margaret Phipps Audi-
       torium, Wells College; Linda Sullivan, soprano;
       Jean Green and Alpha Hockett, oboes; Julie Green,
       Frank Purdy and Edward Gobrecht, bassoons, Martha
       Moor, harp; Crawford R. Thoburn, conductor

>   Other selected performances

W129b. 1968 (December 18): New York, N. Y.; St. Thomas
       Church; Wells College Choir; Linda Sullivan, so-
       prano; Martha Moor, harp; Peter Joseph and Joel
       Maragella, oboes; Beverly Thomas and Charles Nuss-
       baum, bassoons; Crawford R. Thoburn, conductor

W129c. 1975 (May 30): Detroit, Mich.; Wayne State Univer-
       sity; University Women's Chorale; Daniel Pinkham,
       conductor

W129d. 1981 (December 13): Pasadena, Calif.; Neighborhood
       Church; Neighborhood Chorus; JoAnn Turovsky, harp;
       Anne Thompson, soprano; Edward Low, conductor

W130. **The Passion of Judas** (1976, c1978; Ione; 30 min.)

>   For SMzTBB soli, narrator, mixed chorus and instru-
>   mental ensemble (clarinet, harp, viola, double bass
>   and organ)
>   Text based on the Bible, Psalm 1; Psalm 15:1-3, 5;
>   Psalm 51:1, 2, 5-8, 10-12; Matthew 26:14-16, 20-26;
>   Matthew 27:3-5; Mark 14:43-46; Luke 22:47, 48; John
>   13:2 and John 18:1, 2; and poems by Norma Farber,

James Wright and playet by R. C. Norris
Commissioned by the National Presbyterian Church,
Washington, D. C., Ernest E. Legon, Choirmaster
Contents: Psalm 1: Happy is the Man; Lection 1: Tell
Me About the Mother of Judas (Norma Farber); Lection
II; Choral; Lection III; Rescue of the Innocents
(R. C. Norris); Lection IV; Saint Judas (James
Wright); Psalm 51: Be Gracious to Me
See: BG7, B130d

Premiere

W130a. 1976 (June 6): Washington, D. C.; National Presbyte-
rian Church; Church Choir; Susan Roberts, soprano;
Manuel Melendez, tenor; Nan Muntzing, contralto;
Fred Davison, baritone; Allen Crowell, bass;
Daniel Pinkham, conductor
See: B130e

Other selected performances

W130b. 1976 (June 20): Boston, Mass.; King's Chapel; Pamela
Gore, contralto; John Franklin, tenor; King's
Chapel Choir; Daniel Pinkham, conductor
See: B130b

W130c. 1976 (December 31): Pasadena, Calif.; American Guild
of Organists Midwinter Conclave; Neighborhood
Church; Neighborhood Choir; Daniel Pinkham, conductor
See: B130c

W130d. 1980 (March 30): San Diego, Calif.; First Unitarian
Church; Neighborhood Chorus and Instrumental Ensemble of Pasadena; Brandoch L. Lovely, narrator;
Cara Clove, soprano; Priscilla Phillips, mezzo-
soprano; Thomas Yeakle, baritone; Gordon Ramsey,
bass; Marvin Neumann, tenor; Daniel Pinkham, conductor

W130e. 1984 (October 29): Cambridge, Mass.; Sanders Thea-
tre, Harvard University; Barbara Wallace, soprano;
Pamela Gore, mezzo-soprano; Richard Benefield,
baritone; Howard Chadwick, bass; Kim Scown, tenor;
William Cavness, narrator; King's Chapel Choir;
Daniel Pinkham, conductor
See: B130a

W131. **Psalm Set** (1968, c1969; Peters; 7 min.)

For mixed chorus, 2 trumpets, 2 trombones, optional
tuba, timpani and organ, or with organ or piano
Text: Bible, Psalms 134, 117 and 47
Commissioned in observance of the Centennial of the

Episcopal Church Diocese of Central New York
Contents: Fanfare; Benediction; Jubilation

Premiere

W131a. 1968 (November 1): Syracuse, New York; Centennial
of the Episcopal Church Diocese of Central New
York

W132. **The Reproaches** (1960, c1960; AMP; 18 min.)

For mixed chorus a cappella or with organ or with
flexible instrumentation (wind quintet and/or string
quintet)
Text: Liber Usualis, English translation by Jean
Lunn
Dedicated to Lorna Cooke deVaron and the Chamber
Singers of the New England Conservatory of Music

Premiere

W132a. 1960 (March 16): Boston, Mass.; Jordan Hall, New
England Conservatory of Music; Conservatory Chamber Singers and Chamber Orchestra; Lorna Cooke
deVaron, conductor

Other selected performances

W132b. 1960 (August 9): Lenox, Mass.; Berkshire Music Center; Tanglewood Choir and Chamber Orchestra; Lorna
Cooke deVaron, conductor

W132c. 1966 (November 20): Washington, D. C.; National
Chamber Singers; Harlan C. Snow, conductor
See: B132a

W133. **Requiem** (1963, c1963; Peters; 15 min.)

For contralto and tenor soli, mixed chorus, brass
sextet and double bass or with organ or piano
Commissioned by Contemporary Music Society, Leopold
Stokowski, president
Dedicated to the memory of the composer's younger
brother W.W.P. 1926-1962
Contents: Requiem Aeternam; Kyrie Eleison; Absolve,
Domine; Domine Jesu Christe; Sanctus; Agnus Dei

Premiere

W133a. 1963 (January 24): New York, N.Y.; Museum of Modern
Art; Betty Lou Austin, contralto; Richard Conrad,
tenor; members of King's Chapel Choir; members of
the New York Brass Quintet; Daniel Pinkham, con-

ductor
See: B133a, B133b

Other selected performances

W133b. 1963 (March 13): Boston, Mass.; Jordan Hall, New
England Conservatory of Music; Betty Lou Austin,
contralto; Richard Conrad, tenor; King's Chapel
Choir; New England Conservatory of Music Brass
Ensemble; Daniel Pinkham, conductor
See: B133c

W133c. 1965 (February 26): Berea, Ohio; Fanny Nast Gamble
Auditorium, Baldwin Wallace College Conservatory
of Music; Pamela Curry, mezzo-soprano; George
Thomas, tenor; College Choir and Instrumental
Ensemble; Maurice Casey, conductor

W134. **Saint Mark Passion** (1965, c1966; Peters; 33 min.)

For STBarB soli, mixed chorus, brass sextet, double
bass, timpani, harp and percussion or with organ or
piano
Text: Bible, Psalm 2:2; Psalm 22:1-2, 14-19; Psalm
35:11; Psalm 60:1-3; Psalm 62:1, 5; Psalm 69:3, 8,
20; Psalm 83:5; Psalm 109:2; Isaiah 53:7; Isaiah 57:
1; Jeremiah 9:1; Lamentations 1:16; Lamentations 4:
13; Mark 13, 14, 15
Commissioned by St. Mark's School, Southboro, Mass.
on the occasion of its 100th anniversary
See: B134b, B134e, B134g

Premiere

W134a. 1965 (May 22): Southboro, Mass.; St. Mark's School;
Barbara Wallace, soprano; Richard Conrad, tenor;
Walter Brassert, baritone; Harris Poor, bass;
Chorus Pro Musica; members of the Cambridge Festi-
val Orchestra; Alfred Nash Patterson, conductor
See: B134c, B134d

Other selected performances

W134b. 1968 (March 28): Pasadena, Calif.; Neighborhood
Church; Anne Coons, soprano; Reuben Moulton,
tenor; Thomas Yeakle, baritone; Errol Horne, bass;
Neighborhood Chorus; Daniel Pinkham, conductor
See: B134a

W134c. 1976 (June 7): Boston, Mass.; Old South Church;
Chorus Pro Musica; Barbara Wallace, soprano; Ray
DeVoll, tenor; Alfred Nash Patterson, conductor
See: B134f

W135. **The Seven Last Words of Christ on the Cross** (1971,
c1971; Ione; 12 min.)

For tenor, bass-baritone and bass soli, mixed
chorus, organ and electronic tape
Text: Bible, Mark 15:33-35; Luke 23:33-34, 39-43,
46; John 19:25-30
Dedicated to St. Norbert College

Premiere

W135a. 1971 (February 19): DePere, Wisc.; St. Norbert College; College Concert Choir and Brass Ensemble;
Marshall Moss, Patrick Liebergen, Darrell Gilow,
vocal soli; Daniel Pinkham, conductor
See: B135a

Sinfonia Sacra See: **Christmas Cantata** W114

W136. **Stabat Mater** (1964, c1964; Peters; 16 min.)

For soprano solo, mixed chorus, organ or piano or
orchestra 1-1-1-1, 1-1-1-0, timpani, percussion,
harp, celesta and strings
Written for the Festival of Contemporary American
Music sponsored by the Berkshire Music Center in
cooperation with the Fromm Music Foundation
Dedicated to Erich Leinsdorf and the Berkshire Music
Center
See: BG35, BG42, B136a, B136b, B136c

Premiere

W136a. 1964 (August 10): Lenox, Mass.; Theatre-Concert
Hall, Berkshire Music Center; Frances Riley, soprano; Tanglewood Festival Choir; Fromm Fellowship
Players; members of the instrumental department
of the Berkshire Music Center; Thomas Sokol, conductor

Other selected performance

W136b. 1965 (February 27): Berea, Ohio; Fanny Nast Gamble
Auditorium, Baldwin Wallace College Conservatory
of Music; Marilyn Meier, soprano; Baldwin Wallace
College Choir and Chamber Orchestra; Daniel Pinkham, conductor

W137. **To Troubled Friends** (1972, c1974; Ione; 18 min.)

For mixed chorus, string orchestra and electronic

tape
Text: poems by James Wright
Commissioned for B. R. Henson by students and
friends at Texas Christian University
Contents: To a Troubled Friend; Father; A Fit
Against the Country; Evening
See: B137a, B137b

Premiere

W137a. 1972 (December 9): Ft. Worth, Texas; Texas Christian
University; Schola Cantorum; University Chamber
Orchestra; Victor Alessandro, conductor

Other selected performance

W137b. 1982 (March 28): Pasadena, Calif.; Neighborhood
Church; Neighborhood Chorus; Daniel Pinkham, conductor

W138. **Wedding Cantata** (1956, c1959; Peters; 10 min.)

For mixed chorus, optional soprano and tenor soli,
and piano or organ or orchestra (2 horns, celesta,
strings)
Text: Bible, Song of Songs 2:10-12; 4:16; 6:1-3;
8:6, 7
Dedicated to Lotje and Arthur Loeb for their wedding
Contents: Rise Up, My Love, My Fair One; Many Waters
Cannot Quench Love; Awake, O North Wind and Come
Thou South; Epilogue: Set Me as a Seal Upon Thine
Heart
See: BG1

Premiere

W138a. 1956 (November 6): Boston, Mass.; Jordan Hall, New
England Conservatory of Music; Conservatory Alumni
Chorus; Lorna Cooke deVaron, conductor
See: B138b

Other selected performances

W138b. 1957 (June 16): Boston, Mass.; Boston Arts Festival;
Public Gardens; Patricia Lee, soprano; Cambridge
Festival Orchestra; New England Conservatory Stu-
dent and Alumni Chorus; Daniel Pinkham, conductor
See: B138a

W138c. 1960 (February 18): Waltham, Mass.; Recital Hall,
Brandeis University; University Choir and Colle-
gium Musicum; Alfred Nash Patterson, conductor

W138d. 1962 (February 28): Philadelphia, Pa.; Music Teach-

ers National Association Biennial Convention;
Sheraton Hotel; Temple University Concert Choir,
Brass Ensemble and String Ensemble; Robert Page,
conductor

W138e. 1962 (March 14): Boulder, Colo.; Phipps Auditorium,
University of Colorado; The Modern Choir; Denver
Symphony Orchestra; Saul Caston, conductor

W138f. 1964 (January 26): Boston, Mass.; Old South Church;
Chorus Pro Musica; Allan Sly, piano; Alfred Nash
Patterson, conductor
See: B138d

W138g. 1973 (March 2): Notre Dame, Ind.; O'Laughlin Audi-
torium, St. Mary's College; College Madrigal
Singers; Arthur Lawrence, conductor
See: B138c

W138h. 1978 (May 11): Bemidji, Minn.; Thompson Recital
Hall, Bemidji State University; University Concert
Choir and Varsity Choir; Norma Bicek, piano;
Daniel Pinkham, conductor

W138i. 1979 (September 14): Cleveland Heights, Ohio; St.
Paul's Episcopal Church; Chamber Choir; Frances
Bermeister, organ; Daniel Pinkham, conductor

W138j. 1983 (May 1): Washington, D. C.; Terrace Theater,
Kennedy Center; Washington Singers; Paul Singer,
conductor
See: B138e

W138k. 1984 (October 29): Cambridge, Mass.; Sanders Theatre, Harvard University; Barbara Wallace, soprano;
Kim Scown, tenor; King's Chapel Choir; John Finney, piano; Daniel Pinkham, conductor

W138l. 1986 (February 21): Durant, Okla.; Montgomery Auditorium, Southeastern Oklahoma State University;
University Chorale; Daniel Pinkham, conductor

W139. **What Do You Want From Me?** (1978; unpublished)

For mixed chorus, small orchestra and electronic
tape
Text: poems by James Wright
Commissioned by Phillips Academy, Andover, Mass.,
on the occasion of its Bicentennial
Contents: This Morning My Beloved Rose Before I
Did; Beginning; My Grandmother's Ghost; Milkweed;
A Breath of Air

Premiere

W139a. 1978 (June 10): Andover, Mass.; Phillips Academy

W140. **When God Arose** (1979, c1982; Ione; 7 min.)

For mixed chorus, SSATB soli, harpsichord, organ, timpani, and percussion
Text: Bible, Psalm 76:9, 10; Matthew 28:1-7; Colossians 3:1-4
Commissioned by the University of Oklahoma School of Music
Dedicated to Dennis Schrock
See: B140a

Premiere

W140a. 1980 (February 15): Norman, Oklahoma; Oklahoma Festival of Contemporary Music; Holmberg Hall Auditorium, University of Oklahoma; Anne Richardson, Patricia McGlothlin, Grace Reilly, Terry Cook and James Hawkins, soli; Daniel Pinkham, conductor

Other selected performance

W140b. 1982 (March 28): Pasadena, Calif.; Neighborhood Church; Judy Montgomery, Anne Thompson, Sara Willard, sopranos; Thomas Yeakle, baritone; Clarence Treat, tenor; Neighborhood Chorus; Daniel Pinkham, conductor

W141. **You Shall Have a Song** (1986; Ione; 4 min.)

For mixed chorus, symphonic wind orchestra 2-2-2-2, 4-3-3-1, double bass, timpani and percussion
Commissioned by the Choral Society of Pensacola on the occasion of its 50th anniversary

Premiere

W141a. 1985 (November 18): Pensacola, Florida; Choral Society of Pensacola

MUSIC FOR MIXED CHORUS

W142. "Alleluia" from **Fanfares** (1975, c1975; Ione)

For SSATBB chorus and organ
See: B142a

W143. **Alleluia, Acclamation and Carol; An Easter Set**
       (1973, c1975; Ione; 10 min.)

       For mixed chorus, several sopranos, timpani,
       percussion and electronic tape
       Text of Carol: Isaac Watts' "Now Is the Hour of
       Darkness Past"
       Commissioned by St. Mary's College in honor of the
       retirement of Edwyn Hames as conductor of the South
       Bend Symphony Orchestra

       Premiere

W143a. 1973 (March 2): Notre Dame, Ind.; O'Laughlin Audi-
       torium; St. Mary's College; Collegiate Choir;
       Susan Stevens, soprano; Daniel Pinkham, conductor
       See: B143a

       Other selected performance

W143b. 1979 (April 7): Ft. Collins, Colo.; Rocky Mountain
       Contemporary Music Festival; Lincoln Community
       Center Auditorium; Colorado State University
       Chorus; Robert Garretson, conductor

W144. **Amens** (1975; Ione; 3 min.)

       For mixed chorus and electronic tape
       Commissioned by Delta Iota Chapter (Western Michigan
       University) of Phi Mu Alpha Sinfonia Fraternity

       Premiere

W144a. 1976 (March 25); Kalamazoo, Mich.; Western Michigan
       University; Southwestern Michigan Vocal Festival
       Chorus of 1370 voices; Daniel Pinkham, conductor

       Other selected performance

W144b. 1976 (February 28): Lexington, Mass.; Lexington
       High School Auditorium; Bethesda-Chevy Chase, Md.
       High School Concert Choir; John Preston, conductor
       See: B144a

W145. **And Peace Attend Thee** (1983; Ione; 2 min.)

       For mixed chorus
       Text: poem by Norma Farber

W146. **Ave Verum Corpus** (1973; Ione; 3 min.)

       For mixed chorus with optional organ

Text: <u>Liber</u> <u>Usualis</u>

W147.   "Be Gracious to Me, O God" from **The Passion of Judas**
        W130   (1976, c1978; Ione)

        For SMzTBarB soli, mixed chorus and organ
        Text: Bible, Psalm 51:1, 2, 5-8, 10-12

W148.   **Behold, How Good and How Pleasant**   (1966, c1967;
        Peters; 2 min.)

        Psalm Motet V
        For mixed chorus with optional organ or piano
        Text: Bible, Psalm 133:1
        Dedicated to Dennis and Hope Ehn
        <u>See</u>: B148a

W149.   **Burning Bright**   (1976, c1979; Ione; 2 min.)

        For unaccompanied mixed chorus
        Text: poem by Howard Holtzman

W150.   **The Call of Isaiah**   (1971, c1971; Ione; 3 min.)

        For mixed, men's or women's chorus, organ, elec-
        tronic tape and optional timpani and percussion
        Text: Bible, Isaiah 6:1-9
        Dedicated to Lorna Cooke deVaron

        <u>Premiere</u>

   W150a. 1971 (May 7): Boston, Mass.; A Festival of New
           England Composers Past and Present; Jordan Hall,
           New England Conservatory of Music; Conservatory
           Chorus; Lorna Cooke deVaron, conductor

        <u>Other</u> <u>selected</u> <u>performance</u>

   W150b. 1972 (November 5): Pasadena, Calif.; Neighborhood
           Church; Neighborhood Chorus; Edward Low, conductor

W151.   **Canticle of Praise**   (1965, c1965; Ione; 13 min.)

        For mixed chorus, soprano solo, brass ensemble and
        percussion
        Text: Bible, Apocrypha, Song of the Three Holy
        Children v. 29-68
        Commissioned by War Memorial Auditorium Dedication
        Committee, Boston, Mayor John F. Collins, Honorary
        Chairman

71

See: B151a, B151b, B151c, B151f, B151i

Premiere

W151a. 1965 (February 24): Boston, Mass.; Dedication of
War Memorial; Beverly Sills, soprano; combined
choruses: Boston University Chorus, Chorus Pro
Musica, Handel and Haydn Society, Harvard Glee
Club, Radcliffe Choral Society, M.I.T. Choral
Society and Glee Club, New England Conservatory
Chorus; Cambridge Festival Orchestra; G. Wallace
Woodworth, conductor
See: B151d, B151g, B151h

Other selected performances

W151b. 1965 (March 28): New York, N. Y.; Town Hall; New
England Conservatory of Music Chorus; Lorna Cooke
deVaron, conductor
See: B151e

W151c. 1966 (May 15): New York, N. Y.; St. George's
Church; Church Choir; Charles N. Henderson, conductor

W152.   **A Carol for New Year's Day**   (1973; Ione; 2 min.)

For mixed chorus with optional keyboard accompaniment
Anonymous Latin medieval text

W153.   **A Christmas Carol**   (1948; unpublished)

For mixed chorus
Text: poem by Robert Hillyer

W154.   **Christmas Eve**   (1947, c1956; Ione; 2 min.)

For unaccompanied mixed chorus
Text: poem by Robert Hillyer
See: D154a

Selected performances

W154a. 1960 (December 19): Cambridge, Mass.; Memorial
Church, Harvard University; University Choir;
John Ferris, conductor

W154b. 1974 (December 24): Pasadena, Calif.; Neighborhood
Church; Neighborhood Chorus; Edward Low, conductor

72

W155. **Come, Love We God** (1970, c1970; Ione; 2 min.)

For mixed chorus and guitar or harp or piano
Text: Old English macaronic carol
Dedicated to Robert Paul Sullivan
See: D155

Selected performances

W155a. 1970 (December 24): Pasadena, Calif.; Neighborhood
Church; Neighborhood Chorus; Edward Low, conductor

W155b. 1975 (February 13): Winchester, Va.; Shenandoah
College and Conservatory of Music; Handley High
School Hilltop Singers; Douglas Russell, conductor

W156. **Communion Service** (1957; ACA; 4 min.)

For mixed chorus

W157. **Dallas Anthem Book** (1984, c1986; Ione; 20 min.)

Ten short anthems for small choir and organ
Commissioned by Dallas Chapter, American Guild of
Organists
Contents: Be Alert, Be Wakeful; Hosanna to the Son
of David; Now at Last; We Have Seen His Star; O
Steadfast Cross; Alleluia, Tell the Tidings; God Has
Gone Up; O God, the King of Glory; Peace is My
Parting Gift; Amen! Praise and Glory

Premiere

W157a. 1985 (April 16): Dallas, Texas; Walnut Hills Presbyterian Church; Occasional Singers of First
Presbyterian Church; Mary Preston, organ

W158. **De Profundis** (1986; Ione; 4 min. 30 sec.)

For mixed chorus and viola
Text: Bible, paraphrase of Psalm 130 by Thomas Campion

Premiere

W158a. 1986: Shippensburg, Pa.; Shippensburg State University; David Sills, viola; Daniel Pinkham, conductor

Other selected performance

73

W158b. 1987 (March 22): Pasadena, Calif.; Neighborhood
       Church; Neighborhood Chorus; Jane Levy, viola;
       Daniel Pinkham, conductor

W159. **Draw Near with Faith and Benediction** (ACA; 2 min.)

For unaccompanied mixed chorus

An Easter Set See: **Alleluia, Acclamation and Carol**
W143

W160. **Elegy** (1947, c1956; ACA, assigned to Ione; 2 min.)

Title sometimes listed as **Folk Song**
For unaccompanied mixed chorus
Text: poem by Robert Hillyer
Composed for the Randolph Singers
Dedicated to Iva Dee Hiatt
See: D160a

Premiere

W160a. 1956 (January 19): New York, N. Y.; New York Uni-
       versity; Randolph Singers; David Randolph, con-
       ductor

Other selected performances

W160b. 1957 (May 19): Boston, Mass.; Isabella Gardner
       Museum; Randolph Singers; David Randolph, con-
       ductor

W160c. 1973 (March 2): Notre Dame, Ind.; O'Laughlin Audi-
       torium, St. Mary's College; College Madrigal
       Singers; Arthur Lawrence, conductor

W161. **Eternal Are Thy Mercies, Lord** (1956; ACA; 3 min.)

For mixed chorus and organ

Selected performance

W161a. 1956 (February 19): North Easton, Mass.; Unity
       Church; Unity Church Choir

W162. **Farewell, Vain World** (1959, c1964; Ione; 2 min.)

For unaccompanied mixed chorus
Text: epitaph on tomb of Edward Carter (d. 1749)

in Granary Burying Ground, Boston
Dedicated to Edward Low

W163.   **Festival Magnificat and Nunc Dimittis** (1962, c1963;
        Peters; 5 min.)

        For mixed chorus unaccompanied or with organ or
        piano and optional brass
        Text: Bible, Luke 1:47-55 and Luke 2:29-32
        Dedicated to John Festerman and the Old North
        Singers

        Selected performances

W163a. 1971 (November 19): Manhattan, Kan.; Kansas State
        University Auditorium; Colby Community College
        Choir; Vaughn Lippoldt, conductor

W163b. 1982 (March 18): Farmville, Va.; Wygar Recital Hall,
        Longwood College; Camarata Singers; Wanda Morris,
        piano; David Pook and Daphne Tipton, trumpets;
        Richard Durham, French horn; Eric Lee, baritone;
        Peter Tideman, trombone; Louard Egbert, conductor

W163c. 1987 (July 3): Irvine, Calif.; University Concert
        Hall, University of California, Irvine; Chamber
        Singers and Summer Symposium Chorus; Howard Swan,
        conductor

W164.   "Fill Every Glass" from **The Beggar's Opera** (1956;
        ACA) W1

        For mixed chorus, tenor solo and piano

        Folk Song: Elegy See **Elegy** W160

W165.   **For Thee Have I Waited** (1983, c1983; Peters; 1
        min.)

        Psalm Motet XII
        For mixed chorus and organ or piano
        Text: Bible, Psalm 25:5, 6
        Dedicated to Rebecca C. Bradford
        See: B165a

        Four Poems for Music See: **Christmas Eve** W154, **Elegy**
        W160, **The Leaf** W183 and **Piping Anne and Husky Paul**
        W203

W166. **Four Poems of Norma Farber**   (1974, c1978; Ione; 5 min.)

For unaccompanied mixed chorus and soprano solo
Commissioned by the Wall Chamber Choir, Frederic Woodbridge Wilson, director
Contents: The Hatch; Dancer, How Do You Dare?; Fawn Bridge; The Star and Pulsar Discovered Waltzing

Premiere

W166a. 1974 (May 24): Wall, N. J.: Wall High School

W167. **The Gate of Heaven**   (1986; Ione; 1 min. 30 sec.)

For mixed chorus and/or brass choir and organ

W168. **Glory Be To God; Motet for Christmas Day**   (1955, c1966; ACA, released to Ione; 2 min.)

For double mixed chorus with optional organ
Dedicated to Alfred Nash Patterson
See: B168a, B168b, D168a

Premiere

W168a. 1955 (December 6): Boston, Mass.; Church of the Advent; Chorus Pro Musica; Alfred Nash Patterson, conductor

Other selected performance

W168b. 1955 (December 18): Malden, Mass.; First Baptist Church; Church Choir; Edward Low, conductor

W169. **God Is a Spirit**   (1961, c1966; ACA, released to ACA)

For mixed chorus and organ
Text: Bible, John 4:24
Commissioned by South Church, Andover, Mass. on the occasion of its 250th anniversary

Selected performance

W169a. 1964 (September 27): Boston, Mass.; King's Chapel; Chapel Choir; Daniel Pinkham, conductor

W170. **Grace is Poured Abroad**   (1970, c1971; Peters; 2 min.)

Psalm Motet VII
For mixed chorus and optional organ or piano

Text: Bible, Psalm 45:2, 4, 6
Commissioned by California Junior College Music
Educators Association, Southern Division
See: B170a

Premiere

W170a. 1970 (August 16): Long Beach, Calif.; Long Beach
City College; College Choir; Daniel Pinkham,
conductor

W171.   "Happy Is the Man" from **The Passion of Judas** W130
(1976, c1978; Ione)

For mixed chorus and organ
Text: Bible, Psalm 1
Commissioned by National Presbyterian Church,
Washington, D. C.

W172.   **The Heavens Tell Out the Glory of God**   (1984;
Peters; 1 min.)

Psalm Motet XIII
Text: Bible, Psalm 97:6
For mixed chorus and organ
Dedicated to Neighborhood Chorus and Edward Low
on the 20th anniversary of the Chorus

Selected performance

W172a. 1986 (March 23): Pasadena, Calif.; Neighborhood
Church; Neighborhood Chorus; Daniel Pinkham,
conductor

W173.   **Henry Was a Worthy King**   (1957, c1963; ACA, released
to Ione; 2 min.)

For unaccompanied mixed chorus
Old English text
See: D173a

Selected performances

W173a. 1957 (November 20): Brookline, Mass.; Brookline
Public Library; Low Madrigal; Edward Low, conductor

W173b. 1973 (March 2): Notre Dame, Ind.; O'Laughlin Auditorium, St. Mary's College; College Madrigal
Singers; Arthur Lawrence, conductor

W174. **Here Repose, O Broken Body**   (1956, c1959; Highgate;
       4 min. 30 sec.)

       Earlier title: **On the Deposition of Our Saviour,
       Jesus Christ**
       For unaccompanied mixed chorus or with optional
       strings doubling the voices
       <u>See</u>: B174a

       <u>Premiere</u>

W174a. 1957 (March 11): Malden, Mass.; First Baptist
       Church; Church Choir; Edward Low, conductor

       <u>Other</u> <u>selected</u> <u>performances</u>

W174b. 1957 (March 30): Brockton, Mass.; St. Paul's
       Church; Church Choir; Arnold Johnstad, conductor

W174c. 1971 (October 31): Manhattan, Kan.; Kansas State
       University; University Concert Choir; Rod Walker,
       conductor

W175. **How Precious Is Thy Loving Kindness**   (1967, c1968;
       Peters; 2 min.)

       Psalm Motet VI
       For mixed chorus with optional organ or piano
       Text: Bible, Psalm 36:7-9
       Dedicated to Carl Scovel
       <u>See</u>: B175a

       <u>Selected</u> <u>performance</u>

W175a. 1975 (February 13): Winchester, Va.; Shenandoah
       College and Conservatory of Music; James Wood
       High School Concert Choir; Paul Thompson, conduc-
       tor

       Hymn No. 1 <u>See</u>: W231

       For unison chorus and organ or mixed chorus with op-
       tional organ

       Hymn No. 2 <u>See</u>: W232

       For unison chorus and organ or mixed chorus with op-
       tional organ

W176. **I Have Preached Righteousness**   (1967, c1972; Peters;
       1 min.)

Psalm Motet VIII
For mixed chorus and organ or piano
Text: Bible, Psalm 40:9, 10
Dedicated to Morris Calhoun

W177. **I Saw An Angel** (1974, c1974; Ione; 4 min.)

For SATB soli, mixed chorus and electronic tape
Text: Bible, Revelations
Commissioned by Florida Vocal Association 1975
All-State Junior High School Chorus

W178. **I Was Glad** (1962, c1963; AMP; 1 min. 30 sec.)

For mixed chorus with optional organ or piano
Text; Bible, Psalm 122
Commissioned for the 275th anniversary of King's
Chapel, Boston

W179. **In the Beginning of Creation** (1970, c1970; Ione; 3
min.)

For mixed chorus and electronic tape
Text: Bible, Genesis 1:1-3
Commissioned by Westminster Choir College, Prince-
ton, New Jersey
See: B179a

Premiere

W179a. 1970 (June): Princeton, N. J.: Westminster Choir
College; Daniel Pinkham, conductor

Other selected performances

W179b. 1971 (February 19): DePere, Wisc.; Pennings Hall,
St. Norbert College; College Concert Choir; Daniel
Pinkham, conductor
See: B179c

W179c. 1972 (November 5): Pasadena, Calif.; Neighborhood
Church; Neighborhood Chorus; Edward Low, conductor

W179d. 1973 (March 2): Notre Dame, Ind.; O'Laughlin Auditorium, St. Mary's College; Collegiate Choir;
James McCray, conductor

W179e. 1979 (April 7): Ft. Collins, Colo.; Rocky Mountain
Contemporary Music Festival; Lincoln Community
Center Auditorium; Colorado State University
Chorus; Robert Garretson, conductor

W179f. 1982 (October 24): St. Louis, Mo.; Christ Memorial
       Lutheran Church; Webster College Choir
       See: B179b

W180. **Jubilate Deo; O Be Joyful in the Lord** (1964, c1966;
       Ione; 3 min. 30 sec.)

       For mixed chorus, SSA chorus, optional treble
       unison chorus and organ
       Text: Bible, Psalm 100
       Commissioned by Trinity Parish, Southport, Conn.,
       James H. Litton, Choirmaster

       Premiere

W180a. 1964 (June 21): Southport, Conn.; Trinity Parish;
       Church Choir; James H. Litton, conductor

       Other selected performance

W180b. 1971 (February 19): DePere, Wisc.; Pennings Hall,
       St. Norbert College; College Chamber Singers;
       Women's Ensemble; Daniel Pinkham, conductor

W181. **The Kings and the Shepherds** (1974, c1978; Ione;
       3 min.)

       For mixed chorus with optional keyboard doubling
       Text: poem by Robert Hillyer
       See: B181a, D181a

       Selected performance

W181a. 1974 (December 24): Pasadena, Calif.; Neighborhood
       Church; Neighborhood Chorus; Edward Low, conductor

W182. **The Lament of David** (1972, c1974; Ione; 5 min.)

       For mixed chorus and electronic tape
       Text: Bible, II Samuel 1:19-27
       Dedicated to Lorna Cooke deVaron on the occasion
       of her 25th year as choral conductor of the New
       England Conservatory of Music

       Selected performances

W182a. 1974 (March 6): Charleston, Ill,; Eastern Illinois
       University; University Mixed Chorus and Concert
       Choir; Daniel Pinkham, conductor

W182b. 1978 (May 11): Bemidji, Minn.; Thompson Hall,

Bemidji State University; College Concert Choir;
Daniel Pinkham, conductor

W182c. 1985 (March 9): Cleveland, Ohio; Cleveland State
University; University Chorale; Daniel Pinkham,
conductor
See: B182a

W183. **The Leaf** (1955, c1956; Ione; 2 min.)

For unaccompanied mixed chorus
Text: poem by Robert Hillyer
Dedicated to Vose Greenough
See: D183a

Selected peformances

W183a. 1957 (November 20): Brookline, Mass.; Brookline
Public Library; Low Madrigal; Edward Low, conductor

W183b. 1968 (November 24): Manhattan, Kan.; All Faiths
Chapel, Kansas State University; University Madrigal Singers; Rod Walker, conductor

W183c. 1973 (March 2): Notre Dame, Ind.; O'Laughlin Auditorium, St. Mary's College; College Madrigal
Singers; Arthur Lawrence, conductor

W184. **The Lord Has Established His Throne** (1974, c1975;
Peters; 1 min.)

Psalm Motet X
For mixed chorus with optional organ or piano
Text: Bible, Psalm 103:19-22
Dedicated to Robert Fiske Bradford

W185. **The Lord My Shepherd Is** (1986; Ione; 2 min. 30 sec.)

For mixed chorus, oboe and organ
Text: Bible, paraphrase of Psalm 23 by Sir Philip
Sidney

W186. **Love Came Down at Christmas** (1973; Ione; 2 min.)

For mixed chorus with optional organ
Text: poem by Christina Georgina Rossetti

W187. **Love Can Be Still** (1975, c1978; Ione; 8 min.)

For mixed chorus with optional piano

Text: poems by Norma Farber
Commissioned by Kansas State University Concert
Choir; Rod Walker, director
Contents: Take Me Walking in Your Mind; After the
Storm a Star; Da Capo; Love, Bone-Quiet, Said
See: BG8, B187a, D187a

Selected performances

W187a. 1978 (May 11): Bemidji, Minn.; Thompson Recital
Hall, Bemidji State University; University Chamber Singers; Daniel Pinkham, conductor

W187b. 1981 (October 13): Boston, Mass.; Jordan Hall, New
England Conservatory of Music; Patti Dell and
Barbara Wallace, sopranos; Pamela Gore, contralto;
Richard Conrad, tenor; Bryan McNeil, baritone;
Gary Wedow, piano

Madrigal See: **Piping Anne and Husky Paul** W203

W188. **The Martyrdom of Saint Stephen** (1967, c1970; Ione)

For mixed chorus and guitar or piano
Text: Bible, Acts 7:55-60
Commissioned by Southern Illinois University, Ed-
wardsville, Concert Chorale, Leonard Van Camp, con-
ductor
Guitar part edited by Robert Paul Sullivan
See: B188a

Premiere

W188a. 1967 (April 28): Edwardsville, Ill.; Southern Illinois University; University Concert Chorale; David
Engelke, guitar; Daniel Pinkham, conductor

Other selected performance

W188b. 1968 (March 28): Pasadena, Calif.; Neighborhood
Church; Neighborhood Chorus; Dennis Schuck,
guitar; Daniel Pinkham, conductor

W189. **Mass of the Word of God** (1966, c1966; Ione)

For mixed chorus, congregation and organ
Text: official American translation of the Mass as
approved by the National Conference of Bishops of
the U. S. 1964
Commissioned by the Church Association of America
Contents: Lord, Have Mercy; I Believe in One God;
Holy, Holy, Holy; Lamb of God

See: B189a

Premiere

W189a. 1966 (August 27): Milwaukee, Wisc.; St. John's
Cathedral

W190. **The Message** (1968, c1973; Ione)

For mixed chorus and guitar or piano
Text: poem by Siegfried Sassoon "Toward Sunset This
November Day"
Guitar part edited by Robert Paul Sullivan
See: B190a

Selected performance

W190a. 1968 (March 28): Pasadena, Calif.; Neighborhood
Church; Neighborhood Chorus; Dennis Schuck,
guitar; Daniel Pinkham, conductor

W191. **Most Glorious Lord of Life** (1974; unpublished, registered with Ione; 1 min. 30 sec.)

For mixed chorus

W192. **My Heart Is Steadfast** (1977, c1979; Peters; 1 min.
30 sec.)

Psalm Motet XI
For mixed chorus with optional organ or piano
Text: Bible, Psalm 57:7-10
Dedicated to Adrian College, John H. Dawson, Presi-
dent

Premiere

W192a. 1977 (May 22): Adrian, Mich.; Adrian College; Adrian Singers; Dr. Arthur Jones, conductor

W193. **Nativity Madrigals** (1981, c1981; rev. 1982, c1983;
Ione; 10 min.)

For mixed chorus and piano or organ
Text: poems by Norma Farber
Commissioned by Holland Community Chorale, Inc.,
Calvin Langejans, conductor
Contents: Guardian Owl; Get Up! Said Mary; What Did
the Baby Give the Kings?; How They Brought the Good
News by Sea; After

Premiere

W193a. 1982 (March 13): Holland, Mich.; Dimnent Chapel; Holland Community Chorale; Central Michigan University Chamber Orchestra; Daniel Pinkham, conductor

Other selected performances

W193b. 1982 February 7): Laguna Beach, Calif.; Laguna Museum of Art; Neighborhood Chorus of Pasadena; Edward Low, conductor

W193c. 1982 (October 24): St. Louis, Mo.; Christ Memorial Lutheran Church; Webster College Chorus; Daniel Pinkham, conductor

Nunc Dimittis See: **Festival Magnificat and Nunc Dimittis** W163 and **Song of Simeon** W212

W194. **O Beautiful! My Country** (1975, c1976; Ione; 8 min.)

For mixed chorus with optional piano
Commissioned by the Siena Alumni Association for the Bicentennial Festival of the American Arts
Text: poems by Philip Morin Freneau, Anne Bradstreet and James Russell Lowell
Contents: Take Warning, Tyrants (Philip Morin Freneau): The Happy Flood (Anne Bradstreet); The Promised Land (James Russell Lowell)

Premiere

W194a. 1976 (May 7): Loudonville, N. Y.; Siena College; combined choruses of Siena Schola Cantorum and the Capitol Hill Chorus Society of Albany; W. Judson Rand, conductor

W195. **O Depth of Wealth** (1973, c1974; Ione; 4 min.)

For mixed chorus, organ and electronic tape
Text: Bible, Romans 11:33-36
Commissioned by Trinity Lutheran Church, Worcester, Mass. on the occasion of its 25th anniversary

W196. **O Lord God, to Whom Vengeance Belongeth** (1961, c1962; Peters; 2 min.)

Psalm Motet I

For mixed chorus with optional organ or piano

Text: Bible, Psalm 94:1, 2
Dedicated to Edward Low

Selected performance

W196a. 1962 (September 24): Boston, Mass.; King's Chapel;
    King's Chapel Choir; Daniel Pinkham, conductor

O Praise the Lord Alleluia See: "Psalm: O Praise the
Lord Alleluia" W206

W197. **On Secret Errands** (1981; Ione; 5 min.)

For mixed chorus, flute and clarinet
Text: poems by Howard Holtzman
Commissioned by Longwood College, Farmville, Va.
Dedicated to Longwood College Camerata Singers,
Louard Egberg, Director
Contents: The Grey Above the Green; After-Song;
Soaring

Premiere

W197a. 1982 (March 18): Farmville, Va.; Wygar Recital Hall;
    Longwood College; Camerata Singers; Louard Egbert,
    conductor

W198. **On That Day** (1975; Ione)

For mixed chorus, 2 trumpets, 2 trombones, and optional organ doubling
Text: Bible, Isaiah

W199. **On the Dispute About Images** (1969, c1974; Ione; 7
    min.)

For mixed chorus, SATB soli and guitar or piano
Commissioned by the Unitarian Church of All Souls,
New York, N. Y., Walter Donald Kring, minister
Text: Maximus of Tyre (English translation)
See: B199a

W200. **One Shade** (1982; Ione; 2 min.)

For mixed chorus
Text: poem by Howard Holtzman

W201. **Open to Me the Gates of Righteousness** (1966, c1966;
    Peters; 1 min.)

Psalm Motet IV
For mixed chorus with optional organ or piano
Text: Bible, Psalm 118:19
Dedicated to Joseph Barth

W202. **Pater Noster** (1969, c1972; Ione; 2 min.)

For mixed chorus, doubling by oboe, English horn
and 2 bassoons or with optional organ
Dedicated to Putnam Aldrich

W203. **Piping Anne and Husky Paul** (1955; c1956; Ione; 2
min.)

Title sometimes listed as **Madrigal**
For unaccompanied mixed chorus
Text: poem by Robert Hillyer
Dedicated to David Randolph and the Randolph Singers
See: D203a, D203b

Selected performances

W203a. 1957 (May 19): Boston, Mass.; Isabella Stewart
Gardner Museum; Randolph Singers; David Randolph,
conductor

W203b. 1968 (November 24): Manhattan, Kan.; All Faiths
Chapel, Kansas State University; University Madrigal Singers; Rod Walker, conductor

W204. **Psalm 81** (1959; ACA; 3 min.)

For two antiphonal choruses and organ or brass (2
trumpets, 2 trombones)
Commissioned by Phillips Academy, Andover, Mass.

W205. **Psalm 96** (1951; ACA; 2 min.)

For unaccompanied mixed chorus

W206. "Psalm: O Praise the Lord Alleluia" from **Fanfares**
W121 (1975, c1975; Ione)

For mixed chorus and organ, optional unison chorus
and/or congregation
Text: Bible, Psalm 150

W207. **Sacred Service** (1967, c1967; Ione)

For cantor or baritone and SATB soli, mixed chorus
and organ
Commissioned by the Temple, Cleveland, Ohio

Premiere

W207a. 1968 (April 21): Cleveland, Ohio: The Temple;
Bernita Bricker Smith, soprano; Ilona Strasser,
contralto; Charles Smith, tenor; Melvin Hakola,
baritone; David Gooding, organ; Daniel Pinkham,
conductor

W208. **The Sheepheards Song; A Caroll or Himne for Christmas**
(1971, c1972; Ione; 4 min.)

For solo soprano, mixed chorus and optional elec-
tronic tape
Text from England's Helicon, 1600
Dedicated to Richard Felciano

Premiere

W208a. 1971 (December 13): Cambridge, Mass.; Harvard Memorial Church; John Ferris, conductor

Other selected performance

W208b. 1980 (February 13): Norman, Okla.; Oklahoma Festival
of Contemporary Music; Holmberg Hall, University
of Oklahoma; Debra Hays, soprano; University Concert Choir; Howard Woodard, conductor

W209. **Signs Will Appear** (1974; unpublished, registered
with Ione)

For mixed chorus, organ and electronic tape

W210. **Slumber Now** (1982; unpublished, registered with Ione;
2 min.)

For unaccompanied mixed chorus
Text: poem by Howard Holtzman

W211. **Sometimes the Soul** (1955, c1970; Ione)

For mixed chorus and guitar or piano
Text: poem by Norma Farber
Commissioned by the First Unitarian Church, Cincin-
nati, Lewis E. Whikehart, Director of Music
Guitar part edited by Robert Paul Sullivan

87

Works and Performances

See: B211a

Selected performance

W211a. 1968 (March 28): Pasadena, Calif.; Neighborhood
Church; Neighborhood Chorus; Dennis Schuck,
guitar; Daniel Pinkham, conductor

W212. **Song of Simeon (Nunc Dimittis)** (1952; ACA; 5 min.)

For mixed chorus and organ
Text: Bible, Luke 2:29-32

Selected performance

W212a. 1964 (April 12): Boston, Mass.; King's Chapel;
King's Chapel Choir; Daniel Pinkham, conductor

W213. **Songs of Peaceful Departure** (1967, c1970; Ione; 5
min.)

For mixed chorus and guitar or piano
Text: Bible, Isaiah 40:6, 8; Psalm 103:16
Commissioned for Southern Illinois University
Concert Chorale, Edwardsville, Illinois
Contents: All Flesh is Grass; Lord, Make Me To
Know Mine End; Lord, Thou Hast Put Gladness in My
Heart

Premiere

W213a. 1967 (April 28): Edwardsville, Ill.; Communications
Building Auditorium, Southern Illinois University;
University Concert Chorale; David Engelke, guitar;
Daniel Pinkham, conductor

Other selected performance

W213b. 1968 (March 28): Pasadena, Calif.; Neighborhood
Church; Neighborhood Chorus; Dennis Schuck, guitar; Daniel Pinkham, conductor

W214. **Star-Tree Carol** (1949, rev. 1983; Row, released to
C. Fischer; 2 min.)

For unaccompanied mixed chorus
Text: poem by Robert Hillyer
Dedicated to Theodore Chanler

W215. **Statement of Faith** (1961; unpublished, registered
with ACA; 7 min.)

For SATB soli and mixed chorus

W216. **The Temptations in the Wilderness** (1972; unpublished, registered with Ione)

For mixed chorus, solo baritone, organ and electronic tape
Text: Bible, Luke 4

Premiere

W216a. 1972 (November 19): Des Moines, Iowa; Fine Arts Center, Drake University; College Choir and Chamber Chorale; Carl Staplin, organ; Lowell Accolo, baritone; Allan Lehl, conductor

W217. "This Is the Day" from **Easter Cantata** W119 (1960, c1962; Peters; 2 min. 30 sec.)

For mixed chorus, 4 trumpets, 3 trombones, tuba and timpani
Text: Bible, Psalm 68:32-34 and Psalm 118:24

Premiere

W217a. 1960 (August 16): Cambridge, Mass.; Sanders Theatre, Harvard University; Summer School Chorus; members of the Summer School Orchestra; Harold Schmidt, conductor
See: B217a, B217b

Other selected performance

W217b. 1960 (Dec.2): Stanford, Calif.; Dinkelspiel Auditorium, Stanford University; University Chorus and Brass Ensemble; Harold Schimdt, conductor

W218. **Thou Hast Loved Righteousness** (1963, c1964; Peters; 3 min.)

Psalm Motet III
For mixed chorus with optional organ or piano
Text: Bible, Psalm 45:7, 17
Dedicated to the First Presbyterian Church, Oyster Bay, N. Y.

Premiere

W218a. 1964 (Janury 12): Boston, Mass.; King's Chapel; King's Chapel Choir; Daniel Pinkham, conductor

89

W219. **Thou Hast Turned My Laments Into Dancing** (1973,
      c1975; Peters; 1 min.)

      Psalm Motet IX
      For mixed chorus with optional organ or piano
      Text: Bible, Psalm 30:11, 12
      Dedicated to Evelyn Hinrichsen, president, on the
      25th anniversary of C. F. Peters Corp.

W220. **Three Campion Poems** (1981; Ione; 7 min.)

      For mixed chorus, suspended handbells and xylophone
      Text: poems by Thomas Campion
      Commissioned by Waldorf College in honor of its 70th
      anniversary
      Contents: Author of Light; To Music Bent Is My Re-
      tiring Mind; Come, Let Us Sound With Melody

      Premiere

  W220a. 1987 (April 26): Forest City, Iowa; Immanuel Luther-
      an Church; Waldorf College Choir; Marc A. Hafso,
      conductor

W221. **Three Lenten Poems of Richard Crashaw** (1963, c1965;
      Ione; 5 min.)

      For mixed chorus with string quartet (optional
      double bass) or with string orchestra and handbells
      (or celesta or harp) or with keyboard accompaniment
      (optional handbells)
      Also scored for women's chorus See: W258
      Contents: On the Still Surviving Marks of Our
      Savior's Wounds; Upon the Body of Our Blessed Lord,
      Naked and Bloody; O Save Us Then

      Selected performance

  W221a. 1982 (March 18): Farmville, Va.; Wygal Recital Hall,
      Longwood College; College Concert Choir; Pauline
      Haga, director; Catherine Ballard, piano

W222. **Thy Statutes Have Been My Songs** (1965, c1970; Ione)

      For SAB chorus and organ
      Text: Bible, Psalm 119:54

W223. **Time of Times** (1975, c1980; Ione; 8 min.)

      For mixed chorus and piano

Text: poems by Norma Farber
Commissioned in memory of Ruth D. Brandes by the
Abington, Pa., Choral Club
Contents: On Going; Long Lullabye; A Quiet Gospel;
The Tree in the River; A Cage of Half-Light; In the
Counting-House; Time of Aster
See: BG8, D223a

Selected performance

W223a. 1987 (February 14): Boston, Mass.; Concert Hall,
Boston University; Jayne West, soprano; Karen
Lykes, mezzo soprano; William Hite, tenor; Mark
Aliapoulios, baritone; Gary Wedow, piano
See: B223a

W224. **To Think of Those Absent** (1969, c1970; Ione; 2 min.)

For mixed chorus and guitar or harp or piano
Text: poem by Norma Farber
Dedicated to Thomas Dunn
See: D224a

W225. **A Tunnel in the Leaves** (1978; Ione; 8 min.)

For mixed chorus with optional doublings of piano
or string orchestra
Text: poems by Howard Holtzman
Commissioned by Colorado State University
Contents: A Tunnel in the Leaves; Fast Winter
Friends

Premieres

W225a. 1979 (March 25): Pasadena, Calif.; Neighborhood
Church; Neighborhood Chorus; Daniel Pinkham,
conductor

W225b. 1979 (April 7): Ft. Collins, Colo.; Rocky Mountain
Contemporary Music Festival; Lincoln Community
Center; Colorado State University Oratorio
Chorus; Daniel Pinkham, conductor
See: B225a, B225b

W226. **Twentieth Century** (1948; unpublished, registered
with ACA; 1 min.)

For unaccompanied mixed chorus
Text: poem by Robert Hillyer

W227. **Versicle: Call to Prayer** (1956; ACA; 1 min.)

91

For mixed chorus with optional organ

W228. "Who May Lodge in Thy Tabernacle?" from **The Passion of of Judas** W130 (1976, c1978; Ione)

For mixed chorus and organ
Text: Bible, Psalm 15:1-3, 5

W229. **Why Art Thou Cast Down?** (1955, c1962; Peters; 2 min.)

Psalm Motet II
For mixed chorus with optional organ or piano
Text: Bible, Psalm 42:11
Dedicated to Edward Low

MUSIC FOR UNISON CHORUS

Elegy see: W271

For voice and piano or for unison chorus

W230. **Evergreen** (1973, c1974; Ione; 3 min.)

For unison chorus and one or more of the following instruments: organ, piano, harpsichord, harp or 2 guitars and optional handbells, glockenspiel or celesta
Text: poem by Robert Hillyer
Commissioned by Forest Hills Presbyterian Church, Tampa, Florida
See: B230a, D230a

Selected performances

W230a. 1975 (December 4): Manhattan, Kan.; All Faiths Chapel, Kansas State University; combined University Glee Clubs

W230b. 1981 (April 12): Waterville, Me.; Lorimer Chapel, Colby College; selected members of the Chapel Choir

W230c. 1982 (October 24): St. Louis, Mo.; Christ Memorial Lutheran Church; Webster College Choir

W231. **Hymn No. 1** (unpublished)

For unison chorus and organ or mixed chorus with
optional organ
Text: poem by Norma Farber "Why Sleepest Thou?"

W232.   **Hymn No. 2**   (1955; in <u>American</u> <u>Hymns</u> <u>Old</u> <u>and</u> <u>New</u>
published by Columbia University Press, 1980)

For unison chorus and organ or mixed chorus with
optional organ
Text: poem by Norma Farber "Bow Down Mountain"
Commissioned by Albert Crist-Janer

W233.   **In Youth Is Pleasure**   (1953, rev. 1968; Row, released
to Ione; 2 min.)

For unison chorus and guitar or piano or for medium
voice and piano
Text: poem by Robert Wever
Dedicated to Hugues Cuenod

W234.   **Introit for Thanksgiving Day**   (1958; ACA; 1 min.
30 sec.)

For unison chorus and organ

W235.   **Mass of the Good Shepherd**   (1966, c1970; Ione)

For unison chorus and organ
Contents: Threefold Kyrie Eleieson; Ninefold Kyrie
Eleieson; Trisagion; Gloria in Excelsis; Sanctus;
Benedictus Qui Venit; Agnus Dei; Anthem

W236.   **Mass of the Holy Eucharist**   (1966; Ione; 8-10 min.)

For unison chorus, congregation and organ

Prelude, Adagio and Chorale   <u>See</u>: W44

For brass quintet and optional unison chorus

W237.   **We Have Seen His Star**   (1957; ACA; 1 min.)

For unison chorus and organ

<u>Premiere</u>

W237a. 1957 (December 29): Jamaica Plain, Mass.; Central
Congregational Church; Church Choir

Other selected performance

W237b. 1964 (January 5): Boston, Mass.; King's Chapel;
      King's Chapel Choir; Daniel Pinkham, conductor

Wellesley Hills Psalm Book See: W304

For medium voice or unison choir and organ

W238. **Ye Watchers and Ye Holy Ones** (1956, c1957; ACA; 3
      min.)

For unison chorus, 2 violins, violoncello and
organ

MUSIC FOR WOMEN'S OR CHILDREN'S CHORUS

W239. **Alleluia** (1984; Ione; 3 min.)

For SSA or TTB chorus and piano

W240. **Angelus ad Pastores Ait; Shepherd, Awake** (1959,
      c1959; King; 2 min. 30 sec.)

For four part chorus of women's voices, 3 trombones,
tuba, optional trumpets and optional organ
Text: Liber Usualis
Commissioned by the Cecilia Society, Boston

Premiere

W240a. 1959 (December 4): Boston, Mass.; Jordan Hall, New
      England Conservatory of Music; Cecilia Society;
      Boston Brass Choir; Max Miller, organ; Theodore
      Marier, conductor
      See: B240a, B240b, B240c, B240d

W241. **Ave Maria** (1960, c1962; AMP; 2 min.)

For unaccompanied two-part chorus of treble voices
Dedicated to Pine Manor Choir, Edward Low, conductor

Premiere

W241a. 1960 (Dec. 4): Wellesley, Mass.; Bardswell Audito-
      rium; Pine Manor Junior College Choral Society;
      Edward Low, conductor

W242. **Baptism Canon** (1974, c1977; Peters; 2 min.)

For three-part chorus of treble voices and organ
Text: Bible, Matthew 28:19
Dedicated to David Bradford Osgood

W243. **A Biblical Book of Beasts** (1985; Ione; 8 min.)

For two-part chorus of treble voices and string
quartet or piano
Text by Daniel Pinkham

The Call of Isaiah See: W150

For mixed, men's or women's chorus, organ, electronic tape and optional timpani and percussion

W244. **Clear Mirrors** (1980; unpublished, assigned to Ione;
7 min.)

For two-part chorus of treble voices, 2 horns and
harp
Text: poem by Ben Jonson
Commissioned by Dana Hall School for its 100th anniversary

Premiere

W244a. 1981 (May 22): Wellesley, Mass.; Bardwell Auditorium; Dana Hall Chorus

W245. **Company at the Creche** (1977, c1978; Ione; 9 min.)

For treble voices, handbells or glockenspiel and
piano or organ
Text: poems by Norma Farber
Commissioned by United Methodist Church, Worthing-
ton, Ohio, Maurice Casey, Director of Music
Contents: Stork; Dove; Caterpillar; Rooster; Spider;
Porcupine; Lion
See: BG8, B245b, D245a, D245b

Premieres

W245a. 1977 (June 23): Boston, Mass.; Emmanuel College;
Cambridge Boys' Choir; Carl Swanson, harp; Theo-
dore Marier, conductor
See: B245a

W245b. 1977 (December 19): Worthington, Ohio; United Methodist Church

Other selected performance

W245c. 1985 (October 25): Newark, Del.; University of Delaware; University Singers; Neal Kurz, piano; Helen
Carnevale, glockenspiel; Ruth Oatman, conductor

W246. **Five Canzonets** (1958, c1960; AMP; 5 min.)

For unaccompanied two-part chorus of treble voices
Text: Old English nursery rhymes and poems by
William Blake and John Donne
Dedicated to the Pine Manor Junior College Choral
Society, Edward Low, conductor
Contents: The Nut Tree; The Blossom (William Blake);
Daybreak (John Donne); Calico Pie; Spring (William
Blake)

Premiere

W246a. 1960 (spring): Wellesley, Mass.; Pine Manor Junior
College; College Choral Club; Mary Ann Harris and
Ann Houghton, vocal soli; Edward Low, conductor

Other selected performance

W246b. 1973 (September 23): Boston, Mass.; Isabella Stewart
Gardner Museum; Barbara Wallace, soprano; Pamela
Gore, contralto

W247. **Going and Staying** (1975, c1975; Ione; 3 min.)

For women's chorus, electric guitar and electronic
tape or celesta or harp or offstage bells or piano
Text: poem by Norma Farber
Commissioned by Wayne State University Women's
Chorale, Douglas K. Belland, conductor

Premiere

W247a. 1975 (May 30): Detroit, Mich.; Wayne State University; University Women's Chorale; Daniel Pinkham,
conductor

W248. **If Ye Love Me** (1963, c1964; Ione; 3 min.)

For three-part chorus of women's voices and organ
Text: Bible, John 14:15, 16, 18, 21

Premiere

W248a. 1964 (May 17): Boston, Mass.; King's Chapel

In Grato Jubilo <u>See</u>: W14

For soprano, women's chorus, wind orchestra 1-1-1-1, 1-3-2-0 and double bass

The Lamb <u>See</u>: W279

For unison chorus of treble voices or solo high voice and piano or guitar
piano or guitar

Lauds <u>See</u>: W128

For two-part chorus (SA, TB or ST/AB) 2 horns, oboe, organ and percussion

W249. **Let Us Now Praise Famous Men** (1966, c1970; Ione; 8 min.)

For two-part chorus of treble voices unaccompanied or with optional instrumental doubling
Text: Bible, Apocrypha, Ecclesiasticus 45:1, 3, 6, 7, 9; 47:3-5, 7, 8, 11, 13, 14, 16, 17; 48:1, 3, 9
Contents: The Lord Brought Forth Moses; The Lord Exalted Aaron; David Played with Lions; Solomon Reigned in Days of Peace; The Prophet Elijah Rose
<u>See</u>: B249a

W250. **Listen to Me; Five Motets** (1965, c1965; Ione; 5 min.)

For two-part chorus of treble voices with optional instrumental doubling
Text: Bible, Apocrypha, Ecclesiasticus 1:11-12; 18:9-11; 32:3-9; 39:13-14; 43:17, 18
Commissioned by Chicago Children's Choir
Contents: Listen to Me; Hinder Not Music; The Number of Man's Days; He Scatters the Snow; The Fear of the Lord

<u>Premiere</u>

W250a. 1966 (February 15): Boston, Mass.; New England Con-servatory of Music; New England Youth Chamber Singers; Lisa Frederick, conductor

<u>Other</u> <u>selected</u> <u>performances</u>

97

W250b. 1973 (March 2): Notre Dame, Ind.; O'Laughlin Audi-
        torium, St. Mary's College; Corrine Birkovich,
        Suzanne Kellow, Carol Dzikowski and Paula Homer,
        soli

W250c. 1975 (February 13): Winchester, Va.; Shenandoah
        College and Conservatory of Music; Conservatory
        Women's Chorus; James Laster, conductor

A Litany See: W281

For two sopranos or two-part chorus of women's
voices and piano or organ

W251.   **Love's Yoke** (1979; Ione; 7 min.)

For two-part chorus of treble voices and 2 horns
Old English text
Contents: The Solitary Shepherd's Song; We Love;
Merrily, Cheerily

Selected performances

W251a. 1981 (April 21): Boston, Mass.; New England Conser-
        vatory of Music; Conservatory Recital Chorus;
        Johanna Hill Simpson, conductor

W251b. 1982 (March 28): Pasadena, Calif.; Neighborhood
        Church; Westridge Glee Club; Daniel Pinkham, con-
        ductor

Magnificat See: W129

For soprano solo, chorus of women's voices, 2 oboes,
2 bassoons, and harp, or with piano accompaniment

W252.   **Manger Scenes** (1980, c1985; Ione; 7 min.)

For two-part women's chorus or solo medium voice and
piano
Text: poems by Norma Farber
Commissioned by Peter P. Papesch for Barbara Papesch
on their 20th wedding anniversary
Contents: A Lamp in the Manger; The Foundling; The
Queens Came Late, But the Queens Were There

Selected performances

W252a. 1981 (December 10): Boston, Mass.; St. Botolph's
        Club

W252b. 1984 (October 29): Cambridge, Mass.; Sanders Thea-
    tre, Harvard University; King's Chapel Choir;
    Daniel Pinkham, conductor
    See: B252a

W253. **Memory, Hither Come** (1959, c1979; ACA, released to
    Ione; 2 min.)

    For unaccompanied two-part chorus of women's voices
    Text: poem by William Blake
    Dedicated to Pine Manor Junior College Choral Soci-
    ety, Edward Low, conductor

W254. **Pleasure It Is** (1973, c1974; Ione; 6 min.)

    For unison chorus of treble voices, and optional ob-
    bligato melody instruments and organ
    Text: poems by William Randolph Cornish, Christopher
    Smart, Queen Elizabeth I (?)
    Dedicated to Alice Parker, Helen Willard, Nancy
    Joyce, David Carney
    Contents: Pleasure It Is (William Randolph Cornish);
    For Saturday (Christopher Smart); Christ Was the
    Word (sometimes attributed to Queen Elizabeth I);
    Hallelujah

W255. **The Sick Rose** (1959; ACA; 2 min.)

    For unaccompanied two-part chorus of women's voices
    Text: poem by William Blake

    The Song of Jephtha's Daughter See: W296

    For soprano and piano or soprano and baritone soli,
    chorus of women's voices and piano

W256. **Take Life** (1978; Ione; 5 min.)

    For four-part chorus of women's voices
    Text: poem by Norma Farber

W257. **Te Deum** (1959, c1959; King; 3 min.)

    For two-part chorus of women's or men's voices, 3
    trumpets and organ
    Text translated by John Dryden
    Commissioned by the Southern New England Unitarian
    Council Junior Choir Festival 1960

Premiere

W257a. 1960 (May 22): Boston, Mass.; Jordan Hall, New England Conservatory of Music; Southern New England
Unitarian Junior Choir; Natalo Paella, Robert
Mogilnicki, and John Rhea, trumpets; Daniel Pinkham, organ; Allen C. Lannom, conductor

Other selected performance

W257b. 1975 (July 25): Columbus, Ohio; Ohio State University; Maurice Casey, conductor

W258.   **Three Lenten Poems of Richard Crashaw**   (1963, c1965;
Ione; 5 min.)

For women's chorus, string quartet (optional double
bass), or string orchestra and handbells (or celesta
or harp) or with keyboard accompaniment and optional
handbells
Also scored for mixed chorus See: W221
Commissioned by Wheelock Alumnae Association Glee
Club for the 75th anniversary of the college
Contents: On the Still Surviving Marks of Our Sa-
vior's Wounds; Upon the Body of Our Blessed Lord,
Naked and Bloody; O Save Us Then
See: BG44

Premiere

W258a. 1964 (April 1): Boston, Mass.; Jordan Hall, New Eng-
land Conservatory of Music; Wheelock College Glee
Club; Leo Collins, conductor
See: B258a

Other selected performances

W258b. 1975 (May 30): Detroit, Mich.; Wayne State University; University Women's Chorale; Daniel Pinkham,
conductor

W258c. 1979 (April 7): Ft. Collins, Colo.; Rocky Mountain
Contemporary Music Festival; Lincoln Community
Center; Colorado State University Women's Chorus;
Joe Jennings, conductor

W259.   **Three Motets**   (1947, rev. 1975, c1979; Peters; 5 min.)

For three-part chorus of women's voices and organ or
piano with optional violoncello, double bass and
bassoon
Text: Bible, Psalm 96:11-13; Psalm 115:1; Psalm 9:

1-4
Dedicated to Leo Preger, Robert Brawley and Robert
Shaw
Contents: Laetentur Coeli (Let the Heavens Rejoice);
Non Nobis Domine (Not to Us, O Lord); Celebrabro Te
Domine (I Will Praise Thee, O Lord)

Selected performance

W259a. 1982 (March 18): Farmville, Va.; Wygal Recital Hall,
    Longwood College; College Concert Choir; Pauline
    Haga, conductor; Catherine Ballard, piano

W260. **Two Poems of Howard Holtzman** (1975, c1979; Ione;
    4 min.)

    For women's chorus and electronic tape
    Contents: I Sought That Land; On Beachy Head

    Premiere

W260a. 1982 (March 18): Farmsville, Va.; Longwood College;
    College Women's Choir; Daniel Pinkham, conductor

W261. **Witching Hour** (1975, c1979; Ione)

    For women's chorus, electric guitar or piano and
    electronic tape
    Text: poem by Norma Farber "Fire, Sleet and Candle-
    light"
    Commissioned by Wayne State University Women's
    Chorale, Douglas K. Belland, conductor

    Premiere

W261a. 1975 (May 30): Detroit, Mich.; Wayne State Univer-
    sity; University Women's Chorale, Daniel Pinkham,
    conductor

MUSIC FOR MEN'S CHORUS

Alleluia See: W239

    For SSA or TTB chorus and piano

The Call of Isaiah See: W150

    For mixed, men's or women's chorus, organ, elec-
    tronic tape and optional timpani and percussion

101

Lauds <u>See</u>: W128

For two-part chorus (SA, TB or ST/AB), 2 horns, oboe, organ and percussion

W262. **Mizma L'Asaph** (1968; Ione; 7 min.)

For men's chorus, flute, horn, guitar, double bass, vibraphone and percussion

<u>Premiere</u>

W262a. 1969 (March 29): Boston, Mass.; Jordan Hall, New England Conservatory of Music; Colgate University Chorus; David Pelton, conductor

Te Deum <u>See</u>: W257

For two-part chorus of women's or men's voices, 3 trumpets and organ

MUSIC FOR SOLO VOICE

W263. **Alleluia** (1984; Ione)

For soprano and piano or string quartet

W264. **Antiphons** (1987; Ione; 7 min. 30 sec.)

For medium voice and guitar or harp or piano
Version for alto flute and guitar added in Aug. 1987
Text: Gregory's <u>Liber</u> <u>Responsalis</u>

<u>Premieres</u>

W264a. 1987 (March 1): Boston, Mass.; Jordan Hall, New England Conservatory of Music; Richard Conrad, tenor; John Curtis, guitar

W264b. 1987 (July 6): Hanover, N. Hamp.; Rollins Chapel, Dartmouth College; Pamela Gore, mezzo soprano; Carol Baum, harp

W265. **Ave Regina Coelorum; Antiphon in Honor of the Blessed Virgin** (1944; c1952; ACA; 2 min.)

For soprano or tenor solo and piano
To be danced and sung

Selected performances

W265a. 1973 (March 2): Notre Dame, Ind.; O'Laughlin Audi-
        torium, St. Mary's College; Alicia Purcell, so-
        prano; Ronald Morebello, piano; Joan Zimmerman,
        dancer

W265b. 1983 (August 31): Boston, Mass.; Church of the Im-
        maculate Conception; Boston Academy of Music;
        Barbara Wallace, soprano

W266. **Beauty** (1946, c1946; ACA; 3 min.)

       For high voice and piano
       Text: poem by Elinor Wylie

W267. **Bridal Morning** (1970; unpublished, registered with
       ACA)

       For soprano and piano
       Anonymous medieval English text

W268. **Charm Me Asleep** (1977, c1978; Ione; 18 min.)

       Earlier title: **Nine Songs on Old English Texts**
       For medium voice and guitar or piano
       Text: poems by Robert Herrick, William Strode, Nich-
       olas Breton, William Shakespeare, Owen Felltman,
       Fulke Greville, Lord Brooke and Sir Walter Raleigh
       Commissioned in memory of Deborah J. Piazza by fac-
       ulty and friends of Eastern Illinois University
       School of Fine Arts
       Dedicated to Linda McIntosh, Mark Pearson, Theodore
       John Schultz, Susan Brodie, Eugene A. Green, Julia
       Sutton, Charles Robert Stephens and Pamela Gore
       Guitar part edited by Robert Paul Sullivan
       Contents: To Music, to Becalm His Fever (Robert Her-
       rick); In Commendation of Music (William Strode);
       Say That I Should Say (Nicholas Breton); Absence
       (William Shakespeare); Chloris in the Snow (William
       Strode); Upon a Rare Voice (Owen Felltman); A Report
       in a Dream Between a Shepherd and His Nymph (Nicho-
       las Breton); Man, Dream No More (Fulke Greville,
       Lord Brooke), The Conclusion (Sir Walter Raleigh)

       Premiere

W268a. 1977 (December 31): Boston, Mass.; King's Chapel;
        Pamela Gore, contralto; Robert Paul Sullivan,

guitar

Other selected performances

W268b. 1979 (February 28): Boston, Mass.; Jordan Hall, New
England Conservatory of Music; Charles Robert
Stephens, baritone; Frank Wallace, guitar
See: B268a

W269. **The Death of the Witch of Endor**   (1981, c1981; Ione;
10 min.)

For contralto, harpsichord and percussion
Text based on Bible, I Samuel 28
Commissioned by John Grimes and Larry Phillips in
memory of Albert D. Hubbard

Premiere

W269a. 1981 (October 13): Boston, Mass.; Jordan Hall, New
England Conservatory of Music; Pamela Gore, contralto; Larry Phillips, harpsichord; John Grimes,
percussion
See: B269b

Other selected performances

W269b. 1981 (December 10): Boston, Mass.; St. Botolph's
Club; Pamela Gore, contralto; John Grimes, percussion; Larry Phillips, harpsichord

W269c. 1986 (September 16): New York, N.Y.: Merkin Concert
Hall; Pamela Gore, contralto; William Hanley, per-
cussion; Daniel Pinkham, harpsichord
See: B269a

W270. **Eight Poems of Gerard Manley Hopkins**   (1964, c1970;
Ione, 15 min.)

For baritone or tenor baritone and viola
Commissioned by Harvard Musical Association
Contents: Jesus to Cast One Thought Upon; Spring;
Heaven-Haven (also published separately See: W276);
Pied Beauty; Strike, Churl; Spring and Fall; Christ-
mas Day; Jesu That Dost in Mary Dwell
See: B270a

Selected performance

W270a. 1978 (May 9): Bemidji, Minn.; Thompson Recital
Hall, Bemidji State University; Joseph Vene, baritone; Abigail Riley, viola

W271. **Elegy** (1949, c1964; Ione; 2 min.)

>   For voice and piano or for unison chorus
>   Text: poem by Robert Hillyer
>   Dedicated to Nell Tangeman
>
>   Selected performances

W271a. 1956 (January 15): Boston, Mass.; Jordan Hall, New England Conservatory of Music; Eleanor Davis, mezzo soprano; Felix Wolfes, piano

W271b. 1973 (March 2): Notre Dame Ind.; O'Laughlin Auditorium, St. Mary's College; Alicia Purcell, soprano; Ronald Morebello, piano

W271c. 1978 (May 9): Bemidji, Minn.; Thompson Recital Hall, Bemidji State University; Linda Spicher, mezzo soprano; Norma Bicek, piano

W272. **The Faucon** (1945, c1949; Row, released to C.Fischer; 3 min.)

>   For high voice and piano or orchestra
>   Old English text
>   Dedicated to Janet Fairbank
>
>   Selected performances

W272a. 1961 (April 14): New York, N. Y.; Donnell Library; Eva Gauthier Song Society; Lois Hartzell, soprano; Millard Altman, piano

W272b. 1962 (May 4): Boulder, Colo.; University of Colorado; Arthur Shoep, tenor; Ramona Kuemmich, piano

W273. **Four Epigrams** (1953; ACA; 3 min.)

>   For high voice and piano
>   Text: poems by Gerard Manley Hopkins

W274. **Hairs of Gods Are Valuable** (1944; ACA; 2 min.)

>   For medium voice and piano
>   Text: poem by Robert Hillyer

W275. **He Standing Hushed** (1985; Ione; 2 min.)

>   For medium voice and piano
>   Text: poem by A. E. Housman
>   Dedicated to Richard Conrad on his 50th birthday

W276.   **Heaven-Haven/World Welter**   (1947 Heaven-Haven; 1975
        World Welter; c1983; Ione, 2 min.)

        For high or medium voice and piano
        Caption title: "Heaven-Haven; A Nun Takes the Veil"
        "World-Welter; A Nun Removes the Veil"
        Text: Gerard Manley Hopkins "Heaven-Haven" and
        Norma Farber "World Welter"
        Dedicated to Nancy Trickey
        See: B276a

        Selected performances

W276a. 1961 (November 16): Brookline, Mass.; Brookline Li-
        brary Music Association Exhibition Hall; Barbara
        Wallace, soprano; Daniel Pinkham, piano (Heaven-
        Haven only)

W276b. 1975 (May 8): Boston, Mass.; Jordan Hall, New Eng-
        land Conservatory of Music; Students in Eleanor
        Steber Seminar

W277.   **The Hour Glass**   (1956, c1964; Ione; 2 min.)

        For high or medium voice and piano
        Text: poem by Ben Jonson
        Dedicated to Eleanor Davis

        Selected performance

W277a. 1961 (November 16): Brookline, Mass.; Brookline Li-
        brary Music Association Exhibition Hall; Barbara
        Wallace, soprano; Daniel Pinkham, piano

        In Youth Is Pleasure   See: W233

        For unison chorus and guitar or piano, or for medium
        voice and piano

W278.   **Intreat Me Not to Leave Thee**   (1961; ACA; 2 min.)

        For two sopranos and strings

W279.   **The Lamb**   (1952, c1970; ACA, released to Ione; 2 min.)

        For unison chorus of treble voices or solo high
        voice and piano or guitar
        Text: poem by William Blake
        Dedicated to Janet Hayes

Selected performances

W279a. 1960 (March 18): New Brunswick, N.J.; Rutgers Uni-
       versity; Linda Stover, soprano

W279b. 1961 (April 14): New York, N. Y.; Donnell Library;
       Eva Gauthier Song Society; Lois Hartzell, soprano;
       Millard Altman, piano

W280. **Letters From Saint Paul** (1965, c1971; Ione; 10 min.)

       For high voice and organ or piano or string orches-
       tra
       Text: Bible, Hebrews 12:1, 2; Romans 8:35-39; Co-
       lossians 3:16; I Thessalonians 5:1-6; Philippians
       4:4-7; Romans 8:8
       Dedicated to Richard Conrad
       Contents: Wherefore Seeing We Are Also Compassed
       About; Who Shall Separate Us From the Love of
       Christ?; Let the Word of Christ Dwell in You Richly;
       But of the Times and the Seasons; Rejoice in the
       Lord Alway; Now It Is High Time to Awake
       See: B280b

Selected performances

W280a. 1965 (November 10): Boston, Mass.; Jordan Hall, New
       England Conservatory of Music

W280b. 1967 (January 13): South Byfield, Mass.; Governor
       Dummer Academy; Barbara Wallace, soprano; Cam-
       bridge Festival Orchestra; Daniel Pinkham, conduc-
       tor

W280c. 1968 (April 13): New York, N. Y.; Town Hall; Mar-
       jorie Madey, soprano; Paul Beri, piano
       See: B280a

W280d. 1980 (February 13): Norman, Okla.: Oklahoma Festival
       of Contemporary Music; Holmberg Hall Auditorium,
       University of Oklahoma; Catiana McKay, soprano;
       Sam Daniel, organ

W281. **A Litany** (1961, c1965; AMP; 2 min.)

       For two sopranos or two-part chorus of women's
       voices and piano or organ
       Text: poem by Phineas Fletcher
       Dedicated to Jean Lunn and Barbara Wallace

Selected performance
W281a. 1964 (December 14): Boston, Mass.; Jordan Hall, New

England Conservatory of Music; Ann Marie Obressa, soprano; James Miller, tenor

W282. **Man That Is Born of a Woman** (1966, c1971; Ione)

For mezzo soprano and guitar
Text: **The Book of Common Prayer**
Dedicated to Miriam Boyer
Guitar part edited by Robert Paul Sullivan
Contents: Man, That is Born of a Woman; In the Midst of Life; Thou Knowest, Lord, the Secrets of Our Hearts

Premiere

W282a. 1966 (February 15): Boston, Mass.; Jordan Hall, New England Conservatory of Music; Miriam Boyer, mezzo soprano; Robert Paul Sullivan, guitar

Manger Scenes See: W252

For two-part women's chorus or solo medium voice and piano

W283. **Music in the Manger** (1981; Ione; 10 min.)

For medium voice and harpsichord or piano
Text: poems by Norma Farber
Commissioned for Rodney Hardesty and Judith Norell
Contents: What's That Music in the Manger?; Mary, Did You Falter?; A Summoning Hosanna!

Selected performance

W283a. 1984 (October 29): Cambridge, Mass.; Sanders Theatre, Harvard University; Pamela Gore, contralto; Gregory Hayes, piano

W284. **Music, Thou Soul of Heaven** (1953, rev. 1977, c1978; ACA, released to Ione; 3 min.)

For high or medium voice and piano
Anonymous text from Christchurch, Oxford, Ms. 87 dated May 6, 1663
Dedicated to Ned Rorem
See: B284a

Premiere

W284a. 1954 (April): New York, N. Y.; CBS Radio Network; Nell Tangeman, mezzo soprano

Other selected performance

W284b. 1982 (March 19): Farmville, Va.; Wygal Recital Hall,
Longwood College; Natalie Thompson, soprano; Sue
Wilkinson, piano

Nine Songs on Old English Texts See: **Charm Me Asleep**
W268

W285. **Nocturne** (1945; ACA; 4 min.)

For high voice and piano
Text: poem by Robert Hillyer

W286. **O Wholesome Night** (1982, rev. 1987; Ione; 4 min.)

For medium voice and guitar; also scored for flute
and guitar
Text: poem by Norma Farber

W287. **A Partridge in a Pear Tree** (1945, c1948; Row, released to C. Fischer; 4 min.)

For high voice and piano
Old English text
Dedicated to Janet Hayes

Selected performances

W287a. 1961 (April 14): New York, N. Y.; Donnell Library;
Eva Gauthier Song Society; Lois Hartzell, soprano;
Millard Altman, piano

W287b. 1961 (November 16): Brookline, Mass.; Brookline Library Music Association Exhibition Hall; Barbara
Wallace, soprano; Daniel Pinkham, piano

W288. **Pastoral XVII from Thirty Pastorals** (1944; unpublished; 2 min.)

For voice and piano
Text: poem by Robert Hillyer
Dedicated to Isabel French

W289. **Psalm 79 (80)** (1946, c1952; ACA; 2 min.)
For tenor and piano
Dedicated to Romolo de Spirito

W290. **Safe in Their Alabaster Chambers** (1972, c1974; Ione;
       7 min.)

>   For medium voice and electronic tape
>   Text: poems by Emily Dickinson
>   Commissioned by Merrimack College for its 25th
>   anniversary
>   Contents: Safe in Their Alabaster Chambers; There's
>   a Certain Slant of Light; These Are The Days When
>   Birds Come Back
>   See: BG21, B290b

>   Premiere

W290a. 1972 (October 29): North Andover, Mass.; Merrimack
        College; Rosalind Elias, contralto

>   Other selected performances

W290b. 1973 (September 23): Boston, Mass.; Isabella Stew-
        art Gardner Museum; Pamela Gore, contralto

W290c. 1979 (April 7): Ft. Collins, Colo.; Rocky Mountain
        Contemporary Music Festival; Lincoln Community
        Center Auditorium; John Lueck, baritone
        See: B290a

W291. **The Sea Ritual** (1955; ACA; 3 min.)

>   For low voice and piano
>   Text: poem by George Darley
>   Dedicated to Donald Gramm

Set Me As a Seal See: "Wedding Song" W303

W292. **Seven Epigrams** (1944; unpublished; 10 min.)

>   For medium voice and piano
>   Text: poems by Robert Hillyer
>   Dedicated to Isabel French

W293. **Shout for Joy** (1956; ACA; 3 min.)

>   For mixed voices and instruments

W294. **Sing Agreeably of Love** (1948, c1949; Row, released
        to C. Fischer; 2 min.)

>   For medium voice and piano or string quartet

Also part of **Three Lyric Scenes** W299
Text: poem by W. H. Auden

Selected performances

W294a. 1960 (May 24): Wellesley, Mass.; Pine Manor Junior
College; Mary Ann Harris, soprano; Bryan Sturm,
piano

W294b. 1961 (December 4): New York, N. Y.; Town Hall;
Eunice Albert, contralto

W294c. 1962 (May 4): Boulder, Colo.; University of Colorado; Arthur Schoep, tenor; Ramona Kuemmich,
piano

W295. **Slow, Slow Fresh Fount** (1949, c1961; Peters; 2 min.)

For high, medium or low voice and piano
Text: poem by Ben Jonson
Dedicated to Verna Osborne
See: B295a, D295a

W296. **The Song of Jephtha's Daughter** (1963, c1966;
Peters; 13 min.)

For soprano and piano or soprano and baritone soli,
chorus of women's voices and piano
Text: poems by Robert Hillyer
Dedicated to Alice Esty
Contents: Twilight Among the Vineyards; My Father
Came As a Stranger; What Was My Sin?; With Timbrels
and Dancing; Alas, My Daughter; Time Is a Long
Valley; I Turned to My Father; The Tidings of My
Fate; Forever Year By Year
See: B296a

Premiere

W296a. 1965 (April 23): New York, N. Y.; Carnegie Recital
Hall; Alice Esty, soprano

Other selected performances

W296b. 1966 (July 17): Boston, Mass.; Isabella Stewart
Gardner Museum; Barbara Wallace, soprano; Daniel
Pinkham, piano

W296c. 1973 (April 6): Houghton, N. Y.; Houghton College;
Nazareth College Chamber Choir; Daniel Pinkham,
conductor

W296d. 1985 (March 9): Cleveland, Ohio; Cleveland State

University; Elizabeth Unis, soprano; Diane Marazzi, piano

W297. **Songs of Innocence** (1947; ACA, withdrawn except "The Lamb")

For soprano, flute and piano
Text: poems by William Blake
Dedicated to Lois Schaefer, Ned Rorem, Janet Hayes, Nancy Trickey
Contents: Prelude; Infant Joy; The Lamb (also published separately See: W279); Piping Down the Valleys Wild

Selected performance

W297a. 1964 (December 9): Chicago, Ill.; Chicago Chamber Music Society; Eileen Deneen, soprano; Joane Bennett, flute; William Browning, piano

W298. **Stars, I Have Seen Them Fall** (1973, c1983; Ione; 2 min.)

For medium voice and piano
Text: poem by A. E. Housman
Dedicated to Zelda Goodman

W299. **Three Lyric Scenes** (1948; Row; 10 min.)

For voice and string quartet
Text: poems by W. H. Auden
Contents: Look, Stranger, On This Island Now; Let The Florid Music Praise; Sing Agreeably of Love (also published separately See: W294)

W300. **Three Songs from Ecclesiastes** (1960, c1963; ACA, assigned to Ione; 7 min.)

For high, medium or low voice and piano or string quartet or string orchestra
Text: Bible, Ecclesiastes 1, 3, 9
Commissioned by Phyllis Curtin
Contents: Vanity of Vanities; Go Thy Way, Eat Thy Bread With Joy; To Everything There is a Season

Selected performances

W300a. 1962 (August 7): Ventnor, N. J.; Beth Judah Auditorium; Phyllis Curtin, soprano

W300b. 1962 (November 1): Philadelphia, Pa.; Philadelphia

Art Alliance; Jean Lunn, soprano; Lawrence Smith,
piano

W300c. 1963 (April 17): Poughkeepsie, N. Y.; Vassar College; Hope Handloff, soprano

W300d. 1979 (April 7): Ft. Collins, Colo.; Rocky Mountain
Contemporary Music Festival; Lincoln Community
Center; Kathleen Harris, soprano; Colorado State
University Chamber Orchestra; Dave Harman, conduc-
tor

W300e. 1986 (July 29): Nantucket, Mass.; First Congrega-
tional Church; Vernon Hartman, baritone; Ted
Taylor, piano
See: B300a

W301. **Transitions** (1979, c1980; Ione; 14 min.)

For medium voice and piano or bassoon
Text: poems by Howard Holtzman
Commissioned by Pamela Gore and Linda Smith
Contents: Grey; I Like the Light Diffused; Lullaby
for a Shrouded Figure; Home Movies; Aubade; Near
This Stone; So, One by One
See: B301b

Premiere

W301a. 1979 (September 30): New York, N. Y.; Carnegie Recital Hall; Pamela Gore, contralto; Linda Smith,
bassoon
See: B301a

Other selected performance

W301b. 1981 (October 13): Boston, Mass.; New England Conservatory of Music; Pamela Gore, contralto; Gary
Wedow, piano

W302. **Two Motets** (1960, c1971; ACA, released to Ione; 5
min.)

For soprano or tenor, flute and guitar or harpsi-
chord
Text: Bible, John 14:19, 28; Latin hymn attributed
to St. Ambrose, translated by John Mason Neale
Dedicated to Jean Lunn and Julio Prol
Contents: Non Vos Relinquam Orphanos (I Will Not
Leave You Comfortless); Te Lucis Ante Terminum
(Before the Ending of the Day or Evening Hymn)

Premieres

W302a. 1959 (June 15): New York, N.Y.; Carnegie Recital
Hall; Connie McNeil, soprano; Julio Prol, guitar;
Ralph Freundlich, flute (Te Lucis Ante Terminum)

W302b. 1960 (April 24): Cambridge, Mass.; Radcliffe Graduate Center; Jean Lunn, soprano; Howard Brown,
flute; Edward Low, harpsichord

W303. "Wedding Song: Set Me As a Seal" from **Wedding Cantata** W138 (1956, c1975; Peters; 2 min.)

For high or medium voice and organ

W304. **Wellesley Hills Psalm Book** (1983, c1984; Ione; 20
min.)

For medium voice or unison choir and organ
Text: Bible, 16th and 17th century paraphrases of
Psalms 136, 6, 25, 23, 149, 121, 68, 130, 148
Commissioned by Wellesley Hills Congregational
Church for the inauguration of an organ built by
Fritz Noack
Contents: O Praise the Lord Benign; O Lord Rebuke
Me Not; His Mercy is Full, Sweet; The Lord My Shep-
herd Is; Let All his Saints Rejoice; Up to Those
Bright and Gladsome Hills; Let God Arise; Out of the
Deep; Call to Remembrance; The Lord of Heaven Con-
fess
See: B304b

Premiere

W304a. 1984 (April 22); Wellesley, Mass.; Wellesley Hills
Congregational Church; S. Mark Aliapoulios, baritone; James David Christie, organ

Other selected performance

W304b. 1984 (July 22): Nantucket, Mass.; Old North Church;
Howard Chadwick, bass; Andrew Paul Holman, organ
See: B304a

W305. **Winter Nights** (1986; Ione; 18 min.)

For mezzo soprano or contralto, oboe and harp
Text: poems by Thomas Campion
Contents: Your Fair Looks; Oft Have I Sighed;
Though You Are Young; It Fell on a Summer's Day;
Follow Follow; My Love Hath Vowed; Fain Would I Wed;
Now Winter Nights Enlarge

Premiere

W305a. 1986 (September 16): New York, N.Y.; Merkin Hall;
      Pamela Gore, contralto
      See: B305a

MUSIC FOR FILM AND TELEVISION

W306. **International Geophysical Year** (1957; unpublished,
      registered with ACA; 36 min.)

      For 2 horns, celesta, harpsichord and string orches-
      tra
      Music for Film series

W307. **Invention No. 1** (1959; ACA; 2 min.)

      For English horn, bass clarinet and string orchestra
      Film score
      Orchestral arrangement of part of **Partita** W107

W308. **Invention No. 2** (1959; ACA; 2 min.)

      For English horn, bass clarinet and string orchestra
      Film score
      Orchestral arrangement of part of **Partita** W107

W309. **Land of White Alice** (1959; unpublished, registered
      with ACA; 17 min.)

      For contralto, TTBB chorus and orchestra (flute,
      oboe, 2 horns, strings and harpsichord)
      Film score with book and lyrics by Norman Rosten
      Commissioned by General Electric

W310. **Layman's Guide to Modern Art** (1958?; unpublished)

      For harpsichord
      Score for unreleased film
      Subsequently published as **Partita** W107

W311. **MIT Science Reporter** (1961; unpublished, registered
      with ACA; 1 min. 30 sec.)

      For celesta and harpsichord
      Music for television film

W312. **Planet Earth** (1961; unpublished, available from
        McGraw Hill Book Co.)

        Music for a series of 13 half-hour films

W313. **Reaching for the Moon** (1960; unpublished, registered
        with ACA; 16 min.)

        For orchestra 2(pic)-1(Ehn)-1-1, 2-0-2-1, timpani,
        piano, celesta, harpsichord, strings and percussion
        CBS Television film originally titled Man and the
        Moon, hosted by Walter Cronkite

W314. **Structures** (1963; unpublished, registered with ACA;
        15 min. 30 sec.)

        For timpani, percussion (11), celesta and piano
        Film score for documentaries on the work of R. Buck-
        minster Fuller

MISCELLANEOUS

W315. **Aspects of the Apocalypse** (1972, c1972; Ione; 7 min.)

        For electronic tape

        Selected performances

  W315a. 1973 (April 6): Houghton, N. Y.; Houghton College

  W315b. 1982 (October 24): St. Louis, Mo.; Webster College
         See: B315a

W316. **Dithyramb** (1946; ACA; 2 min. 30 sec.)

        For carillon

W317. **Little Bell Book** (1979; unpublished, registered with
        Ione; 6 min.)

        For carillion

W318. **Song for the Bells** (1961, c1962; Peters; 3 min.)

        For carillon or handbells
        Dedicated to Laurence Apgar

Discography

The Discography includes all commercially released records, regardless of current availability. "D" numbers correspond to "W" numbers in the **Works and Performances** section of this volume.

D3. **Garden of Artemis**

  D3a.   Cambridge Festival Recording XTV 14448

D9. **Concertante No. 1**

  D9a.   CRI 143 and SD-143. Originally released as MGM E3245
         (1950)
         Robert Brink, violin; Claude Jean Chiasson, harp-
         sichord; Edward Low, celesta; MGM String Ensemble;
         Izler Solomon, conductor
         Program notes by Carl Sigmon on container
         Also includes works by W. Flanagan, A. Berger and
         I. Heilner
         See: B9a, B9b, B9f, B9g, B9i

D19. **Signs of the Zodiac**

  D19a.   Louisville LS 673 and LOU 673. 1967
         Louisville Symphony Orchestra; David McCord,
         narrator; Robert Whitney, conductor
         Louisville Orchestra First Editions Records
         Program notes by Dudley Fitts on container
         Also contains a work by R. Rohe
         See: B19c, B19d, B19e, B19f

D21. **Symphony No. 2**

D21a. Louisville LOU 652. 1965
Louisville Symphony Orchestra; Robert Whitney,
conductor
Louisville Orchestra First Editions Records
Also includes a work by L. R. Finney
See: B21a, B21b, B21c, B21d

D29. **Cantilena and Capriccio**

D29a. CRI 109 and SD 109. 1956?
Daniel Pinkham, harpsichord; Robert Brink, violin
Notes by Lester Trimble on container
Also includes his **Concerto for Celesta and Harpsi-
chord**, and works by H. Cowell and A. Hovhaness
See: B29a

D61. **Diversions**

D61a. Northeastern NR 205. 1983
James David Christie, organ; Carol Baum, harp
Album title: Sounds of New England
Program notes in part by the composer on container
Recorded at Cochran Chapel, Phillips Academy, Ando-
ver, Mass. in October 1981
Also includes his **Miracles** and **Proverbs**

D62. **For Evening Draws On**

D62a. Golden Crest NEC 114. 1975
Larry Phillips, organ; Kenneth Roth, English horn
New England Conservatory Recording Series
Also includes his **Liturgies** and **Toccatas for the
Vault of Heaven** and a work by D. Martino

D65. **Liturgies**

D65a. Golden Crest NEC 114. 1975
Larry Phillips, organ; John Grimes, timpani
New England Conservatory Recording Series
Also includes his **For Evening Draws On** and **Toccatas
for the Vault of Heaven** and a work by D. Martino

D66. **Miracles**

D66a. Northeastern NR 205. 1983
James David Christie, organ; Doriot Anthony Dwyer,
flute
Album title: Sounds of New England
Program notes in part by the composer on container
Recorded at Cochran Chapel, Phillips Academy,

Recorded at Cochran Chapel, Phillips Academy,
Andover, Mass. in October 1980
Also includes his **Diversions** and **Proverbs**

D68. **Nebulae**

  D68a. Golden Crest CBDNA-77-3. 1977
National Conference of College Band Directors
Recorded at the University Methodist Church, College
Park, Md. on March 10, 1977

D69. **The Other Voices of the Trumpet**

  D69a. Crystal S365. 1982
Bryon Pearson, trumpet; Arthur Vidrich, organ
Album title: <u>The Voice of Trumpet and Organ</u>
Notes by Arthur Vidrich on container
Recorded at First Baptist Church of Detroit
Also includes works by T. Torelli, A. Hovhaness,
H. L. Schilling, L. Nuckolls and J. Langlais
<u>See</u>: B69a, B69c

D80. **Toccatas for the Vault of Heaven**

  D80a. Golden Crest NEC 114. 1975
Larry Phillips, organ
New England Conservatory Recording Series
Also includes his **For Evening Draws On** and **Liturgies**
and a work by D. Martino

D86. **Epiphanies**

  D86a. Gothic 18313. 1983
Joan Lippincott, organ
Recorded on Fisk organ, House of Hope Presbyterian
Church, St. Paul, Minn.
Also includes his **Man's Days Are Like the Grass** and
Revelations

D87. **Five Voluntaries for Organ Manuals**

  D87a. Ethos ES 1002. 1973
Robert Thompson, organ
Album title: <u>Robert Thompson at the Positiv Organ</u>
Recorded at the Chapel of the School of Good
Counsel in Mankato, Minn. in August 1973
Voluntaries included: "Quiet and Cheerful", Wistful"
and "Nimble

Discography

D90.   **Man's Days Are Like the Grass**

  D90a. Gothic 18313. 1983
         Joan Lippincott, organ
         Recorded on Fisk organ, House of Hope Presbyterian
         Church, St. Paul, Minn.
         Also includes his **Epiphanies** and **Revelations**

D91.   **Pastoral on a Morning Star**

  D91a. R-A Recording CO 1023. 1962
         Daniel Pinkham, organ
         Album title: Organ Historical Society, 7th National
         Convention
         Recorded at St. Mary's Roman Catholic Church,
         Auburn, N. Y. on July 9, 1962

D96.   **Proverbs**

  D96a. Northeastern NR 205. 1983
         James David Christie, organ
         Album title: Sounds of New England
         Program notes in part by composer on container
         Recorded at Cochran Chapel, Phillips Academy, Ando-
         ver, Mass. in October 1981
         Also includes his **Diversions** and **Miracles**

D97.   **Revelations**

  D97a. Gothic 18313. 1983
         Joan Lippincott, organ
         Recorded on Fisk organ, House of Hope Presbyterian
         Church, St. Paul, Minn.
         Also includes his **Epiphanies** and **Man's Days Are
         Like the Grass**

  D97b. Wealden WS 142
         Jack Hindmarsh, organ
         Recorded on Haileyburg College organ
         "Litany" and "Toccata" only
         Also includes works by Arne, Bach, Johnson, Jongen,
         Langlais, Salome, Vierne and Whitlock

D100. **Concerto for Celesta and Harpsichord**

  D100a. CRI 109 and SD109. 1956?
         Daniel Pinkham, harpsichord; Edward Low, celesta
         Program notes by Lester Trimble on container
         Also includes his **Cantilena and Capriccio** and works
         by H. Cowell and A. Hovhaness
         See: B100a, B100b, B100d, B100f

D107. **Partita**

D107a. Cambridge CRS 412 and CRM 412. 1962
Daniel Pinkham, harpsichord
Album title: Works by Organists of King's Chapel
Also includes works by W. Selby and V. Thomson
See: B107a, B107b

D114. **Christmas Cantata; Sinfonia Sacra**

D114a. Angel S-36016. 1967
Roger Wagner Chorale; Roger Wagner, conductor
Album title: A Christmas Festival
See: B114a, B114b, B114e, B114g

D114b. Augsburg 23-1961. 1982
Dale Warland Singers; Ronald Hasselman and Merrimon
Hipps, Jr., trumpets; Ronald Ricketts and Steven
Zellmer, trombones; John Ferguson, organ; Dale War-
land, conductor
Album title: Sing Noel, Christmas Music of Daniel
Pinkham
Also includes his **Christmas Eve, Company at the
Creche, Evergreen, Fanfares, The Kings and the
Shepherds, Magnificat,** and **To Think of Those Absent**
See: BG 14, B114l

D114c. Delta DRS 69 676
St. Charles High School Choir
Album title: Cantique de Noel

D114d. Northeastern NR 103. 1980
Northeastern Choral Society; Joshua Jacobson, con-
ductor
Album title:The Road Not Taken; Twentieth Century
American Choral Music
Recorded in Jordan Hall, New England Conservatory of
Music in May 1980

D114e. Northeastern NR 229. 1985
John Oliver Chorale; John Oliver, conductor
Album title: Christmas Antiphonies
Recorded at Houghton Memorial Chapel, Wellesley,
Mass. in January 1985
Also includes works by H. Schutz, M. Praetorius,
A. Bax and S. Scheidt

D121. **Fanfares**

D121a. Augsburg 23-1961. 1982

Dale Warland Singers; William Rollie, tenor; Dale
Warland, conductor
Album title: Sing Noel, Christmas Music of Daniel
Pinkham
Also includes his **Christmas Cantata, Christmas Eve,
Company at the Creche, Evergreen, The Kings and the
Shepherds, Magnificat,** and **To Think of Those Absent**

D129. **Magnificat**

D129a. Augsburg 23-1961. 1982
Dale Warland Singers; Linda Steen, soprano; Rhadames
Angelucci and Richard Killmer, oboes; Carol Smith
and Charles Ullery, bassoons; Kathy Kienzle, harp;
Dale Warland, conductor
Album title: Sing Noel, Christmas Music of Daniel
Pinkham
Also includes his **Christmas Cantata, Christmas Eve,
Company at the Creche, Evergreen, Fanfares, The
Kings and the Shepherds,** and **To Think of Those Absent**

D154. **Christmas Eve**

D154a. Augsburg 23-1961. 1982
Dale Warland Singers; Dale Warland, conductor
Album title: Sing Noel, Christmas Music of Daniel
Pinkham
Also includes his **Christmas Cantata, Company at
the Creche, Evergreen, Fanfares, The Kings and the
Shepherds, Magnificat,** and **To Think of Those Absent**

D155. **Come, Love We God**

D155a. Marquis ERA 107. 1970
Vancouver Chamber Choir; John Washburn, conductor
Album title: Sweet Was the Song
Also includes works by D. Gurney and K. Korte

D160. **Elegy**

D160a. CRI 102. 1956
Randolph Singers; David Randolph, conductor
Album title: Lament for April 15 and Other Modern
Madrigals
Also includes his [**Madrigal:**] **Piping Anne and Husky
Paul** and works by A. Claflin, C. Mills, H. Stevens,
U. S. Kay, K. List, J. M. Dvorkin, E. T. Canby and C.
Harman

D168. **Glory Be To God; Motet for Christmas Day**

D168a. CRI 191. 1964
Mid-America Chorale; John Dexter, conductor
Album title: <u>Sing Unto the Lord a New Song, Choral
Music for Today's Worship</u>
Program notes by David Hall on container
Also includes works by A. Stout, H. Stevens, N.
Lockwood, G. Brinkerd, R. Woolen, E. Kohs, J. Av-
shalamov
<u>See</u>: B168a

D173. **Henry Was a Worthy King**

D173a. Orion ORS 75205. 1975?
The King Chorale; Gordon King, conductor
Album title: <u>American Songs for a Capella Choir</u>
Recorded at All Saints Episcopal Church, Ft. Worth,
Texas
Also includes his **The Leaf** and **Piping Anne and
Husky Paul** and works by S. Barber, M. Hennagin, N.
Rorem, H. Stevens, R. Thompson, J. Berger, P. Mennin,
V. Persichetti, S. Adler and J. Chorbajin

D181. **The Kings and the Shepherds**

D181a. Augsburg 23-1961. 1982
Dale Warland Singers; Dale Warland, conductor
Album title: <u>Sing Noel, Christmas Music of Daniel
Pinkham</u>
Also includes his **Christmas Cantata, Christmas Eve,
Company at the Creche, Evergreen, Fanfares, Magni-
ficat**, and **To Think of Those Absent**
<u>See</u>: B181a

D183. **The Leaf**

D183a. Orion ORS 75205. 1975?
The King Chorale; Gordon King, conductor
Album title: <u>American Songs for a Capella Choir</u>
Recorded at All Saints Episcopal Church, Fort
Worth, Texas
Also includes his **Henry Was a Worthy King**, and **Piping
Anne and Husky Paul** and works by S. Barber, M. Hen-
nagin, N. Rorem, H. Stevens, R. Thompson, J. Berger,
P. Mennin, V. Persichetti, S. Adler and J. Chorbajin

D187. **Love Can Be Still**

D187a. Northeastern NR 201. 1981
Patti Dell and Barbara Wallace, sopranos; Pamela
Gore, contralto; Richard Conrad, tenor; Bryan

McNeil, baritone; Gary Wedow, piano
Album title: <u>Love</u> <u>Can</u> <u>Be</u> <u>Still</u>, <u>Verses</u> <u>by</u> <u>Norma</u>
<u>Farber</u>
Program notes by the composer on container
Recorded at the Church of Our Saviour, Brookline,
Mass. on Nov. 7 and 8, 1980
Also includes his **Company at the Creche** and **Time
of Times**
<u>See</u>: BG8, B187a

D203.   **[Madrigal] Piping Anne and Husky Paul**

D203a. CRI 102. 1956?
Randolph Singers; David Randolph, conductor
Album title: <u>Lament</u> <u>for</u> <u>April</u> <u>15</u> <u>and</u> <u>Other</u> <u>Modern</u>
<u>Madrigals</u>
Also includes his **Elegy** and works by A. Claflin,
C. Mills, H. Stevens, U. S. Kay, K. List, J. M.
Dvorkin, E. T. Canby and C. Harman

D203b. Orion ORS 75205. 1975?
The King Chorale; Gordon King, conductor
Album title: <u>American</u> <u>Songs</u> <u>for</u> <u>a</u> <u>Capella</u> <u>Choir</u>
Recorded at All Saints Episcopal Church, Ft. Worth
Texas
Also includes his **Henry Was a Worthy King** and **The
Leaf**, and works by S. Barber, M. Hennagin, N. Rorem,
H. Stevens, R. Thompson, J. Berger, P. Mennin, V.
Persichetti, S. Adler and John Chorbajin

D223.   **Time of Times**

D223a. Northeastern NR 201. 1981
Patti Dell and Barbara Wallace, sopranos; Pamela
Gore, contralto, Richard Conrad, tenor; John McNeil,
baritone; Gary Wedow, piano
Album title: <u>Love</u> <u>Can</u> <u>Be</u> <u>Still</u>, <u>Verses</u> <u>by</u> <u>Norma</u>
<u>Farber</u>
Program notes by the composer on container
Recorded at the Church of Our Saviour, Brookline,
Mass. on November 7 and 8, 1980
Also includes his **Company at the Creche** and **Love
Can Be Still**
<u>See</u>: BG8

D224.   **To Think of Those Absent**

D224a. Augsburg 23-1961. 1982
Dale Warland Singers; Jeffrey Van, guitar; Dale War-
land, conductor
Album title: <u>Sing</u> <u>Noel</u>, <u>Christmas</u> <u>Music</u> <u>of</u> <u>Daniel</u>
<u>Pinkham</u>
Also includes his **Christmas Cantata, Christmas Eve,**

Company at the Creche, Evergreen, Fanfares, The
Kings and the Shepherds, and Magnificat

D230.   **Evergreen**

D230a. Augsburg 23-1961. 1982
Dale Warland Singers; John Ferguson, organ; Kathy
Kienzle, harp; Jay Johnson, handbells; Dale Warland,
conductor
Album title: <u>Sing Noel, Christmas Music of Daniel
Pinkham</u>
Also includes his **Christmas Cantata, Christmas Eve,
Company at the Creche, Fanfares, The Kings and the
Shepherds, Magnificat,** and **To Think of Those Absent**
<u>See</u>: B230a

D245.   **Company at the Creche**

D245a. Augsburg Records 23-1961. 1982
Dale Warland Singers; Kathy Kienzle, harp; Jay John-
son, handbells; Dale Warland, conductor
Album title: <u>Sing Noel, Christmas Music of Daniel
Pinkham</u>
Program notes by the composer on container
Also includes his **Christmas Cantata, Christmas Eve,
Evergreen, Fanfares, The Kings and the Shepherds,
Magnificat,** and **To Think of Those Absent**

D245b. Northeastern NR 201. 1981
Patti Dell and Barbara Wallace, sopranos; Pamela
Gore, contralto; Bryan McNeil, baritone; Robert W.
Cross, glockenspiel
Album title: <u>Love Can Be Still, Verses by Norma
Farber</u>
Recorded at the Church of Our Saviour, Brookline,
Mass. on November 7 and 8, 1980
Also includes his **Love Can Be Still** and **Time of
Times**
<u>See</u>: BG8, B245b

D295.   **Slow, Slow Sweet Fount**

D295a. Desto D411-412 and DS 6411-6412. 1968
John McCollum, tenor
Album title: <u>Songs of American Composers</u>
Also includes many other songs by various composers

Bibliography

The Bibliography provides a view of how Daniel Pinkham's music has been received while also giving access to a general body of contemporary opinion and scholarship concerned with the composer. Most annotations take the form of quotations from the sources cited. Where lengthier passages are quoted, it was felt that this was the best way to illuminate the often differing perspectives of various writers and critics.

In the two sections ("BG" denoting general references and "B" specific works), "see" references are guides to the individual works and particular performances described in the **Works and Performances** section of this volume.

GENERAL REFERENCES

BG1. Avery, Scott A. The Choral Music of Daniel Pinkham. M.M. thesis, Ball State University, 1985.
    Brief observations on Pinkham's compositional style based on his **Wedding Cantata** and other choral works (1958-1963). The study was prepared in connection with an all-Pinkham choral recital conducted by the author at Ball State University, November 5, 1984.

BG2. Blackwell, Patrick. "Hit of the Week: Organ Album." Boston Globe, March 24, 1983.
    "Pinkham's music always sounds. He writes with particular discretion and imagination for the combination of music's potentially loudest instrument with other, frailer vessels." [Review of disc NR 205]

BG3. Chien, George. "The Spirit of Christmas Past." Fanfares 6:67 (January/February 1983)
    "The style is accessible, which is to say harmonically spicy but not overly dissonant, and demonstrates the composer's considerable rhythmic inventiveness." [Review of

disc Augsburg 23-1964]

BG4. Chipman, Abram. "Classical." <u>High</u> <u>Fidelity</u> 26:85 (June 1976)
"The overside three pieces by Daniel Pinkham, written between 1972 and 1974, lean heavily on aleatoric and electronic effects. Except for the 1973 setting of **For Evening Draws On**, where the lovely English-horn soliloquy is impressively spectral in the context of all that tape background, it is rather arid stuff." [Review of disc NEC 114]

BG5. Christiansen, Larry A. "The Choral Music of Daniel Pinkham." <u>Choral</u> <u>Journal</u> 9:18 (September-October 1968)
Brief but apposite remarks on Pinkham's choral style without reference to individual works.

BG6. Corzine, Michael Loyd. <u>The</u> <u>Organ</u> <u>Works</u> <u>of</u> <u>Daniel</u> <u>Pinkham</u>. D.M.A. dissertation, Eastman School of Music, 1979.
Precise analysis from the performer's point of view of thirty Pinkham works for organ solo and in various combinations. The study was prepared in close contact with the composer, who is quoted frequently. Corzine reviews the Pinkham <u>oeuvre</u> for its pedagogical values. An appendix provides complete stoplists for four organs closely connected with Pinkham the organist, viz. the Busch-Reisinger Museum in Cambridge, King's Chapel in Boston, the Riverside Church in New York City, and the Memorial Church at Harvard.

BG7. Cox, Dennis Keith. <u>Aspects</u> <u>of</u> <u>the</u> <u>Compositional</u> <u>Styles</u> <u>of</u> <u>Three</u> <u>Selected</u> <u>Twentieth-Century</u> <u>American</u> <u>Composers</u> <u>of</u> <u>Choral</u> <u>Music:</u> <u>Alan</u> <u>Hovhaness,</u> <u>Ron</u> <u>Nelson,</u> <u>and</u> <u>Daniel</u> <u>Pinkham</u>. D.M.A. dissertation, University of Missouri, Kansas City, 1978.
Stylistic analysis of Pinkham's choral music, with particular reference to his **Passion of Judas** (1976). Pinkham's brand of eclecticism is seen as deriving from his mastery of the musical forms and conventions of the past.

BG8. Crumb, Rupert. "Pinkham: **Time of Times, Company at the Creche,** and **Love Can Be Still.**" <u>New</u> <u>Records</u> v.52 (April 1983)
"The works are interesting for their unusual but appealing harmonies and for the harmonic tension that Pinkham creates by weaving the music into and out of dissonance." [Review of disc NR201]

BG9. Daniel, Oliver. "The New Festival." <u>American</u> <u>Composers</u> <u>Alliance</u> <u>Bulletin</u> 5:20 (#1,1955)
"There is something bright and shining about 'Danny' Pinkham; and while he may never be a formidable personality in the world of music, he should become one of the most pleasant, agreeable, entirely enjoyed composers of the lot. Don't misunderstand--he is not a 'small-time' composer. He is a real natural talent. He is positively top-notch!"

BG10. Driver, Paul. "Somewhere, Someone's Playing His Music." Boston Globe, October 26, 1983.
"Simplicity and complexity combine in Pinkham to produce a spare-textured music with directness of appeal. His style is one in which rigorous argument supports a bright fanfare-like surface that, in the organ pieces at least, may have a decorative quality resembling Messiaen's writing for the instrument."

BG11. Durgin, Cyrus. "Music by Pinkham at Jordan Hall." Boston Globe, May 9, 1958.
"Everything on the list was in admirable taste; all had been created with care for no more notes than were necessary to convey the composer's thought; in the case of the songs, the words had been treated with as much concern as the musical setting. But, save for the Concertante No. 2 for violin and strings, which Mr. Pinkham conducted, all was singularly 'head' rather than 'heart' music. All was tidy, and all save this was singularly bloodless."

BG12. Dyer, Richard. "Cecilia Joyful Holiday Package." Boston Globe, December 16, 1976.
"Two of his works, the Christmas Cantata from 1957 and Fanfares from 1974, which adapt the techniques of Renaissance works to a more modern harmonic and rhythmic language in order to say something new about things that are timeless."

BG13. Dyer, Richard. "Concert Spans 29 Years of Daniel Pinkham's Works." Boston Globe, October 31, 1984.
"These instrumental pieces show Pinkham's sureness of craftsmanship, his delight in quality and variety of sound, his consideration for performers and for audience--no Pinkham piece is too long for what it sets out to accomplish."

BG14. Dyer, Richard. "Dale Warland Singers Sing Noel: Christmas Music of Daniel Pinkham." Boston Globe, December 9, 1982.
"Throughout this record one hears again, gratefully, all those qualities one associates with Pinkham's music--the exactness of prosody, the finesse of instrumental ear, the fitness of music for performers, and they sound like so much fun to sing that anyone who has ever sung in a chorus will want to chime into these pieces. And one hears the spirit of Christmas." [Review of disc Augsburg 23-1961]

BG15. Dyer, Richard. "A Natural Musical Resource." Boston Globe, October 4, 1981.
Review of the composer's career, quoting Pinkham extensively on non-technical matters. Dyer is a music critic with the Globe who frequently reviews concerts of Pinkham's music.

BG16. Dyer, Richard. "Pinkham Conducts Own Works." Boston Globe, September 2, 1983.
"Pinkham's style has altered with the passing years,

but the sound, seasoned sweetness of the voice remains unchanged. The earliest works and the latest profit from his studies of medieval and renaissance music, from his discriminating taste in texts, from the exactness of his prosody (among living composers probably only Ned Rorem knows as much about how words move and sound), and from the elegance of his part-writing and unexpected twists of harmony. In more recent years he has spiced the line with dissonance and experimented with electronics (the tape whooshes impressively through the latter half of a piece called **The Other Voices of the Trumpet**), but all of it sounds wonderfully like itself."

BG17. Finn, Robert. "Church Concert Is All Pinkham." Cleveland Plain Dealer, September 24, 1979.

"Even by the very conservative standards that apply in most church choir and organ lofts, there is nothing avant-garde about Daniel Pinkham. He writes in a sturdily tonal, honorably conservative idiom in which expressivity, especially if texts are involved, is paramount. He uses dissonance for pungency and is never afraid to indulge in a good old-fashioned major triad. His music, if it seldom surprises the ear, never offends it either."

BG18. Finn, Robert. "Music Smorgasbord Is Tribute to Composer." Cleveland Plain Dealer, March 11, 1985.

"This is all effective and easily listenable music that serves its texts honorably and would certainly not offend even the most conservatively oriented ears. It has strong melodic profile, it is expressive and it never, never overstays its welcome."

BG19. Fiske, Judy Mayberry. An Analysis of the Solo Organ Works of Daniel Pinkham. M.C.M. thesis, Southern Baptist Theological Seminary, 1979.

Analysis of six pre-1978 works for solo organ: **Five Voluntaries for Organ Manuals** (1965), **Four Short Pieces for Organ Manuals** (1962), **Pastorale on the Morning Star** (1962), **A Prophecy for Organ** (1968), **Revelations** (1956), and **Suite for Organ** (1957).

BG20. Flanagan, William. "Society for Contemporary Music in Varied Program." New York Herald Tribune, March 31, 1960.

"Mr. Pinkham's compositions--as ever--were striking for their sophisticated lack of pretense, their preciseness of expressive intention, and their canny workmanship. And Mr. Pinkham has a live ear for instrumental color that is unusual in a day when such preoccupations are held in low estate, one that transcends, moreover, the relative novelty of the instruments for which he composes."

BG21. Giffin, Glenn. "Rocky Mountain Contemporary Music Festival." High Fidelity/Musical America 29:MA27 (September 1979)

"The all-Pinkham concert revealed a composer of conservative leaning who is willing to experiment and to adapt current practice to his own purposes. Much of his choral music is traditional and straight-forward. This quality marks his electronic accompaniments, as well--the sound, even though manufactured, tending to be a support rather than a competitor with the singing. Still, his **Safe in Their Alabaster Chambers** for solo baritone and tape proved enormously effective."

BG22. Haller, William P. "A Look at Some Recent Organ Works." Clavier 13:33 (January 1974)
   "The music of Daniel Pinkham has represented a needed change in style for American organ music since the publication of his music began in the 60s . . . . While some of the works reveal more individuality than others, all are extremely well written for the organ. His newest experiments show great promise for the future. Pinkham has the ability to succeed at writing short compositions, grasping the mood and intent of a musical statement in a very few bars."

BG23. Henderson, Charles. "Daniel Pinkham." Music: the AGO and RCCO Magazine 8:20-23 (December 1974)
   A general discussion of Pinkham's teaching and the influences on his music. Henderson elicits cogent statements from the composer about his artistic goals. The interview provides a useful background for some of the more technical studies of his work.

BG24. Johnson, Marlowe W. "A Choral Composer for Our Time: Daniel Pinkham." Music: The A.G.O. Magazine 2:30-31+ (June 1968)
   Summary treatment of the Pinkham style and analysis of his musical materials, based on the author's doctoral dissertation.

BG25. Johnson, Marlowe W. "The Choral Writing of Daniel Pinkham." American Choral Review 8:16 (June 1966)
   "Audiences find immediate appeal in the sonorous harmonies, the striking melodies, and the stimulating rhythms of Pinkham's choral music. Pinkham is neither avant-garde nor conservative. While he stands in the middle, he is not standing still, however. He is not given to either cliches or tricks but he will doubtless continue to produce solid works by employing in fresh ways techniques of proven effectiveness."

BG26. Johnson, Marlowe Wayne. The Choral Writing of Daniel Pinkham. Ph.D. dissertation, University of Iowa, 1968.
   Full discussion of theoretical principles and musical materials in Pinkham's pre-1968 choral works. The dissertation served as the basis of two significant periodical articles by Johnson.

BG27. Johnson, Richard L. "Hartt College Workshop." Music: the AGO and RCCO Magazine 6:42 (September 1972)
   "Combining the two highly complementary media of organ

and electronic tape, Pinkham has created works of music which evoke sharp emotional responses, and a deep respect for the composer."

BG28. Kirk, Theron. "Twentieth Century Choral Idioms Discussed by Daniel Pinkham." Choral Journal 6:11 (May-June 1966)
Notes on a Pinkham lecture concerning choral sonorities in pre-baroque music.

BG29. Little, Jeanie R. Serial, Aleatoric, and Electronic Techniques in American Organ Music Published Between 1960 and 1972. Ph.D. dissertation, University of Iowa, 1975.
Detailed analysis of Pinkham's Five Voluntaries for Organ Manuals (1965) and A Prophecy (1968).

BG30. McCray, James. "Daniel Pinkham's Published Music for Chorus and Electronic Tape." Choral Journal 19:10-16 (March 1979)
A detailed discussion of Pinkham's music for chorus and electronic tape, essential for understanding this part of his career. McCray includes details of performance procedures for sixteen choral/tape works written between 1970 and 1979.

BG31. McCray, James. "Pinkham: On Composing." Choral Journal 17:15-17 (October 1976)
An informative musician-to-musician interview in which McCray elicits important statements from the composer on his working habits, musical influences and approach to composing, with particular reference to his music for electronic tape.

BG32. Mellers, Wilfrid. Music in a New Found Land: Themes and Developments in the History of American Music. New York, Oxford University Press, 1987.
"The music of Daniel Pinkham, who was born in 1923, lacks the passionate sensitivity that makes [Lou] Harrison's best work so moving; yet it distils from its prettified medievalism a genuine tenderness and radiance. The tinkling bells and melismatic patterns of the Concerto for Celeste and Harpsichord or the elegantly pure vocal writing of the Easter Cantata (in which the voices are haloed by more bells and by muted brass) are delightful to listen to, and unassuming in their acceptance of their emotional limitations. They are true to their composer's talent, though to most of us they cannot but seem anachronistic." (page 156)

BG33. Osgasapian, John. "Reviews: Records." American Organist 17:22 (November 1983)
"Daniel Pinkham's music has about it a knack for maintaining accessibility to the average listener while utilizing sophisticated structural bases and devices. In this it shares a characteristic of early Messiaen . . . . The music has the added-note chords and clusters, formulaic rhythms (movement II of Proverbs is essentially isorhythmic

in the medieval sense), and colorfully beautiful melodies. The scoring of the instruments against the organ (especially the flute, which can present a whole set of complexities) is smooth and effective. Without a doubt, Pinkham is one of the major creative talents of our time." [Review of disc NR 205]

BG34. Pinkham, Daniel. "Intonation, Dissonance and Sonority." American Choral Foundation Bulletin 3:6-7 (March 1961)
      The composer discusses problems of pitch and intonation encountered in performing unaccompanied choral music.

BG35. Pinkham, Daniel. "New Problems Enlarge Horizons." Music Journal 23:40+ (April 1965)
      The composer illustrates his methods of solving self-imposed technical problems, with reference to his **Stabat Mater, Easter Cantata, Signs of the Zodiac,** and the **Violin Concerto.**

BG36. Raver, Leonard. "The Solo Organ Music of Daniel Pinkham." American Organist 17:37 (June 1983)
      "How fortunate we are to have a composer of Daniel Pinkham's stature writing for the organ. From the very easiest one-page pieces suitable for beginning players to the most brilliant toccatas for virtuosos, here is music for everyone to play and enjoy."

BG37. Robb, Christina. "Music Master." Boston Globe, February 12, 1984.
      A rather full treatment of the composer's life and musical career from an anecdotal rather than a technical point of view. Robb believes that contemporary tastes have caught up with the style Pinkham created thirty years earlier.

BG38. Safford, Edwin. "Collecting New England's Composers." Providence Journal (Rhode Island), January 29, 1984.
      "New England composer Daniel Pinkham is an actively imaginative sort whose ideas seem always to be in ferment. No American today writes for organ more creatively, not in ways that blend tradition and advanced techniques more comfortably." [Review of disc NR 205]

BG39. Scanlan, Roger. "Spotlight on Contemporary American Composers." NATS Bulletin 33:36-37+ (Winter 1976)
      Description, by a professor of voice, of nineteen works for solo voice by Pinkham. Commentary covers choice of text, voice range and difficulty, and elements of style.

BG40. Smith, Warren Storey. "Daniel Pinkham." American Composers Alliance Bulletin 10:9-13 (#1, 1961)
      This first attempt at appraisal of Pinkham's accomplishments includes discussion of his compositional methods based for the most part on his instrumental music written 1950-1960. Pinkham is seen as belonging to a tradition of the musician/composer, equally at home as performer, teacher,

and creator of comprehensible new music.   A detailed list of his early works is appended.

BG41. Stallings, Mark E. Representative Works for Mixed Chorus by Daniel Pinkham, 1968-1983.   D.M.A. dissertation, University of Miami, 1984.
    Extended profile of Pinkham's compositional style, followed by analysis of his **Ascension Cantata** (1970), **Daniel in the Lions' Den** (1972), and **Fanfares** (1975).   Included is an exhaustive catalogue of works through 1983.   The author regarded his study as a continuation of the Johnson disserta- tion (BG26).

BG42.   Sullivan, George Wyndole, Jr.   Cadences in Selected Choral Works of Daniel Pinkham.   M.M. thesis, Southwestern Baptist Theological Seminary, 1986.
    Technical   study   of cadence   technique   in Pinkham's **Christmas Cantata** (1957), **Easter Cantata** (1961), **The Lamenta- tions of Jeremiah**, (1966), **Stabat Mater** (1964), and **Daniel in the Lions' Den** (1972).

BG43. Treggor, Philip. "Harpsichord News." Diapason 59:8 (July 1968)
    Interview with the composer about the harpsichord re- vival, comparing qualities of contemporary and older instru- ments and differing ideas of authenticity in performance approach.

BG44.   Van Alen, Janice Kay.   Stylistic and Interpretive Analysis and Performance of Selected Choral Compositions for Women's Voices by Three American Composers: Vincent Persi- chetti, Virgil Thomson, and Daniel Pinkham.   Ed.D. disserta- tion, Columbia University, 1973.
    Discussion of structure and interpretation of Pink- ham's **Three Lenten Poems of Richard Crashaw** (1963), **Magni- ficat** (1968), and **An Emily Dickinson Mosaic** (1962), prepared in connection with a performance of the three works conducted by the author at Teachers' College, Columbia University, on July 10, 1973.

REFERENCES RELATING TO INDIVIDUAL WORKS

B1.   Beggar's Opera

B1a. Durgin, Cyrus. "New **Beggar's Opera** Has Fine Music and Much Action." Boston Globe, July 29, 1956.
    "Daniel Pinkham's music is melodious, delightful and extremely clever in period suggestion. . . . Here is a score absolutely clear, never too full, piquant in orchestral detail including some ingenious effects for high string har- monics. He uses a string quintet, a wind quintet (no clarinet, for that would have been out of period frame), per-

cussion and harpsichord, which last is very prominent. The degree and quality of melodic invention are remarkably good. These are real tunes that Pinkham has conceived; they sing well and they touch the ear pleasantly. The harmony beneath them is proper to the time (approximately at least), and of original turn." See: W1a

B1b. Durgin, Cyrus. "The Summer Stage: New **Beggar's Opera**." Boston Globe, July 26, 1956.
"As for Mr. Pinkham's score--which, he tells me, has a few snippets from Handel--it is altogether delightful. This music is full of melody--and most ingeniously harmonized according to the period (or just before), and it is brightly orchestrated for a string quintet, a wind quintet, harpsichord and percussion." See: W1a

B1c. T., R. S. **"The Beggar's Opera."** Boston Herald, July 26, 1956.
"Daniel Pinkham's adaptation retains the essential spirit of the delightful ballads and catches and Miles Morgan conducts them with limpid clarity in the pit." See: W1a

B2. The Dreadful Dining Car

B2a. Pinkham, Daniel. Program notes, May 1, 1983 concert.
"The late James Wright initially suggested Mark Twain's short story 'Cannibalism in the Cars' as an entertaining libretto for a one-act comic opera. When Terry Eder proposed that I write a work for the Centennial of the University of North Dakota, I decided that here was the perfect opportunity to use that text. There were a number of cogent reasons. Firstly, the Twain story is set in the American Midwest at roughly the same era as the founding of the University. Secondly, the depiction of a fierce December storm and the snow-bound train would surely be not unfamiliar to residents of North Dakota. And thirdly because the sly fun poked by Mark Twain in his use of Robert's Rules of Parliamentary Procedure (he really goes by the book) would certainly amuse any one obliged--as am I--to do committee work within the walls of a college or university." See: W2a

B3. The Garden of Artemis or Apollo's Revels

B3a. Elie, Rudolph. "Mason Memorial." Boston Herald, October 18, 1948.
"Mr. Pinkham's setting for three solo voices, women's voices, flute, clarinet, violin, viola and cello, stands as one of the most refreshing essays ever to come out of the Piston-Longy circle. Happily enough, not only has the composer, in his mid-20s, a capacity for melody, but no sense of embarrassment at all in using it. The result was music of exceptional freshness, charm, grace and wit entirely unblemished with intellectuality so-called, and of no pretense

whatever. It appeared to have been written for no other reason than to please an audience, to let us hear the amusing lyrics of Mr. Hillyer. It seems to have been written to be sung, played, heard and enjoyed, and I only wish other equally youthful composers would stop being geniuses long enough to do the same. In any case, I feel Mr. Pinkham's piece, the instrumental part of which was exquisite in its texture, will be going the rounds for some time to come." See: W3a

B4. Garden Party

B4a. Dyer, Richard. "Fine **Garden Party**." Boston Globe, March 26, 1977.
"The real reason for celebration yesterday was the premiere of Daniel Pinkham's **Garden Party**, one of those minor, sporting works that makes the world a "more" diverting place to be in. . . . There are some positively slinky harmonic progressions in the best art-trashy French manner; an irresistible gospel song led off by a barbershop quartet; a lovely, sensuous duet of regret; and strong choral settings of Ms. Farber's poems. . . . The trouble is that the piece generates energies and densities and frivolities that don't quite cohere; the ideas and musical events in it are sequential rather than consequential. . . . But the failure of detail to cohere didn't mean that the piece wasn't consistently surprising and absorbing to listen to." See: W4a

B4b. Pfeifer, Ellen. **"Garden Party** World Premiere Is Witty." Boston Herald American, March 26, 1977.
"To underline the texts, the composer provided music of remarkably diverse and apt styles. There were the grave, slightly antique sounding settings of the Farber poems, then the wonderfully funny barbershop quartet with massive choral punctuation on the text 'Don't forget to read the Bible,' and the electronic twitterings accompanying the Voice of God." See: W4a

B4c. Pinkham, Daniel. Program notes, March 25, 1977 concert.
"Norma Farber, my friend, neighbor and colleague for many years, has graciously permitted me to set her sonnets 'Tree of Blame' and 'While Eve', which are sung by the chorus in the third scene, and which provide, in an exact reversal of Shakespeare's practice, a welcome interlude of 'serious relief' before the levity of the finale." See: W4

B5. The Left Behind Beasts

B5a. Dyer, Richard. "East Boston Students Stage World Premiere." Boston Globe, June 15, 1985.
"Like all of his music, Pinkham's score is both practical and challenging, pitched to the capacities of

American schoolchildren of today, but not condescending to them. The tunes are catchy and full of artful dodges; the plot advances through rhythmic speech (and the composer calls on the multilingual abilities of the children). The orchestral writing suggests a less cynical Kurt Weill--and the kids get to play along with the percussion. The piece is both delightful and touching." See: W5a

B5b. Frisbie, Judith. **"Left Behind Beasts** Was a Special Experience." Natick Bulletin (Mass.), June 19, 1986.
   "It was standing room only when Daniel Pinkham's charming opera **The Left Behind Beasts** was performed at Memorial School under the director of the Opera Company of Boston's Jerome Shannon. . . . It tells how the beasts who did not go with Noah on the ark saved themselves from the flood by building Mount Ararat. The opera's sometimes atonal choral pieces and the rhythmic speeches were performed by 35 fourth and fifth graders who elected to take chorus at the school this year. Accompanying the five-piece Opera Company of Boston's orchestra were seven grade school percussionists playing 'found instruments,' which were items such as hub caps and brake drums." See: W5b

B6. **A Mast for the Unicorn**

B6a. Adams, Shirley. "Three Nights of Opera." Martha's Vineyard Times (Mass.), June 19, 1986.
   "A Mast for the Unicorn, by Daniel Pinkham, is, of course, Martha's Vineyard's story of three girls--Maria Allen, Polly Daggett and Parnell Manter--who blew up the Liberty Pole to keep the British Commander from using it to repair his ship which had been dismasted in a gale. This led to the ship's capture by American soldiers since it was helpless in the harbor." See: W6a

B8. **Catacoustical Measures**

B8a. Rich, Alan. "Music Composed to Test Acoustics". New York Times, June 1, 1962.
   "Musical compositions have been commissioned over the centuries to celebrate royal birthdays, river pageants and military victories. This week at Lincoln Center's Philharmonic Hall, however, a piece of music is being performed that was commissioned specifically for trying out new concert halls. The work is Daniel Pinkham's **Catacoustical Measures**, and the young American composer wrote it for the acoustical engineering concern of Bolt, Beranek and Newman. The concern, which is advising on the acoustical problems at Philharmonic Hall, wanted a handy piece for orchestra that would show up the specific problems acoustical engineers want answered--reverberation, clarity, definition and the projection of high and low frequencies--and so it paid Mr. Pinkham to write one. The New York Philharmonic has been playing in

its home this week, while the engineers go through the complex process of 'tuning' the hall, and every time a change is made, Mr. Pinkham's piece is played. It is a work full of thunderclaps followed by silences and tinkly high passages followed by low roars, and a spokesman for the acoustical concern seemed to feel that it filled the bill." See: W8a

B8b. "Pinkham's Problem." American Composers Alliance Bulletin 10:7 (#4, 1962)
        "If a poll were taken among composers with the object of finding the most unusual reason behind the commissioning of a work, Daniel Pinkham would probably lead the field. The acoustical engineering firm of Bolt, Beranek and Newman were determined that their latest structure (Philharmonic Hall) would be sonically perfect. Passing up the proverbial pin-dropping, they discovered a more exact method; commission a composer to write a work for the specific purpose of calculating reverberation time, timbre definition and related phenomena. The result was Daniel Pinkham's **Catacoustical Measures**, a four minute work for super-sized orchestra constructed in alternating layers of screaming, whispering, loud-soft antiphony. During the testing of Philharmonic Hall, the Pinkham piece was played again and again and again as conductors Erich Leinsdorf, Leopold Stokowski, Eugene Ormandy and resident maestro Leonard Bernstein roamed the corridors and tiers searching for imperfections (in the concert hall, not the music) while a ghostly audience of hundreds of fibreglass dummies listened attentively. The sounds of 'Pinkham's Problem' floated all the way down to the renowned C. F. Peters Corporation, who promptly published the work and announced three forthcoming performances, a possible recording and a radio broadcast--this time in a hall that presumably needs no testing." See: W8a

B9.   **Concertante No. 1**

B9a. Cohn, Arthur. "CRI, Louisville and New Music." Music Magazine/Musical Courier 164:42 (February 1962)
        "Daniel Pinkham's **Concertante** is warmed with the pre-serial Stravinsky gospel though it reaches toward much more romantic goals; Pinkham's melodic lines are more velvety than the neoclassic knittings of his musical Bishop." See: D9a

B9b. Cohn, Arthur. Recorded Classical Music; a Critical Guide to Compositions and Performance. New York, Schirmer Books, 1981.
        "Pinkham's work features the violin and harpsichord as the solo voices, with the celesta functioning as a part of the orchestral forces. The music is in turn thoughtful and robust; the creative recipe is classicism salted with neat frictions and peppered with sharply defined coloration. Deucedly attractive writing. The sound is exceedingly bright and open." (p. 1375) See: D9a

B9c. Elie, Rudolph. "Festival Orchestra." Boston Herald, December 17, 1954.
     "The first, a **Concertante** for violin and harpsichord with strings and celeste displayed in its first movement an ingenious and piquant contrast in sonorities, the use of the celeste being of particular novelty and effect. In the cantilena Mr. Pinkham again demonstrated his feeling for charming lyricism, the solo violin, excellently played by Robert Brink, emerging over the sound of the strings in a captivating way. The burlesca, following immediately, presented highly contrasted rhythms and materials that seemed not to build to any solid conclusion and so diminished somewhat the overall effect of these brief but well fashioned pieces." See: W9a

B9d. Finch, Everett. "Delightful Finale Given by Tri-City Symphony." Union Star (Schenectady, N. Y.), May 22, 1957.
     "Daniel Pinkham's **Concertante** (for Violin and Harpsichord Soli, Celeste and String Orchestra) proved to be an immensely ingratiating inclusion in the Tri-City Symphony Orchestra's program last night. . . . The **Concertante**, composed as recently as 1954, has a wealth of striking tonal effect holding one in rapt delight." See: W9d

B9e. Flanagan, William. "WNYC Music Festival Opens with Concert at Town Hall." New York Herald Tribune, February 13, 1958.
     "The most fetching work on the program was not one of those tagged with any kind of 'first performance' claim. Daniel Pinkham, born in 1923, has written a **Concertante** for violin, string orchestra, harpsichord and celeste that has a shapely and stylish musical texture (a pretty one, too), an easy lyricism, and that makes lovely sounds with its unusual combination. It bears heavily for source on the late-Stravinsky--it is much less dry a wine, however--and your reporter felt that Mr. Pinkham had been somewhat disinclined to stick by his more animated music, had promised us this contrast, only to ease us back into the luxury of the slow lyrical music which, in the end, dominates the piece rather excessively. It's a lovely work, all the same, and an unusual one." See: W9e

B9f. Frankenstein, Alfred. "Recitals and Miscellany." High Fidelity 6:103 (December 1956)
     "The delightful **Concertante** of Daniel Pinkham, a 'study in sonorities' of the lightest and wittiest kind." See: D9a

B9g. Persichetti, Vincent. "Reviews of Records." Musical Quarterly 48:272 (April 1962)
     "Pinkham is hypnotized by the harpsichord's and celesta's sound possibilities." See: D9a

B9h. Robb, Christina. "Music Master." Boston Globe, February 12, 1984.

"The harpsichord veers from a muscular, pounding modernism to a cheery bar or two that sound like fugitives from Haydn. But the violin sings, whether poignant or brilliant. The unashamed melodiousness of the soaring violin against a clearly punctuated background is Pinkham's distinctive style adapted for violin." See: W9

B9i. Sigmon, Carl. Notes from record album CRI 143.
"Daniel Pinkham's choice of instruments could scarcely be more exotic. The celesta and harpsichord are disarmingly so, yet the atmosphere of our time is present everywhere. . . . Each unfolding bar of the Burlesca at the same time redefines and reshapes the movement preceding. If one is unfamiliar with this observation, be assured that it is worth a trial. The form, additive and open, is strikingly improvisatory. The violin is impassioned and its assertions bump squarely into the melodies and accompanying figures. Burlesca? I think so. The seeds that were planted in the introduction have germinated and the work is resultingly unified." See: D9a

B9j. Wolffers, Jules. "Daniel Pinkham Conducts Own Works in Jordan Hall." Christian Science Monitor (Atlantic edition), December 17, 1954.
"Mr. Pinkham's own Concertante for violin and harpsichord solo with strings and celesta proved a fascinating work, especially for its timbres. Intriguing combinations of instruments--plucked, bowed and struck--produced altogether novel effects." See: W9a

B10.   Concertante No. 2

B10a. Cooke, Francis Judd. "Philharmonia Concert Is Good Experience for All, Says Cooke." Lexington Minute-Man, (Mass.), April 9, 1959.
"Next came Daniel Pinkham's Concertante No. 2, composed last year for Robert Brink, who played the modest solo violin parts. It proved to be no path-breaker but a straightforward, soberly-scored work, unwittingly almost a period-piece circa 1925. A jolting Allegro was followed by a slow movement neo-Romantic in cast, too long and surprisingly like Sibelius' Fourth in spots. The Finale disconcertingly evoked Stravinsky wedded to the six-eight plus three-four bear-dancing of Sibelius, but it swept to a spirited and sonorous end. The composer, who was also the evening's harpsichordist, was warmly acclaimed." See: W10b

B10b. Durgin, Cyrus. "Music by Pinkham at Jordan Hall." Boston Globe, May 9, 1958.
"The Concertante is a fine work for eight accompanying strings and the solo instrument; it is music of substance and an easy, pleasant flow. So far as one might judge at first hearing, since this performance was the first, it was well played, with Mr. Pinkham's longtime associate, Robert Brink,

Bibliography

as soloist." <u>See</u>: W10a

B11.   Concertino in A for Small Orchestra and Obbligato Pianoforte

B11a.   A., R. "Ensemble Concert." <u>Boston Herald</u>, May 4, 1950.
   "Mr. Pinkham's **Concertino for Small Orchestra and Piano Obbligato** was enthusiastically received. While offering little of novelty to contemporary music, nevertheless it showed the composer's sympathy for the melodic aspect of the musical craft. There can be little doubt that this approach has found a response in certain listeners." <u>See</u>: W11a

B11b.   Rogers, Harold. "Pinkham's New Work at Harvard." <u>Christian Science Monitor</u> (Atlantic edition), May 4, 1950.
   "Mr. Pinkham leans to the classic in form, to the impressionistic in mood, all the while articulating his ideas in a contemporary tongue that is intelligible, furthermore, to the majority of contemporaries. This is no mean accomplishment." <u>See</u>: W11a

B12.   Divertimento

B12a.   Buell, Richard. "A Matter of Consciousness Raising." <u>Boston Globe</u>, May 31, 1983.
   "Daniel Pinkham's **Divertimento** for soprano recorder and string orchestra was up to a trickier business altogether, some of it having an ominously musing Shostakovich-like quality (very odd on a recorder), but giving way in the concluding Processional to a lewd evocation of morris dancing." <u>See</u>: W12b

B13.   Five Short Pieces

B13a.   Elie, Rudolph. "Festival Orchestra." <u>Boston Herald</u>, December 17, 1954.
   "The **Five Short Pieces**, each in its own way of a very pleasant character, were also a little too brief to sink in though the first, which was a little reminiscent of a section of Schoenberg's **Verklaerte Nacht** was particularly grateful to hear. Succinctness is, of course, an admirable quality, but one felt Mr. Pinkham had perhaps been a little too concise in developing these very musical miniatures." <u>See</u>: W13a

B13b.   Riley, John William. "Pinkham Conducts Chamber Music." <u>Boston Globe</u>, December 17, 1954.
   "His tunes have an easy turn of phrase, ingratiating melody, little distinction in either conception or technique. They are not pretentious, and are not intended to set the world afire. But they are pleasant, which is a worthy

accomplishment in this age of hyperthryroid music." See:
W13a

B13c. Wolffers, Jules. "Daniel Pinkham Conducts Own Works
in Jordan Hall." Christian Science Monitor (Atlantic edition), December 17, 1954.
        "The high standard of performance was continued for
another work by Mr. Pinkham--**Five Short Pieces for String
Orchestra.** The players tossed the little items off with the
right amount of dash and humor. Easily accessible at first
hearing--as the composer intended--the audience thoroughly
enjoyed the music." See: W13a

B15. **Masks**

B15a. Dyer, Richard. "A Pinkham Premiere." Boston Globe,
October 15, 1981.
        "An entertaining and disturbing piece for harpsichord
and chamber ensemble. . . . **Masks** is a group of four character pieces in which there is something wistful about the
comedy, something hopeful about the tragedy, something bittersweet about the reminiscence, and something horribly true
about the deceptions. It works on a small scale, and says
reverberant things." See: W15c

B16. **Now the Trumpet Summons Us Again**

B16a. Steinberg, Michael. "JFK Prose-in-Music Tasteful,
Intelligent." Boston Globe, December 15, 1964.
        "It is a brief and restrained treatment of just a
couple of sentences, and while the composer has gone about
his task with taste and intelligence, he could not make one
forget the intrinsic difficulty of convincingly setting to
music a piece of prose, even though it is very rhetorical
prose, longs to move faster, and more simply than musical
speed permits." See: W16a

B17. **Organ Concerto**

B17a. Dwyer, John. "Wednesday Evening in Keinhans Music
Hall." Buffalo Evening News (N. Y.), July 2, 1970.
        "The four-movement Pinkham work is based on a tone-
row, worked out in considerable coloristic variety and dynamic contrasts. Episodes were lively, contemplative, tender
or reverential on the composer's demand, with a complex grace
and thrust in line and color. Snare drum, vibraphone, bells,
tambourine, timpani, syncopated trumpet and bristling strings
make it a virtuoso orchestra, matched by rippling coloratura
and energetic declamation at the console." See: W17a

B18. **Seven Deadly Sins**

B18a. Abell, Kathy. "Pinkham Concert Worth Every Cent Paid." Eastern News (Eastern Illinois University), March 8, 1974.
"Pinkham follows the modern 20th century style of music and likes to use special devices, such as unusual percussion combinations and eerie sound effects." See: W18a

B19. **Signs of the Zodiac**

B19a. Brown, Harrison. "International Flavor Predominated at Portland Symphony's Concert." Portland Evening Express, (Maine), November 11, 1964.
"A highly interesting piece indeed. Everyone is entitled to his opinion. Mine is that the Pinkham work is one-tenth serious experimentation into far-out sound and nine-tenths delightful spoof, all of it extremely well orchestrated." See: W19a

B19b. Bryant, Marshall F. "Concert Program Here Salutes Oslo, Norway." Press Herald (Portland, Maine), November 11, 1964.
"The poems and the music are companions in impressionism, warmed over the same fires of imagination, and end up as dual spirits floating blissfully in a kaleidoscope of shimmering sound, now blustery, now humorous or pompous, but perhaps suggesting spheres in endless flight. It was a tremendously absorbing piece and should find favor elsewhere. Certainly it is worth hearing again." See: W19a

B19c. Cohn, Arthur. Recorded Classical Music; a Critical Guide to Compositions and Performances. New York, Schirmer Books, 1981.
"Pink-pilled by programmaticism, though not of the play-by-play variety. Each of the twelve signs is musically ascertained. Aries the 'rambunctious Ram' is brassy, instruments are paired for Gemini, the twins, etc. For music of this sort the pinpointed subject lends enchantment, and Pinkham is successful." (p. 1374) See: D19a

B19d. Fitts, Dudley. "A Note on the Poems," from record album LOU-673
"There is no question here of literal description, either in the music or in the poetry. Rather, the celestial Twelve are conceived of as influences, as points of departure for the imagination." See: D19a

B19e. Frankenstein, Alfred. "Other Classical Reviews." High Fidelity 17:150 (October 1967)
"The pieces themselves are very tuneful, very dissonant, very brilliantly orchestrated, and totally enchanting in every dimension." See: D19a

B19f. Kroeger, Karl. "Music Reviews." Music Library

Association Notes 25:827 (June 1969)
"Without David McCord's witty poems, Pinkham's **Signs
of the Zodiac** is nothing more than twelve miniatures--sonic
microcosms of twenty to thirty measures each, containing some
interesting ideas but hardly amounting to an organized and
satisfying whole. . . . The music is intended to be descrip-
tive of the poetry, but they do not fuse and become one."
See: D19a

B20. **Symphony No. 1**

  B20a. Kroeger, Karl. "Music Reviews." Music Library
Association Notes 20:122 (Winter 1962-63)
"Daniel Pinkham has produced a very promising **First
Symphony**. . . . Pinkham shows excellent craftsmanship in his
handling of the orchestra and is sensitive to orchestral
colors. Though his is a tonal language, his music tends to
be highly chromatic and occasionally polytonal." See: W20

B21. **Symphony No. 2**

  B21a. Barker, John W. "Other Reviews." American Record
Guide 31:986 (June 1965)
"It is an interesting example of how a highly individ-
ualistic composer can make use of 12-tone technique in his
own way without surrendering to any doctrinaire theoretical
commitment. . . . This is not ingratiating nor simple music,
but it is rich in ideas and it merits close study and acqain-
tance." See: D21a

  B21b. Cohn, Arthur. Recorded Classical Music; a Critical
Guide to Compositions and Performances. New York, Schirmer
Books, 1981.
"Definition of content meaning neither removes a work
from the absolute-music category nor cancels the composer's
decision to term it a symphony. One hears and recognizes the
elegiac tone and symphonicism of Pinkham's twelve-tone
work. . . . Pinkham's work speaks clearly and, more impor-
tantly, eloquently. That significant artistic result is
evidence that practice must go beyond theoretical commitment
and that when it does, it thereby proves the absolute
validity of the latter. Point of evidence: the marvelous
trumpet phrases edged by rhythmic persistence in the 'Ballade.' There's plenty more." (p. 1374) See: D21a

  B21c. Dumm, Robert. "Period Discs Tune the Ear."
Christian Science Monitor, (New England ed.) September 13,
1965.
"The Pinkham symphony is all control, but not cool.
It has a lean palette that invites the ear and a lucidity
that intrigues the mind. Delicate motor rhythms oil the
wheels of movement and a melodic (praise be) use of tone-rows
in tuneful wisps and banners fall extra clearly on the ear."

Bibliography

See: D21a

    B21d.   Flanagan, William.   "Classical."   Hi Fi/Stereo
Review 15:86 (October 1965)
       "Pinkham. . . has attempted a free, tonally "anchored"
adaptation of twelve-tone techniques without sacrificing the
essentially neo-classic ideals of subtlety and delicacy of
texture that characterize his previously more diatonic music.
At the same time, he has built clearly recognizable thematic
ideas from his serial materials and treated them in an
essentially traditional manner. . . . The result is a piece
that is still all Pinkham, and one that in its clearly
elegiac and lyrical gesture is both touching and individual."
See: D21a

    B21e. "Symphony No. 2." Notes from record album LOU 652
       "His second symphony was composed in 1963 for the
Lansing (Mich.) Orchestra, and demonstrates the flexibility
of the twelve-tone technique--it contains little of the
difficulty for players or audiences usually associated with
serial (so-called twelve-tone) music. The four movements are
based mostly upon two closely related tone-rows, used, as the
composer says, in a personal way--frequent pedal-points and
ostinato-like repetitions plus occasional departures from the
strict pursuit of the row give feelings of tonal anchor-
age." See: W21

    B21f. Notes from the score.
       "The Pinkham Symphony No. 2 is essentially a lyrical,
elegiac work; its orchestral texture is simple and unclut-
tered, and its thematic material is very clear. The opening
'Aria' and concluding 'Envoy' are contemplative and serene.
The 'Epigrams' are terse statements, as the name suggests,
and are of contrasting character.   The 'Ballade' is the most
aggressive and rhythmic movement as it begins, but becomes
the most soaring and impassioned at its climax." See: W21

    B21g.   Wintermute, Edwin. "Alter Symphony Program to Fit
Nation's Grief." Lansing State Journal (Mich.), November 25,
1963.
       "Second on the program came the world premiere of
Daniel Pinkham's Second Symphony in modern idiom, but
fortunately, rather in keeping, than not, with the spirit of
lamentation. . . . The composition began with the 'urban and
industrial' sounds, including the suggestion of river traffic
and blasts of the air whistles of diesel-powered tugboats,
and it proceeded by means of melody purposely distorted, and
half-finished musical statements--always avoiding flat decla-
rations--to puzzle and to disturb. Second Symphony. . . has
a distinct flavor as of pickled walnuts or of tarmarind: it
is not, however, devoid of beauty. It will be published and
will take its place on the shelves of modernity, along with
the similar achievements of Sessions, Piston, and yes, Bartok, Berg, Schoenberg, and Milhaud." See: W21a

B22.   Symphony No. 3

B22a.   Couture, Michael. "Superb Premiere by Philharmonic." Brockton Enterprise (Mass.), February 12, 1986.
     "Pinkham's **Symphony Number Three**, receiving its world premiere, proved to be a multi-faceted work that at times was fragmented and seemingly without direction in its perspective.   Although diverse in its makeup, the piece, which attempts to combine 20th century theories with that of the masters, appeared too thinly spread in spots, although the first section began with a dronelike mood and had a nice subtlety.   The string section was a commanding influence in the second section, while the epilogue was pulsating, solidly defined and certainly pleasant to the ear." See: W22a

B22b.   Harper, George W.   "Schlegel Leads Plymouth Philharmonic in Pinkham Premiere and Other Works." The Patriot Ledger (Quincy, Mass.), February 11, 1986.
     "That Pinkham is a man of many parts was amply demonstrated Saturday night with the premiere of his **Third Symphony**, commissioned by the Plymouth Philharmonic on the occasion of its 70th anniversary season.   This composition, a short, segmented work in a single movement, made use of percussion as a sort of punctuation to set off and bind together carefully poised interchanges between choirs of bright woodwinds and somber strings." See: W22a

B23.   Violin Concerto

B23a.   Maddocks, Melvin.   "Pinkham Concerto Presented." Christian Science Monitor, September 10, 1956.
     "Mr. Pinkham's new work is a dramatic piece of music, foreboding rather than brooding, full of electric bits of suspense.   The Introduction and Capriccio are syncopated, suggesting jazz influences.   The phrases are terse, deliberately crowded against one another, allowing little room for thematic development.   The Nocturne begins more calmly but under the same ominous tension which characterized the concerto as a whole.   Oboe, French horns, and harp are featured as well as violin.   But the phrases become abrupt again, the bass is plucked more often than bowed, the harp is heard in sudden pizzicati which play upon the nerves.   The Scherzo-Finale opens with perhaps the concerto's most brilliant passage: a headlong rondo air of gypsy flavor, which successfully releases the tensions pent up by the rhythmic devices of the earlier movements." See: W23a

B26.   Prelude, Epigram and Elegy

B26a.   Woessner, Bob.   "Pinkham, SNC Performers Show Versatility." Green Bay Press-Gazette (Wisc.), February 20, 1971.

"The **Prelude, Epigram and Elegy,** the only Pinkham work written for band, was a bit of brinksmanship. It headed from dissonance into chaos a time or two, but then became rich and full. The treatment was typical of Pinkham, a work with both feet planted firmly--one in traditional music, one in modern. A good combination." See: W26b

B29. Cantilena and Capriccio

B29a.   Cohn, Arthur. Recorded Classical Music; a Critical Guide to Compositions and Performances. New York, Schirmer Books, 1981.
"An expert harpsichordist, Pinkham has composed a large quantity of music using the instrument, including it in a dozen chamber and instrumental pieces. Contemporary classic diction defines Pinkham's **Cantilena and Capriccio;** the latter is athletically graceful, the former curvaceously lyrical." (p. 1375) See: D29a

B29b.   Durgin, Cyrus. "Voltaire and Rabelais Listen to Modern Music." Boston Globe, May 12, 1960.
"Pinkham's music has motion, flow, glinting vitality and a sense of structure." See: W29d

B29c.   Trimble, Lester. **"Cantilena for Violin and Harpsichord, Capriccio for Violin and Harspsichord".** Notes from record cover CRI 109.
"The **Cantilena** and the **Capriccio for Violin and Harpsichord,** both by Daniel Pinkham are concerned with the establishment of moods--in the case of the Cantilena, one of tenderness and warmth; in the Capriccio, one exemplifying energy, boisterousness, and athleticism. Both works, incidentally, have been orchestrated by the composer." See: W29

B40. Inaugural Marches

B40a.   Tommasini, Anthony. "Nadia Boulanger Celebration Opens at Longy." Boston Globe, September 17, 1987.
"The marches are frothy, handsome and filled with neo-classic humor; some deliberately and deliciously clumsy part-writing, and, in the first, a wonderful obbligato, off-beat bass line for the tuba." See: W40c

B50. Serenades

B50a.   Buell, Richard. "Wind Ensemble Gives Lots of Nice Things." Boston Globe, December 15, 1980.
"Daniel Pinkham's **Serenades for Trumpet and Wind Ensemble,** a piece d'occasion turned out for the Harvard Band and former BSO [Boston Symphony Orchestra] honcho Rolf Smedvig, was resourceful, bright, and cheery in a '50s neo-classical way. Its harmonic color was congruent with its

instrumental color. And it played well." <u>See</u>: W50b

B52. **Sonata da Requiem**

B52a. Dyer, Richard. "A Pinkham Premiere." <u>Boston Globe</u>,
October 15, 1981.
"The **Sonata da Requiem** is full of criss-crossing
intensities, wonderfully imagined for the instruments, which
are resolved and brought to peace by the tolling of the
bell." <u>See</u>: W52b

B56. **Vigils**

B56a. Davis, H. "Third Candlelight Concert Provides
Delightful Evening." <u>Inquirer and Mirror</u> (Nantucket, Mass.),
July 26, 1984.
"This is a difficult work which was played with
assured dexterity, particularly in the asymmetric rhythms of
the Presto Scherzando third movement and the rich harmonies
of the final Allegro. If Mr. PInkham does not play the harp
himself, he certainly understands the problems and potential-
ities of the instrument." <u>See</u>: W56c

B56b. Dyer, Richard. "Concert Spans 29 Years of Daniel
Pinkham's Works." <u>Boston Globe</u>, October 31, 1984.
"Pinkham hasn't undergone sweeping changes of style.
Vigils, four episodes for solo harp that were played for the
first time earlier this year is recognizable as the work of
the composer of **Concerto for Celesta and Harpsichord**, which
was written during a single week in November 1955. These
instrumental pieces show Pinkham's sureness of craftsmanship,
his delight in quality and variety of sound, his consideration for performers and for audience." <u>See</u>: W56d

B56c. Henry, Derrick. "Pinkham Premiere at King's Chapel."
<u>Boston Globe</u>, February 7, 1984.
"Pinkham's own **Vigils** for harpist Carol Baum proved to
be a colorful piece whose overriding serenity deepened into
darkness, though for my taste it relied too heavily on those
ubiquitous tools of the harpist's trade, arpeggio and glis-
sando." <u>See</u>: W56b

B56d. Pinkham, Daniel. Program notes, undated.
"In these four brief movements you will hear a myriad
of colors, dynamics, and effects: bell-like harmonics, the
pizzicato effect of <u>sons etouffes</u>, and great sweeping <u>glis-
sandi</u>. But most of all you will hear that in the hands (and
feet!) of a skillful artist the harp can set forth a lyric
and singing cantabile line." <u>See</u>: W56

B58. **Concertante No. 3**

147

B58a. Bingham, Seth. "Recitals and Concerts." <u>American</u> <u>Organist</u> 47:9 (July 1964)
    "Thoroughly modern in the best sense, even making expressive use of a 12-tone row (pronounced roe!), these three contrasted movements, partly due to the striking instrumental combination, proved to be fresh and direct in appeal. This was particularly apparent in the poignantly beautiful elegy which might fittingly echo the expression of national sorrow for the death of a great and beloved leader." <u>See</u>: W58d

B58b. Devine, George F. "Music Reviews." <u>Music Library Association Notes</u> 27:805 (June 1971)
    "Two slower movements, Aria and Elegy, flank a Scherzo in which serial writing is employed to a limited extent. As a whole the piece is moderately dissonant. . . . As an addition to the growing literature in which the organ is part of a chamber ensemble Pinkham's **Concertante** will be found interesting for executants and listeners alike." <u>See</u>: W58

B59. **Concertante No. 4**

B59a. Kerner, Leighton. "Pleasure and Pain." <u>Village Voice</u> (New York, N. Y.), February 6, 1964.
    "Mr. Pinkham's piece might be described as ruggedly conservative. He never seems to lose sight of tonality, but he uses his traditional tools of composition in quite his own way. The three movements ('Canzona', 'Procession' and 'Plaint') are elaborate structures built on terse, extremely energized motifs, and the separations and mixings of the organ, brass (on and off stage), drum, cymbal, and gong timbres are fascinating in themselves." <u>See</u>: W59a

B59b. Monaco, Richard A. "Music Reviews." <u>Music Library Association Notes</u> 24:153 (September 1967)
    "The materials of each movement are drawn from the initial twelve-tone series stated in the first phrase by the organ and brass. The music is, however, tonal and, as one would expect from this composer, the melodic lines are lyrical and idiomatically composed. . . . The piece deserves the many performances it will undoubtedly have." <u>See</u>: W59

B59c. Sly, Allan. "Recitals and Concerts." <u>American Organist</u> 47:7 (April 1964)
    "The new Pinkham piece started out coyly with the notes CBF (initials of builder Charles Fisk), working them into a canzona. The following Procession established a very festive mood and at its conclusion the composer, who was conducting, picked up a large-headed drum stick and swung a wicked fortissimo on a drum strategically concealed nearby. At the end of the Plaint the brass players moved to successively receding stations--behind the organ and finally out in the choir room with the door closed. Very effective. Like Pinkham's other works for organ and instruments, this new

Concertante will find wide acceptance." <u>See</u>: W59a

B61. **Diversions**

B61a. Pinkham, Daniel. Program notes, undated.
"The opening 'Jovial' is a good-natured lyrical movement with frequent changes of meter. The second movement, 'Hushed', combines harp and organ in dissimilar material. The harp plays patterns suggestive of the 'change-ringing' of bells in English cathedrals. The organ moves very slowly in tone clusters of various densities, which in turn suggest large clouds that slowly change shape in the late afternoon sky. The finale, 'Dancing', is a joyous dialogue between the two instruments, ending in a blaze of <u>glissandi</u>." <u>See</u>: W61

B62. **For Evening Draws On**

B62a. Felciano, Richard. "More on a Contemporary Workshop." <u>Music:the</u> <u>AGO</u> <u>and</u> <u>RCCO</u> <u>Magazine</u> 7:28 (October 1973)
"The third premiere of the evening was Daniel Pinkham's **For Evening Draws On** (a reference to Luke 24:29) in which additive descending organ clusters float gently 'like clouds' through a quietly atmospheric tape part. Through this tonal landscape, an English horn soliloquy, played beautifully by Kenneth Roth, winds its way." <u>See</u>: W62a

B65. **Liturgies**

B65a. Albright, William. "Festival of Contemporary Organ Music." <u>Music:The</u> <u>AGO</u> <u>and</u> <u>RCCO</u> <u>Magazine</u> 8:23 (September 1974)
"Daniel Pinkham's **Liturgies** for organ, timpani and tape. . . amply demonstrated two of this composer's attributes: wit and skill. Most attractive was the first movement with its concentration on a few rhythmic and melodic cells." <u>See</u>: W65a

B66. **Miracles**

B66a. Krusenstjerna, Mary. "Music Reviews." <u>Music</u> <u>Library</u> <u>Association</u> <u>Notes</u> 37:147 (September 1980)
"Daniel Pinkham has made a significant contribution to flute repertoire with his **Miracles** for flute and organ. . . . The music is tonal, harmonically boldly dissonant, rhythmically strong with some meter changes and sometimes difficult from the ensemble standpoint, pointillistic when appropriate to the program, and contrapuntal as one would expect from Pinkham. There is a lot of color and contrast throughout and the character of each miracle is quite different. . . . An interesting and exciting work!" <u>See</u>: W66

B66b.   St. George, David.   "Pappoutsakis Remembered."
Boston Globe, January 30, 1980.
     "It is a set of five tone poems, or rather medita-
tions, on New Testament miracles. The harmonic language is
bolder than is often the case with Pinkham, and many of the
movements are extremely effective evocations of their sub-
jects. In one, 'and the crippled shall walk,' high, serene,
vibrato-filled   chords   in   the   organ   are   interrupted
periodically by awkward, stumbling, two-note interjections in
the flute.   In the most vigorous of the pieces, 'The Miracle
in the Country of Gerasenes', unclean spirits are driven from
the mind of an insane man and take refuge in a herd of pigs
who then drown themselves.   It is gauged almost as a war
between flute and organ.   In a very brief coda the opening
music comes back, but, programmatically, with the parts
reversed.   In the last piece a blind man glimpses light for
the first time in the radiance of the work's final C major
chord." See: W66e

B67.   **Mourn for the Eclipse of His Light**

     B67a.   Jones, Bruce. "Florida Conclave." Music: The AGO
and RCCO Magazine 8:35 (February 1974)
     "Daniel Pinkham's **Mourn for the Eclipse of His Light**
for violin, organ and tape is based on a text from Ecclesiastes.   It was described in a statement by the composer as a
work using the idiomatic qualities of each of the instruments, the organ's sustained sound, the violin's lyricism and
the tape's variety of textures.   In fact, the tape in this
work, as is true of many Pinkham works for instruments and
tape, serves as little more than a background surface. Pinkham is particularly fond of tinkling crystalline textures
which appear throughout **Mourn** and other works, creating as
they do a euphoric elevated sensitivity in the listener."
See: W67a

B69.   **The Other Voices of the Trumpet**

     B69a.   Darrell, R. D.   "Recitals and Miscellany." High
Fidelity 31:78 (March 1981)
     "Mildly daring only is Daniel Pinkham's **Other Voices
of the Trumpet**, with its inexplicable interpolation of electronic sound effects." See: D69a

     B69b.   Raver, Leonard.   "Contemporary Organ Music Work-
shop." Music: the AGO and RCCO Magazine 6:50 (January 1972)
     "Pinkham's **The Other Voices**. . . is, like many of his
other recent works, a twelve-tone piece, this one based on
two different rows from which Pinkham has fashioned a
delightful syntax of piquant effects between organ and trumpet for the first half.   A free recitative leads to a
recapitulation of the beginning rondo before the entrance of

the tape begins the final section." See: W69a

B69c. Vidrich, Arthur. Notes from record album Crystal S365.
"Written for the 1971 Hartt College Contemporary Organ Music Workshop, this piece explores the various possible colors of the trumpet accompanied throughout the first part by the organ and adding a uniquely developed sound track near the end." See: D69a

B75. **Signs in the Sun**

B75a. Burkett. John Morris. Music for Two or More Players at One or More Organs. D.M.A. dissertation, University of Illinois at Urbana-Champaign, 1973.
Detailed structural and tone row analysis of Pinkham's **Signs in the Sun** (1967) as part of a larger study of contemporary organ music for two performers. See: W75

B75b. Hickman, Charles. "The Dedication of a Great American Organ." Music: The A.G.O. Magazine 1:35 (October 1967)
"Pinkham achieved his purpose in speaking through modern tonal and rhythmic idioms, basing his practice on the style of the early 17th century Venetian composers." See: W75a

B76. **Sonata for Organ and Brasses**

B76a. Berry, Ray. "Recitals and Concerts." American Organist 41:263 (July 1958)
"The first movement had vitality but gave to this listener a somewhat spotty, "bunched" effect. The Aria had flowing lyricism and was very well written for the organ and four brasses. The Finale's organ opening was strongly reminiscent of a device in a Hindemith organ sonata for a moment, and was again heard in the brasses toward the end of the movement--a movement which proceeded in swift scherzo-like style with great motion and driving rhythmic patterns to a climax of considerable proportion." See: W76a

B81. **Variations**

B81a. Crow, Todd. "Music Reviews." Music Library Association Notes 28:525 (March 1972)
"The continual rhythmic interest (especially the fragmented rhythms of the Scherzo and Finale, and ornamental rhythmic display of the Nocturne), richness of melodic invention, in addition to the composer's impeccable sense of both instruments, reveal the work of a craftsman. The combination of these elements have produced an attractive work which deserves frequent performance." See: W81

B82. When the Morning Stars Sang Together

B82a.   Hoover,   Richard Lee.   An Analysis with Historical Background of Selected Compositions of American Organ Music. M.A. thesis, California State University Long Beach, 1974.
Brief   analysis of Pinkham's When the Morning Stars Sang Together (1972), in connection with the author's recital on April 28, 1974 at First Congregational Church in Long Beach, California. See: W82

B86. Epiphanies

B86a.   Dyer,   Richard.   "Epiphanies in N. E. Premiere." Boston Globe, October 20, 1980.
"Pinkham,   of course, is perhaps the most accomplished miniaturist of today's composers, and Epiphanies, instead of a sustained exercise, is five short pieces, linked by their harmonic language, and by their common inspiration--five encounters with the emanent Divine in the New Testament, events like the appearance of the star in the east and Paul's encounter on the road to Damascus. The pieces exhibit all of Pinkham's usual qualities--a brilliant, imaginative, idio-matic use of the instrument; an exploratory sense that is counterbalanced by a strong sense of tradition and of taste; an unabashed emotional directness; an elegance of craftsman-ship." See: W86b

B86b.   Shuler,   David.   "Music Reviews." Music Library Association Notes 38:944 (June 1982)
"Each movement is a meditation on the text, not unlike the meditations of Messiaen (for instance L'Ascension), and is similar in nature to other Pinkham works such as Blessings for organ. The musical language is, of course, different, as are the techniques of realizing 'affect.' Nonetheless, there are a number of similarities due to the nature of the intent. The music is expressly non-dramatic. While numerous passages in the Pinkham work possess rhythmic vitality and drive, there is no climax in the dramatic sense toward which the music moves. Sections, passages, or ideas exist, rather than move in a directed manner. The music is constructed of blocks, large or small, which are placed next to each other or superimposed. Literal repetition is a fundamental tech-nique as well as devices such as ostinatos and canons. The compositional approach, then, is quite different than that of say, a dramatic tone poem, for the emphasis is placed on the timeless, eternal aspects of the scriptural texts." See: W86

B96. Proverbs

B96a.   Stoeckl,   Rudolf.   "Neue Musik--aus und fuer Franken." Neue Zeitschrift fuer Musik 1:47 (Jan.-Feb. 1980)

"Musikalische Erscheinungsformen des 14. bis 17. Jahrhunderts" greift auch Daniel Pinkham (1923) in seinen **Proverbs** auf: hier aber gewinnen alte Melodien durch intelligente Verarbeitungstechniken und reizvolle Klangmischungen neue Aktualitaet." See: W96

B98. **Suite**

B98a. Rudd, Michael. Stylistic Trends in Comtemporary Organ Music; a Stylistic Analysis of Post-World War II Works 1945-1965. Ph.D. dissertation, Louisiana State University, 1967.
"The **Suite** is a superb example of combining old and new ideas into a setting neither trite nor controversial. A 'bittersweet' quality permeates the composer's attitude. The term 'bittersweet' implies a fusion of common and uncommon harmonic progressions, sonorities, and general harmonic color."

B98b. Rudd, Michael. "Stylistic Features and Compositional Activities in Organ Literature Since World War II." Diapason 59:12 (June 12, 1968)
"Not many Americans write better for the organ than Daniel Pinkham, as illustrated by his **Suite** of 1952. The beautiful use of modality is combined with frequent tonal hamonic changes. . . . The work is well-written and rewarding for the performer." See: W98

B100. **Concerto for Celesta and Harpsichord Soli**

B100a. Cohn, Arthur. Recorded Classical Music; a Critical Guide to Compositions and Performances. New York, Schirmer Books, 1981.
"A unique combination. The suave sonorities match the scrupulous harmonic clarity, the guarantee of neoclassic style. 'Concerto' notwithstanding, the intimacy of the work places Pinkham's communicative piece (three movements) in the chamber-music category." (p. 1375) See: D100a

B100b. Doris, Hubert. "Review of Records." Musical Quarterly 43:416-7 (July 1957)
"In listening to the work, nothing of the Baroque drive, excitement, and tension is present. Is he writing a purely contrapuntal piece in which the harmonic combinations formed by the voices have no significance, or is his procedure to be guided by the principles of harmonic rhythm and vertical combination whose roots are familiar to us? He must decide, so that the ancient problem of verticality versus linearity will be gratifyingly dealt with." See: D100a

B100c. Downes, Edward. "American Works Heard in Concert." New York Times, November 21, 1955.
"The program included one work so new that, according

to Mr. Pinkham, it was not even begun until the week before the concert. This was his **Concerto for Celesta and Harpsichord** written for performance on this occasion and so ingratiating a work that it surely will be heard again. . . . The composer showed striking technical facility, elegance and ease of invention. The immediate attraction of his music stems also from the sheer sensuous appeal of color and sonority. One would guess that Mr. Pinkham is headed for popularity and perhaps much more." See: W100a

B100d. Frankenstein, Alfred. "Records in Review." <u>High Fidelity Magazine</u> 7:64 (March 1957)
"First, however, comes Pinkham's absolutely enchanting **Concerto for Celesta and Harpsichord Soli**, a brilliantly classical piece wherein timbre is used to reinforce line much as Bartok used color to clarify the voices in his edition of Bach's **Well-Tempered Clavier**. The bright and tingly sounds of this concerto are completely delightful in themselves, but that is not why they are employed." See: D100a

B100e. H., A. "Pinkham and Powell Works in Composers' 2d Concert." <u>New York Herald Tribune</u>, November 21, 1955.
"Being a harpsichordist himself, as well as an organist and a former composition pupil of Walter Piston and Nadia Boulanger, Mr. Pinkham is firmly dedicated to the so-called neo-classic way of writing music. But he knows how to season and personalize it with piquant, exotic sonorities, and they divert the listener's attention from what might otherwise become patterns of predictable boredom. Everything is suave and elegant, but everything is listenable, too, especially the novelty for the two keyboard instruments." See: W100a

B100f. Newlin, Dika. "Discs." <u>Pan Pipes of Sigma Alpha Iota</u> 50:29 (January 1958)
"The movements of Pinkham's **Concerto** bear the typically baroque designations of 'Prelude', 'Ricercare', and 'Canzona'. However, the sonorities sometimes suggest Oriental rather than baroque influence--especially the 'Prelude' of Pinkham, which is reminiscent of the sound of a Javanese gamelan orchestra." See: D100a

B100g. Smith, Warren Storey. "Daniel Pinkham". <u>American Composers Alliance Bulletin</u> 10:10 (#1, 1961)
"The first movement marked Allegro . . . is what might be called titillating. Yet for all its modernity of timbre, contemporary rhythmic and tonal structure, the impress of the Baroque is there, thanks alike to the celesta and the way the harpsichord is employed. The first and third movements are 'busy' and wholly impersonal. More expressive by far is the Ricercare. . . . Tonal brilliance and rhythmic energy characterize the final Canzona." See: W100

B100h. Trimble, Lester. Notes from record cover CRI 109.
"The work, dedicated to Henry Cowell, presents a

unique and delightful experience in sonorities. For, the incisiveness of the harpsichord's tone; the ability of the celeste both to blend with and to stand out in contrast against the plucked sounds; and the essential delicacy of both instruments, all serve to create an extrememly beautiful fusion of colors." See: W100

B107. **Partita**

B107a. Flanagan, William. "Classics." Hi Fi/Stereo Review 9:82 (September 1962)
"Pinkham's **Partita for Harpsichord** represents the smooth, controlled and highly idiomatic writing that one has come to expect of this young composer." See: D107a

B107b. Frankenstein, Alfred. "Other Classical Reviews." High Fidelity 12:66 (July 1962)
"The great piece on this disc, however, is the Pinkham, which occupies all of the second side. This is an amazing work, one that used some old forms--toccata, canon, fugue--but in no antiquarian spirit. The harmonic texture is entirely modern, and so is the composer's exploration of instrumental color. . . . The main thing is that this is a tremendous work, one of the finest keyboard sonatas yet written by an American, and it is magnificiently performed by the composer himself." See: D107a

B107c. Fuller, David. "Music Reviews." Music Library Association Notes 22:818-9 (September 1965)
"Daniel Pinkham's **Partita** is a big work, lasting 24 minutes, and it is exclusively for harpsichord, the piano being unmentioned as a possible medium anywhere in the score. . . . The work, if not extraordinarily inventive from the point of view of instrumental sound, is satisfyingly idiomatic. A happy corollary to the lack of flash and surprises is ease of execution. . . . The work is thus well launched toward the success which it highly merits as much for its intrinsic quality as for its utility in helping to fill an important gap in modern harpsichord repertoire." See: W107

B111. **Ascension Cantata**

B111a. McCafferty, James T. "Beethoven Shatters." Columbus Dispatch (Ohio), March 23, 1970.
"Commissioned by the University for the occasion, it proved to be a work of uncommon interest. Pinkham has dared to face the unfashionable when melodiousness seems more desirable, and the result is comprehensive writing of surging impact. The piece is in four movements, sung in incredibly swift Latin. It is dissonant enough to defy casual performance, yet not beyond the reach of groups which would approach it studiously. Time alone will tell of its permanency and

popularity. The important thing is that Pinkham is a composer of unusual promise. His contrasts are striking, his dynamics startling. He knows how to be modern without going overboard. A standing ovation ended the evening. Never was it more deserved." See: W111a

B114. Christmas Cantata; Sinfonia Sacra

B114a. Anderson, William. "Christmas on Disc." Hi Fi Stereo Review 19:4 (December 1967)
"Another delight here is Daniel Pinkham's big, bold Christmas Cantata." See: D114a

B114b. Cohn, Arthur. Recorded Classical Music; a Critical Guide to Compositions and Performances. New York, Schirmer Books, 1981.
"Simple but strong contemporaneous music." (p. 1376) See: D114a

B114c. Duffy, John. "St. Cecilia and Pinkham Go Well." Boston Herald American, December 17, 1976.
"The program Pinkham selected was a festive one, opening with his own Christmas Cantata for chorus and double brass choir. It was an apt choice, for the piece epitomized the entire concert, encompassing the dance-like joyfulness of the occasion and the awe and wonder of the great mystery and miracle of the birth of Christ. The brass ensemble through- out the concert was as responsive as the singers to the spirit of the text." See: W114k

B114d. Durgin, Cyrus. "Pinkham, Hovhaness New Choral Music Heard." Boston Globe, December 11, 1957.
"This is a large work for voices and brass instruments with organ, written in a sort of new baroque manner. The Sinfonia Sacra tells the Christmas story in a Latin text, and is easily the strongest music Pinkham has given us. No matter that the antique brilliance of, say, a Gabrieli, is reflected in the score; it also has its own individuality and to a certain extent contemporary flavor. It is highly sing- able, too, as well as flowing and a little ornate." See: W114b

B114e. Ericson, Raymond. "Recordings: A L'Enfance for All Seasons." New York Times, December 3, 1967.
"Christmas Cantata. . . is a short three-part work, relatively conservative in style, written with taste and sensitivity." See: D114a

B114f. Faber, Bernard. "Chorus at Fine Arts." Clark Scarlet (Clark University, Worcester, Mass.), December 6, 1957.
"Mr. Pinkham is a young composer who has overcome many of the downfalls of contemporary music and has arrived at a substantial and definite style. The audience received the

work with the same gusto and enthusiasm it had exhibited throughout the afternoon." See: W114a

B114g. Hart, Philip. "Recitals and Miscellany." High Fidelity Magazine 17:114 (December 1967)
"The Pinkham Cantata, which apparently here appears on records for the first time, achieves a very successful amalgam of the old and new in musical style. Though harking back to the architectural antiphony of St. Marks, the virtuosity of the vocal and instrumental writing could be conceived and performed only in our time. Moreover, though the harmony often sounds like a modern extension of modal devices, the rhythm owes much to Stravinsky." See: D114a

B114h. Kelly, Kevin. "N. E. Prep Schools' 14th Annual Concert." Boston Globe, April 20, 1959.
"A richly modernized reverential hymn that ended with an exultant 'Gloria in Excelsis Deo,' which was superbly realized." See: W114d

B114i. Morin, Raymond. "Christmas Music Pleases Fine Arts Course Patrons." Worcester Telegram (Mass.), December 2, 1957.
"The high point was perhaps the first performance anywhere of Daniel Pinkham's Sinfonia Sacra, written this year by the Bostonian for the Conservatory Chorus. While it leans securely on contemporary methods, an interesting, even stimulating correlation has been established between words and music. The first and third portions delve into irregular rhythmic formations that might have jarred the serenity of the text had the words not been so clearly pronounced. Greater interest exists in the middle sequence that weaves attractive tonal patterns, and expressive thought over a droned bass." See: W114a

B114j. "Reviews." Brass Quarterly 2:41 (September 1958)
"The first two movements have a rather medieval air about them. The third is more baroque, with its lavish sonority and flourishing trumpets. The harmonic idiom is somewhat dissonant, a favorite device being a triad containing both the major and minor third above the root. . . .All told, it is a very effective work. There are a few spots where the harmony seems a bit strained, and one awkward place in the last movement where the trumpet descant gives a wrench, but the over-all impression is of a very pleasant work. The vocal writing is especially well done, with very few difficult intervals for a modern work." See: W114

B114k. Robb, Christina. "Music Master." Boston Globe, February 12, 1984.
"His greatest hit--Christmas Cantata, a seven-minute celebration in Latin for chorus, organ and trumpets. . . combines the spirit of Giovanni Gabrieli's sixteenth-century echoic choral symphonies with Pinkham's own cheerful, tuneful contemporaneity." See: W114

B1141. Slettom, Jeanyne Bezoier and D. R. Martin. "Music on Record." Minneapolis-St. Paul Magazine 10:54 (December 1982)
"Highlights include **Christmas Cantata**, a three-move-ment work of contrasting moods and engaging, accented rhythms." See: D114b

B114m. Wolffers, Jules. "Festival Brass, Ensemble Chorus Pro Musica." Boston Herald, June 20, 1960.
"Daniel Pinkham's hauntingly beautiful **Sinfonia Sacra** had its genesis in ancient church music chants. . . . Verdi used to say that he wanted tunes that the public would whistle when they left the opera house. Last night I heard a listener whistling the main theme of Dan Pinkham's Sacred Symphony!" See: W114e

B116. A Curse, a Lament and a Vision

B116a. Zuck, Barbara. "Cantari Honors Four." Columbus Dispatch (Ohio), January 28, 1985.
"The world premiere of the Pinkham piece was a smashing success. The singers performed the work a cappella as though they had been singing it for years. Enunciation of the text was especially outstanding. It is set in a declamatory, essentially homorhythmic style identifiably the composer's, and one tired slightly of the spewing out of so much text. Only in the last section did the parts separate. This is an efficient setting of a great amount of material. Yet Pinkham's harmonic style and knack for drama are always a joy." See: W116a

B117. Daniel in the Lions' Den

B117a. Abell, Kathy. "Pinkham Concert Worth Every Cent Paid." Eastern News (Eastern Illinois University), March 8, 1974.
"The third piece on the program, **Daniel in the Lions' Den** used piano, percussion and fine solo performances. . . to blend with Dale Morgan's narration and create a good musical story based on the Biblical tale. In this number, the Concert Choir created interesting background sound effects, such as crowd noise and roaring lions." See: W117d

B117b. Deal, Susan Parr. Conductor's Analysis of Selected Works by Rolande de Lasseu, Johann Herman Schein, George Frederick Handel, Ralph Vaughan Williams and Daniel Pinkham. M.M. thesis, Southwestern Baptist Theological Seminary, 1982.
Analysis of Pinkham's compositional style as exemp-lified by his **Daniel in the Lions' Den**. See: W117

B117c. Giffin, Glenn. "Pinkham Works Intrigue." Denver Post, April 9, 1979.

"A modern composer's answer to the medieval miracle play. Pinkham may or may not have been influenced by 'The Play of Daniel', a 12th century liturgical drama with music, but his **Daniel in the Lions' Den** for two pianos, percussion and tape has a similar naive quality about it." See: W117e

B117d. Hyatt, Willard. "The Journal Reviews." Music Journal 32:47 (April 1974)
"The intensity of the dramatic line mounts rapidly with climactic realistic sound effects augmenting the drama of the story. The score makes arresting use of instrumental color and rhythmic excitement. Baritone, bass and tenor soloists sang with dynamic exactitude and choral tone was at all times massive and vigorous." See: W117e

B117e. Program notes, February 11, 1973 concert.
"Commissioned by the Music for Voices project, **Daniel in the Lions' Den** was written by Mr. Pinkham late in 1972. His text is derived from the sixth chapter of Daniel in which the Old Testament author records God's rescue of Daniel from the pit of lions. The first part of the work, in which the story unfolds, is scored for narrator, mixed chorus, two pianos, percussion, and electronic tape. The work closes with an anthem based on Psalm 116, in which the works of King Darius are heard praising the living God 'whose kingly power shall not be weakened, whose sovereignty shall have no end. Hallelujah'." See: W117

B117f. Wynne, Peter. "Voices Merge in Workshop." Record (Hackensack, N.J.), February 13, 1973.
"The tape aside, there was nothing in the work that could not have been composed anytime in the last 60 years. Nor is this meant as criticism. The piece was dissonant, yet it contained many singable melodies and some jazzy rhythms. Even the electronic music, so often the bane of audiences, should have been within the reach of the layman. The tape sections that accompanied the singers and players at the opening and closing of the work apparently a random assort- ment of bleeps--seemed to add little. However, the sections that provided the solo accompaniment to Daniel's prayers were truly pleasant, like Oriental string and percussion music." See: W117a

B118. **The Descent Into Hell**

B118a. Horne, Barbara. "Exciting Evening of Music." Wesleyan Pharos (West Virginia Wesleyan College), October 22, 1980.
"The text grew out of Pinkham's interest in the extraordinary legends in the Apocryphal New Testament. This 4th century story was particularly exciting to Pinkham because it revealed Hell not as a place, but as a person, swallowing up death and later being cast off by the King of Glory." See: W118a

B119. **Easter Cantata**

B119a.   I.,   Y.   "Reviews."   <u>Music</u> <u>Ministry</u> 4:36 (February 1963)
    "This cantata should strike the fancy of those who want to sing something different.   Indeed, this is strange music!   The opening chorus utilizes two contrasting motifs; one an alternating dissonance of a major and minor second; the other an angular lament in unison.   The next chorus juxtaposes a running sixteenth-note accompaniment against staid block chords for voices.   Then follows a four-part canon, a cappella for the first 35 measures.   The final chorus (there are no solos) is again harmonically conceived, ending with bold 'alleluias'."   <u>See</u>: W119

B119b.   Page, Tim.   "Concert: Musica Sacra Offers Modern Program."   <u>New</u> <u>York</u> <u>Times</u>, April 26, 1987.
    "Mr. Pinkham's **Easter Cantata** proved an apt curtain raiser.   With its bright jangle of mallet instruments, its simple, direct and consonant settings, it brought to mind Orff's Christmas music with a smattering of the pastoral modality of Ralph Vaughan Williams.   It is an attractive, unassuming work that deserves a wider audience."   <u>See</u>: W119c

B119c.   Reyes, James E.   "Music Reviews."   <u>Music</u> <u>Library</u> <u>Association</u> <u>Notes</u> 21:455-6 (Summer 1964)
    "It is marked by the composer's directness of musical expression and his ear for colorful brass and percussion sounds. . . . The present **Cantata** is a succinct dramatic narrative of the Resurrection story in music, rather than an elaborate musical commentary thereon.   The simplicity and brevity of musical gesture in the work, however, may be seen both as virtue and as shortcoming.   The composer's musical intentions are clear, but few of the musical ideas presented here are really distinguished.   One would have preferred to see some of them developed at greater length, to the exclusion of others."   <u>See</u>: W119

B119d.   Woessner, Bob.   "Pinkham, SNC Performers Show Versatility."   <u>Green</u> <u>Bay</u> <u>Press-Gazette</u> (Wisc.),   February 20, 1971.
    "The concluding **Easter Cantata** was a triumphant selection.   It used a wide range of instrumentation.   The first movement, for example, used trumpets, horns, trombones, bass, celeste, timpani and percussion--part of it off stage. It went through the familiar Resurrection story, but the treatment was often modern and lilting."   <u>See</u>: W119a

B120. **An Emily Dickinson Mosaic**

B120a.   George, Collins.   "Pinkham Offers a Treat: His Own Works."   <u>Detroit</u> <u>Free</u> <u>Press</u>, June 1, 1975.

"One cavil might be that his most elaborate work was his setting of the Dickinson poems, which just seemed to call out for the type of simplicity which usually is one of Pinkham's long points." See: W120b

B120b. "Weekend Features **Dickinson Mosaic.**" Mount Holyoke News, (South Hadley, Mass.), June 3, 1962.
"A celesta, a giant tam-tam, a suspended cymbal, a glockenspiel and a timpani were responsible for several special effects which highlighted the piece, the cymbal clash provided emphasis, while the bell-like sound of the celesta balanced the glockenspiel. . . .The dramatic effectiveness of the piece results from rhythmic and chromatic variety; it has been said of Mr. Pinkham that his music 'always sounds well in performance.' Like the poetry of Emily Dickinson, according to Miss Douglass, the music is 'unstereotyped'." See: W120a

B121. **Fanfares**

B121a. Belt, Byron. "Choral Groups Merit Bravos at Carnegie Hall." Star-Ledger (Newark, N. J.), December 16, 1982.
"Daniel Pinkham's **Fanfares** scored impressively in its mixture of brass and voices." See: W121f

B121b. Bernhart, William H. "Centennial No Triumph." Reading Times (Pa.), April 26, 1975.
"Pinkham has an impressive background in music, but **Fanfares** was indicative of none of this. Except for the final 'Psalm', it was weak and uninspiring." See: W121b

B121c. Dyer, Richard. "NEC Chorus: Sweet Tone and Ardent Delivery." Boston Globe, March 11, 1987.
"The Pinkham piece has the advantage of being fun to sing and fun to listen to. The Psalm at the end works up a fine celebratory head of steam, but the most unusual movement is the third, a haunting 'Alleluia' that creates its own internal acoustic by means of hocketing and echo effects." See: W121g

B121d. Kjelson, Lee. "Something for Everyone." School Musician, Director and Teacher 56:38 (December 1984)
"Our Miami Civic Chorale struggled with certain areas of this work. In fact, we lost a small percentage of our membership because of the musical demands it places on individual singers. On the other hand, we achieved through its rehearsal and performance valuable musical experiences dealing with rhythmic and tonal accuracy. I recommend it highly." See: W121

B121e. Kratzensteen, Marilou. "Festival Service of Convocation." Diapason 67:5 (August 1976)
"The climax of the service was Daniel Pinkham's new

anthem, **Fanfares**, for choir, congregation, organ, brass, and percussion. This is very singable music. The refrain ('O praise the Lord, alleluia'), sung by the congregation, haunts me still. The congregational part is easy enough so that it could be learned by an unskilled congregation with a modicum of good will. The work as a whole is a brilliant statement of praise. Participating in this work was a moving religious experience, as well as an artistic one." <u>See</u>: W121c

B122. **Four Elegies**

  B122a. Kratzensteen, Marilou. "Cecilia Society." <u>Diapason</u> 67:5 (August 1976)
    "The **Four Elegies** by Pinkham are an eloquent work, distinguised by expressive, yet refined text setting. While the work has a contemporary ring, one notes that the composer is not afraid of the triad nor of tonal implications. The choral writing is basically homophonic and very idiomatic to the voice. . . . The elegies are connected by three interludes of progressively increasing intensity, performed by tape and various instrumental combinations. For the interludes, the composer utilized fragile, crystalline, sonorities which set a dream-like mood, difficult to describe in words." <u>See</u>: W122b

  B122b. Schwartz, Lloyd. "Teeter [sic] Superior." <u>Boston Herald American</u>, June 16, 1976.
    "Daniel Pinkham's choice was mainly to allow the music to follow the poetry. The rhythms, for the most part, reflect the rhythms of the verses. Sung by a tenor soloist, even with full chorus, most of the words come through with elegant clarity. The settings are more than recitative, but not quite aria. What moves us is the text. More affecting musically are the interludes separating the poems, where solo instruments (bassoon, for example, or English horn--played with wonderful expressivity by Stephen Tramontozzi and Raymond Toubman, respectively) lyrically or searchingly or seductively wind around or rise above tinkly electronics on tape. Here Pinkham seems to release his fullest emotional response to the poems." <u>See</u>: W122a

B123. **Getting to Heaven**

  B123a. Buell, Richard. [Concert Review] <u>Boston Globe</u>, October 27, 1987.
    "Musically it shone with the premiere performace of Daniel Pinkham's Emily Dickinson settings **Getting to Heaven**, which made the texts clear as day, sounded genuine emotional depths, and had a spare, piquant sound not unlike the **Requiem Canticles** of Stravinsky or late Britten." <u>See</u>: W123a

B125. **In Heaven Soaring Up**

B125a. Miller, Nancy. "King's Chapel Marks 300 Years." Boston Globe, January 14, 1986.
"Commissioned for this occasion by King's Chapel, **In Heaven Soaring Up** is based on three poems by Edward Taylor, an orthdox Puritan minister in Westfield for many years until his death in 1729. Within a harmonically rich but predominantly atonal idiom, Pinkham judiciously intersperses passages of a more diatonic character as the poetic context suggests—in the refrain concluding each stanza of 'The Coach for Glory', for example, in the recurrent interlocking of major and minor thirds in 'Thy Spinning Wheele', or in selectively highlighting certain colorful phrases of 'Ascended Up On High' ('Taylor at his most extravagant theatrical baroque,' as Pinkham aptly noted)." See: W125a

B126. Jonah

B126a. Boeringer, James. "Choral Music Reviewed." Music: The A.G.O. Magazine 2:46 (September 1968)
"Pinkham has devised his own brief libretto, and all the music grows directly out of the words, both melodically and rhythmically, though he wrings every syllable dry of its possibilities, requiring ultimate irregular athleticism and technique from the voices." See: W126

B126b. Boswell, Rolfe. "Debut of Pinkham's **Jonah**." Boston Record American, May 18, 1967.
"Acoustically excellent Jordan Hall reverberated with the replicated sounds of this tumultuous and tempestuous music. Add Daniel Pinkham to the brief roster of those composers, American and British, who know how to set the stepmother tongue to music." See: W126a

B126c. Cunkle, Frank. "Choral Music." Diapason 58:17 (November 1967)
"His dramatic cantata, Jonah, used solos in mezzo, tenor and bass-baritone, orchestra and chorus to tell the familiar Old Testament story. . . . The work is of considerable stature." See: W126

B126d. Harris, McLaren. "Concert Features Modernism." Boston Herald, May 18, 1967.
"Much of the vocal writing is well-drawn along lines of natural speech inflection; the work has a fine dramatic peak during the tempest, and a gently-passioned, almost tender prayer of Jonah following. The Psalm sung by Jonah's wife came off more as a recitative than as an arioso, and the market scene cries were a trifle distracting (Sprechstimme may serve better), but the great dynamic range aided by 6 percussion instruments, contributed a decisive effect. Pinkham was warmly congraulated." See: W126a

B126e. Monson, Karen. "Jordan Hall Concert Features 3 Firsts." Boston Globe, May 18, 1967.

163

"Dramatically, the Cantata is a great success. To a degree, this makes up for its lack of musical innovation. The characters of Jonah and his wife are clearly portrayed in the music. . . . The choral parts, though well-performed, are unimaginative, and the market scene, intended to give the illusion of Jonah's progress through the market, doesn't work. Consistently fine, however, is the setting of the text; Pinkham bows to the rhythm of the words, capitalizing on their dramatic impact." See: W126a

B126f. Nadeau, Roland. "Pinkham's **Jonah** Premiere Marks Centennial." Christian Science Monitor, May 26, 1967.
"Daniel Pinkham has a tremendous flair for music imagery. He captures with tone the mood and essence of his text with startling vividness. For example, the storm scene when Jonah is cast away was a blistering howl of furious sound. On the next words, 'The wind again gentle', a floating calm suddenly suffused the orchestra which then dispersed itself into beautiful, open, but streaked sonorities. This was magical. . . . The choral writing throughout, as can be expected with Pinkham, was stunning and the declamatory music for the soloists very good." See: W126a

B126g. Newell, Dorothy. "Cantata in a Whale." Quincy Patriot Ledger (Mass.), May 18, 1967.
"The result is a strong and stirring work, which carries with it all the emotion of Jonah's uncertain destiny, the stormy gale, the whale's belly--and God himself, a conservatory-style John Houston, calling then freeing His servant." See: W126a

B126h. Ottaway, Hugh. "Modern Choral." The Musical Times 109:265 (March 1968)
"Daniel Pinkham's **Jonah** is the sort of biblical cantata I always hope to avoid; declamatory, brow-beating, and sadly predictable in its melodramatic effects. To make matters worse, the composer's obsession with major sevenths and minor seconds and ninths conditions nearly every step he takes. A depressing example of the new academicism." See: W126

B127. **The Lamentations of Jeremiah**

B127a. "ACDA Convention Sets New Goals." Choral Journal 6:26 (May-June 1966)
"This interesting and unusual addition to contemporary choral music exemplifies further the originality and musical perception of this composer." See: W127a

B127b. Jackson, Arthur Wesley. A Conductor's Analysis of Selected Works by Giovanni Pierluigi da Palestrina, Orlando di Lasso, William Byrd, Giovanni Gabrieli, Dietrich Buxtehude, and Daniel Pinkham. M.M. thesis, Southwestern Baptist Theological Seminary, 1976.

Detailed stylistic and tone row analysis of Pinkham's
Lamentations of Jeremiah (1966). See: W127

B129. **Magnificat**

B129a. Thoburn, Crawford R., "Conductor's Reactions on
Preparing First Performance." Wells Courier (Wells College,
Aurora, N. Y.), April 1968.
"I wanted to offer the commission to a composer who
knows the voice and who has had ample experience writing in
this medium. Daniel Pinkham is eminently qualified in this
regard, both as a conductor and as a composer. The results
are a number of 'non-commercial effects' which one would not
often find, but which can be brought off successfully, and
which enhance the interest of the work for both the performers and audience. For instance, Pinkham takes advantage
of our 'famous gutsy alto sound' by writing low alto parts
that range down to D below middle C. He divides the choir
in several places into as many as six parts. This violates
two cardinal laws of commercial arranging; first that alto
parts should not go below A below middle C, and secondly that
one should not write for more than three voice parts in
pieces for women's chorus. The results are most effective,
and if we show that it can be done, perhaps other composers
will follow suit." See W129

B130. **The Passion of Judas**

B130a. Dyer, Richard. "Concert Spans 29 Years of Daniel
Pinkham's Works." Boston Globe, October 31, 1984.
"The most impressive of these works, though, is **The
Passion of Judas**, which uses spoken narration from the Bible,
choral settings from the psalms, poems by James Wright and
Farber for soloists, and a playlet by R. C. Norris. While
Pinkham's music hasn't made major shifts of style, it does
operate at different levels of density, and in this work it
approaches a profound subject, the nature of evil, on a deep
level of engagement. The tolling, solemn final chorus, on
verses from Psalm 51, belongs among Pinkham's most impressive
achievements." See: W130e

B130b. Dyer, Richard. "Pinkham's Newest Work Applauded."
Boston Globe, June 21, 1976.
"The work is distinguished in conception, skillful in
composition, deeply moving in its effect. The music, conducted by the composer, is scored for small instrumental
ensemble, with the chamber organ and the harp playing the
most prominent role. The music for the playlet seemed to me
the least interesting--the text, of necessity, is mostly
expository, and while the music points up the words with
great resourcefulness, there is little opportunity for
emotional expansiveness, for real singing music, until the
end. There the parents sing 'He is the blessing of God on

us, our first born, our pride, our treasure. We have named him Judas.' This is a passage of great and shuddering beauty, and it was fervently sung by Pamela Gore and John Franklin." See: W130b

B130c. Lawrence, Arthur. "AGO Mid-Winter Conclave." Diapason 68:4 (February 1977)
   "Daniel Pinkham then led soloists, chorus, and five instrumentalists in a performance of his recent **The Passion of Judas** (1975). While I would never expect to be disappointed by one of Mr. Pinkham's compositions, I was nevertheless not prepared for the impact a hearing of this work makes. To my mind, it was the most moving event of the conclave, and I predict that this will be judged a major contribution to 20th-century choral literature. Based on an alternation of Biblical texts and three modern texts, the work makes a powerful dramatization of the words by using the same time levels employed in the Bach Passions. The sounds, however, are from the present, and reflect, to my ear, much the same style used by such French masters as Lili Boulanger, Poulenc, and Honegger." See: W130c

B130d. Pinkham, Daniel. Notes from the score.
   "**The Passion of Judas** at once relects my interest in the mystery play of the medieval church (such as **the Play of Daniel**) as well as my interest in the experiments with chronology as found in Bach's two extant Passion settings. The mystery play is didactic even as it entertains--an acted-out sermon. And even if it presents no surprises (everybody, after all, knows the story) we at least see the parade of familiar Biblical characters for a moment clothed in this year's flesh. . . . I conceived the work as a theater piece to be performed in the setting of the chancel of the church. It lends itself, consequently, to a variety of production possibilities: staging in the manner of opera; choreography, as in ballet; or with introduction of lights, slides or with other visual effects. It may also be done effectively as a concert work." See: W130

B130e. Reinthaler, Joan. "Splendid **Passion**." Washington Post, June 7, 1976.
   "In a tradition traceable from the medieval liturgical Easter dramas, through Bach's Passion settings, Pinkham has treated the tragedy of Judas on several levels. Sections straight from the New Testament, unadorned and read with powerful simplicity by Tod Walch, alternated with the musical movements and gave the work structural unity. The three 'solo' movements, settings of poems from different sources, provide both ironic comment and dramatic background to the story. Pinkham has used a familiar contemporary recitative idiom for these sections, but has endowed them with rather more than usual lyricism. The choruses, simple but effective settings of pertinent psalms, reflect on the drama." See: W130a

B132. **The Reproaches**

B132a.   Lowens,   Irving.   "Choral Performances."   American
Choral Review 9:34 (Spring, 1967)
     "The   major effort by this newly organized   group   was
The Reproaches, a setting of Greek and Latin passages from
the liturgy of second-century Constantinople composed by
Daniel Pinkham.   The work can be performed by a variety of
chóral and instrumental combinations--this one was by ten
singers, flute, oboe, clarinet, bassoon, French horn, and
organ. The writing was in traditional vein, rather reminiscent at moments of Messiaen or Vaughan Williams; the performance of it was praised by the critics more than the piece
itself." See: W132c

B133. **Requiem**

B133a.   Chapin, Louis. "Audiences Attracted by Innova-
tions." Christian Science Monitor, January 26, 1963.
     "But communication reached its greatest depths of the
two evenings in Daniel Pinkham's **Requiem**, composed in memory
of his younger brother, and conducted by Mr. Pinkham in its
world premiere. Performed by a small chorus and two soloists
with brass and string bass accompaniment, it warmed a
liturgical tradition with the living desire to crystallize
feelings. The two-lined texture in most of the voice writing
underlines restraint and feasibility, though there is occasional awkwardness in the contrapuntal leaping of the alto
and tenor solists, and extraordinary demands pulling the
latter toward the bass range." See: W133a

B133b.   Johnson, Thomas. "Chamber Music; Some Old and New
Faces." Musical America 83:38 (March 1963)
     "Pinkham's conservative **Requiem** uses brass sextet and
double bass to accompany the voices.   The double bass adds a
softness to produce an effective funereal quality. The instruments move in rather undifferentiated chordal patterns
against the angular vocal lines and often, not much happens
musically. But the work does achieve an appropriately touching, solemn mood." See: W133a

B133c.   M., M.   "Pinkham's **Requiem** Has Local Premiere."
Boston Globe, March 14, 1963.
     "The choral writing is deliberately restrained and is
almost stark with never more than two parts singing their
gentle polyphony. A brass choir (two trumpets, two horns and
two trombones) with double bass provide a rich mass of sound
underlying the vocal lines. . . . The economy of this 15-
minute piece is quite remarkable: even the shortest part
makes a musical statement and sets a mood." See: W133b

B134. **Saint Mark Passion**

B134a.   Arlen,   Walter.   "Pinkham Conducts Own Work."   Los
Angeles Times, March 30, 1968.
        "The Passion was quite in a different class. Given in
less cramped surroundings by more distinctly professional
forces, its dramatically charged stark idiom is sure to leave
an even stronger effect than it did on this occasion.   As a
conductor, Pinkham obviously knows his business." See: W134b

B134b.   Monaco, Richard A. "Music Review." Music Library
Association Notes 24: 360 (December 1967)
        "The harmony is more complex and dissonant than one
has come to expect from Pinkham.   The chorus is, however,
given all too ample support by the instrumental group to the
detriment of the music. There is simply not much of interest
going on in the accompaniment. . . . The music needs rhythmic
vitality which cannot be supplied by changes of tempo." See:
W134

B134c.   Morin, Raymond. "Saint Mark Passion at Southboro."
Worchester Daily Telegram (Mass.), May 24, 1965.
        "The composer combined objectivity with an obvious
sympathy and dedication to the religious text.   His instrumental setting has strong appeal and serves as a stimulus to
thought.   Choral ensemble spans a wide-spread dramatic range
from an almost vitriolic denunciation, 'Crucify Him!' to a
peacefully reflective close, 'My soul, wait.' A startling
enigma is Pinkham's assigning the voice and words of Christ
to the soprano soloist. . . . Musically, Pinkham's score is
eventful with contemporary idioms.   This he has accomplished
without disdaining tradition.   Musical elements remain af-
fixed to the spirit of the text. His use of the solo voice,
however, is at the least, a challenge to credulity."   See:
W134a

B134d.   Owen, Barbara. "Recitals and Concerts." American
Organist 48:15 (August 1966)
        "In the St. Mark Passion he has. . . produced what to
this listener is his most mature writing in this medium. The
spare, dissonant, polyrhythmic punctuations are there, underlying and undergirding the chorus, recitative and solo, yet
never are they obvious or conspicuous, never do they obtrude
or call attention to the means. . . . The St. Mark Passion
represents another milestone in the work of Daniel Pinkham.
Of all his larger choral works, even his Requiem, this
appears to display the greatest sophistication yet."   See:
W134a

B134e.   Pinkham, Daniel.   Program notes, May 22, 1965
concert.
        "My Saint Mark Passion is largely fashioned after the
musical settings of the North German Reformation composers of
the Baroque era.   Thus the role of the Evangelist is sung by
a solo tenor in recitativo secco and the brief dramatic roles
of Judas and Pilate are also sung by solo voices, low bass

and high baritone, respectively. The chorus portrays a variety of active participants in the drama including Roman soldiers, High Priests and the crowd. It also sings one of the Words of Christ on the Cross. In addition it sings passages of commentary, admonition or contemplation, as does the solo soprano. . . . The instrumental forces are divided into two groups. The smaller group consists of chamber organ, harp and double bass and accompanies the Evangelist in a manner which recalls early Baroque bass continuo technique. The brass and percussion are primarily associated with the chorus and the three other solosits." See W134

B134f. Steinberg, Michael. "Chorus Pro Musica Honors Pinkham." Boston Globe, June 7, 1976.
"The music is just a bit neutral, but it does let you through to the text Pinkham has skillfully put together from gospel, psalm, and prophecy. And in a performance as good as yesterday's, the **Passion** provides 35 minutes of absorbed listening and contemplation." See: W134c

B134g. Ulrich, Homer. A Survey of Choral Music. New York, Harcourt, Brace, Jovanovich, Inc., 1973.
"The dramatic moments of the story are treated with skill and imagination, and the effect of the whole is appropriately moving." (page 195) See: W134

B135. **The Seven Last Words of Christ on the Cross**

B135a. Woessner, Bob. "Pinkham, SNC Performers Show Versatility." Green Bay Press-Gazette (Wisc.), February 20, 1971.
"If personal preference is allowed, it was not the best piece of the evening. The dirge-like quality did not make this a piece to be 'enjoyed.' **The Seven Words** lacked the power of other Pinkham's works also performed." See: W135a

B136. **Stabat Mater**

B136a. Moore, James Stanley. A Conductor's Analysis of "Magnificat a 7" from the 1610 **Vespers** by Claudio Monteverdi, **Missa Brevis St. Joannis De Deo** by Franz Joseph Haydn, and **Stabat Mater** by Daniel Pinkham. M. M. thesis, Southwestern Baptist Theological Seminary, 1977.
Very detailed analysis of Pinkham's **Stabat Mater**, especially from the point of harmony and the use of serial technique. Moore is also concerned with prosody and the use of choral densities. See: W136

B136b. Robison, Richard William. Reading Contemporary Choral Literature: an Analytical Study of Selected Contemporary Choral Compositions with Recommendations for the Improvement of Choral Reading Skills. Ph.D. disseration,

169

Brigham Young University, 1969.
      Robison quotes Pinkham: "I am very fussy about the intonation of my singers and although the piece is in twelve tone technique, I have very carefully considered the spelling of the possible enharmonic places with a view to getting the chords in tune. This is also one of the reasons there are so many <u>pedal</u> <u>points</u> and other tonal reference points, to give notes against which the singers can tune up." <u>See</u>: W136

   B136c. Willoughby, Dale Edward. <u>Performance</u> <u>Preparation</u> <u>of</u> <u>Various</u> <u>Choral</u> <u>Works</u> <u>Representing</u> <u>Selected</u> <u>Periods</u> <u>of</u> <u>Music</u> <u>History</u>. D.M.A. dissertation, University of Miami, 1971.
      Discussion of serial structure and performance values of Pinkham's **Stabat Mater** (1964).

B137. **To Troubled Friends**

   B137a. Dovaras, John. "Choral Reviews." <u>Choral</u> <u>Journal</u> 15:35 (February 1975)
      "Highly dissonant treatment of four James Wright poems, utilizing the serial technique. Contains tonal clusters, rhythmic cross relations, wide intervallic leaps in individual voice parts and other traits characteristic of avant garde music. Electronic tape appears in the second and final movements." <u>See</u>: W137

   B137b. Lock, William. "Chamber Choirs." <u>Choral</u> <u>Journal</u> 12:14 (September 1971)
      "If you conduct an ensemble of advanced singers, you may want to consider Daniel Pinkham's settings of four poems by James Wright. **To Troubled Friends** is for SATB chorus, string orchestra and electronic tape. The vocal entries are simplified by the sounding of the same pitches by the instruments, ahead of time. The melodic leaps are difficult. Sometimes they move alternatively up and down sixths and sevenths. The men are instructed to sing falsetto in more than one place. In another place tone clusters are used. Sobering words and serious avante-garde techniques make this a compelling composition." <u>See</u>: W137

B138. **Wedding Cantata**

   B138a. McKinnon, George.   "Music at the Arts Festival." <u>Boston</u> <u>Globe</u>, June 17, 1957.
      "He manages ably to bring both the joy and the solemnity of a wedding into musically winning forms."   <u>See</u>: W138b

   B138b. Riley, John William. "Alumni Chorus Sings Cantata by Pinkham." <u>Boston</u> <u>Globe</u>, November 7, 1956.
      "Based on four brief verses from the 'Song of Solomon', the cantata calls for small chorus, soprano soloist

and small chamber orchestra. The vocal and instrumental combinations are fortuitous ones. The sonorities which Mr. Pinkham draws from the ensemble are attractive. The melodic lines themselves, while not startlingly original, are nicely suited to the sentiment of the verses. Altogether a successful work in a genre not widely cultivated today." See: W138a

B138c. Rust, Dave. "Pinkham Piece Premieres at SMC." Observer (St. Mary's College, Notre Dame, Ind.), March 2, 1973.
"The Chamber Singers perform some of Pinkham's sweetest and most lyrical works. His **Wedding Cantata**, a four movement vehicle which begins joyful, goes solemn, then wild, then reflective, is an especial favorite of his. He wrote it for the marriage of two Dutch friends, and both bride and groom sang it together with a small group at their own wedding." See: W138g

B138d. Siders, Harvey. "Impressive Premieres by Chorus Pro Musica." Boston Globe, January 27, 1964.
"Daniel Pinkham's **Wedding Cantata** was given a rousing performance, enhanced by the able accompaniment of pianist Allan Sly. Much of this 1959 composition has the delightful lilt and propulsive force of a sea chanty, although it is based on the Song of Solomon." See: W138f

B138e. Tuck, Lon. "Stylish Paul Hill Singers." Washington Post, May 2, 1983.
"The group sang another rarity, Daniel Pinkham's **Wedding Cantata**, settings of four songs drawn from the biblical 'Songs of Songs.' A pleasant, modest lyric work, unswervingly diatonic." See: W138j

B140. **When God Arose**

B140a. Cox, Dennis. "Choral Reviews." Choral Journal 24:39 (February 1984)
"The somewhat angular solo writing contributes to this effective, dramatic composition. The choral sections are accessible to a good church choir, but the solo parts are somewhat demanding. A final quick 'Alleluia' section with unison chorus and glockenspiel provides a strong rhythmic thrust to the powerful conclusion." See: W140

B142. "Alleluia" from **Fanfares**

B142a. McCray, James. "Music for Voices and Organ." Diapason 74:19 (September 1983)
"The organ music is challenging, written on three staves and has a single note sustained by the left foot throughout the entire movement. The right foot, additionally, has a separate line. The majority of the eleven-page setting is in less than six parts with some unison and two-

Bibliography

part singing.   Only the title word is employed; it is set in
long lines, brief rhythmic motives and sometimes divided into
syllables for different sections.   The choral music is not
difficult, but will require a good ensemble as they sing
above some extended, mildly dissonant organ chords. Sophisticated music for advanced choirs." See: W142

B143. Alleluia, Acclamation and Carol; an Easter Set

B143a.   Rust, Dave. "Pinkham Piece Premieres at SMC."
Observer (St. Mary's College, Notre Dame, Ind.), March 2,
1973.
"A splendid almost overpowering example of what the
synthesizer can be made to do for serious music." See: W143a

B144. Amens

B144a.   Alexander, Judy.   "Lexington and Bethesda-Chevy
Chase Making Beautiful Music Together." Minute Man (Lexington, Mass.), March 4, 1976.
"Amens by New England Conservatory of Music's Daniel
Pinkham, was conducted with the aid of a stopwatch.   A tape
deck provided accompaniment.   As Mr. Preston explained, the
composer's instructions require that the choral parts be
timed to coincide with the sounds on the tape. 'Sounds' is
the correct word, for what is on the tape is electronic
music. The conductor and choir had fun with this piece."
See: W144a

B148. Behold, How Good and How Pleasant

B148a.   Woodward, Henry. "Sacred Choral Octavos." Music
Library Association Notes 24:602 (March 1968)
"Only nineteen measures long, Behold How Good and How
Pleasant is simple and direct, but by no means obvious, in
its madrigalesque treatment of the text (Ps. 133:1).   Its
clear, essentially diatonic voice-leading (which nevertheless
produces effective dissonance) is a delight to the ear, and
its beautiful construction is most satisfying." See: W148

B151. Canticle of Praise

B151a. Boeringer, James. "Cantatas, Oratorios and Operas
Reviewed." Music: the AGO and RCCO Magazine 2:50 (December
1968)
"Percussion here (as usual with Pinkham stands for
rather more variety than it does with other composers;
tambourine, bass drum, triangle, suspended cymbal and handbells, giant tam tam, glockenspiel, and vibraphone, but what
they do is not hinted at in the vocal score, except for
effects obviously beyond brass. Pinkham is good at that kind

172

of coloration, however, and if the fundamental simplicity of the choral and brass parts is to be offset at all by the percussion, the two players will be busy." <u>See</u>: W151

B151b.   Cameron, Francis.   "New Choir Music."   <u>Musical</u> <u>Times</u> 110:82 (January 1969)
     "**Canticle of Praise**. . . by David [sic] Pinkham shows an assurance in its harmonic blend of the contemporary and the antique, but there could be more rhythmic excitement in this Song of the Three Holy Children." <u>See</u>: W151

B151c.   Cunkle, Frank.   "Choral Music."   <u>Diapason</u> 59:17 (June, 1968)
     "Strong, virile, contemporary stuff, it was written on commission and should see considerable festival and college use." <u>See</u>: W151

B151d.   Cuno, John.   "Auditorium's Choral Salute." <u>Christian</u> <u>Science</u> <u>Monitor</u>, (New England ed.) February 25, 1965.
     "The work has three sections, each built on a litany, and each litany expressing a different mood. The first is stately; and second, rhythmic and angular; the third, lyrical and warm. The singers were accompanied by brass and percussion creating an intriguing pattern of instrumental relationships. Juxtaposed dissonances and harmonies enhanced the choral lines of tension and release. The effect was to produce a mood of urgency at the beginning and divine assurance at the end of each couplet." <u>See</u>: W151a

B151e.   Jacobson, Bernard.   "New Works."   <u>Music</u> <u>Journal</u> 23:80 (May 1965)
     "It was unlucky for Daniel Pinkham's **Canticle of Praise**, which also received its New York premiere, that Copland's **In the Beginning** was on the same program. Copland's masterly economy underlined, by contrast, the arbitrary nature of Mr. Pinkham's piece. Though very professional in its smooth finish, the **Canticle** seemed devoid of real musical impulse. Its first movement leans heavily on Walton in harmonic idiom, its second begins so much like a passage in Stravinsky's **Symphony of Psalms** that I thought for a moment we had strayed into that work by accident." <u>See</u>: W151b

B151f.   McCray, James.   "Music for Voices & Organ." <u>Diapason</u> 70:4 (June 1979)
     "This extended 40-page work will require an advanced choir for performance. There are three movements but the soloist does not appear in the first one. Her material is, at times, rhapsodic and explores the full soprano range. It has many wide intervallic jumps and will need an accomplished singer. The music is dissonant, but usually the choral dissonances are approached so that the difficulty is solved from linear writing." <u>See</u>" W151

B151g.   Steinberg, Michael.   "Choral Blessing on the

House." <u>Boston</u> <u>Globe</u>, February 25, 1965.
"The **Canticle of Praise** is festive, but not pompous.
It was well calculated for the over 600 choristers involved,
sticking to simple rhythmic patterns (except for some rapid
staccato declamation for a semi-chorus) and to intervals and
textures not liable to becoming muddy. The accompaniment is
for brass and percussion, and its effectiveness showed the
composer's good sense in avoiding the inevitably hopeless
struggles of strings and woodwinds to be clearly heard
against so many singers. Moreover, Pinkham served himself
well in that the piece is so written as not to be restricted
to the special performance condition that prevailed this
time." <u>See</u>: W151a

B151h. Taylor, Robert. "6 Choruses Perform at War
Memorial." <u>Boston</u> <u>Herald</u>, February 25, 1965.
"Mr. Pinkham's **Canticle of Praise** turned out to be a
work of harmonic felicity, flecked by delicate orchestral
sound effects to underline the words, a piece fundamentally
conservative, but nevertheless grateful to the ear." <u>See</u>:
W151a

B151i. Wienandt, Elwyn A. "Choral Music." <u>Music</u> <u>Library</u>
<u>Association</u> <u>Notes</u> 25:831 (June 1969)
"Without the contrasting, but otherwise unremarkable,
solo lines, the choral setting would become the victim of its
repetitious text, a problem the composer has wisely minimized
even further by overlapping phrases of text in imitative
entrances, rather than giving each voice the same words at
each point of entry. This piling up of text is most welcome,
for without it the piece might, as the mercy of the Lord
which is apostrophized near its conclusion, seem to endure
forever. The barring is regular throughout, to the detriment
of some unimportant words that fall on strong beats. Except
for the matter of vocal range mentioned above, the work
presents no great problem to the chorus, for it is carefully
supported by the instrumental ensemble. The soprano soloist
must be able to cover wide leaps without such help, for
sustained chords or repeated single pitches often provide the
only foundation for her exposed melodies." <u>See</u>: W131

B160. **Elegy**

B160a. Cohn, Arthur. <u>Recorded</u> <u>Classical</u> <u>Music;</u> <u>a</u> <u>Critical</u>
<u>Guide</u> <u>to</u> <u>Compositions</u> <u>and</u> <u>Performances</u>. New York, Schirmer
Books, 1981.
"The light dissonance that sprays the first of these
pieces is a perfect example of creative good taste and stylistic reasonableness." (p. 1375) <u>See</u>: D160a

B165. **For Thee Have I Waited**

B165a. Goodrich, Herbert A. "Choral Reviews." <u>Choral</u>

Journal 25:38 (September 1984)
    "Though it lasts only one minute, the composer skill-
fully established a five-bar homophonic theme characterized
by ascending parallel thirds, repeats that theme with the
same text, and closed the work with contrasting material that
makes this work excellent as an introductory piece for the
worship service." See: W165

B168. **Glory Be to God; Motet for Christmas Day**

    B168a. Cohn, Arthur. Recorded Classical Music, a Critical
Guide to Compositions and Performances. New York, Schirmer
Books, 1981.
    "A refreshing approach to devotional music, Pinkham's
Motet unaccompanied double chorus used imitation both of
phrases and bell-like sounds. The result is hightly communi-
cable." (p. 1376) See: D168a

    B168b. "Sing Unto the Ford a New Song." Saturday Review
48:60 (January 30, 1965)
    "Daniel Pinkham. . . has written a **Motet for Christ-
mas Day** that turns out to be a fortunate fusion of procedures
both ancient and modern." See: W168

B170. **Grace is Poured Abroad**

    B170a. Schuneman, Robert. "New Choral Music." Diapason
62:16 (November 1971)
    "The Psalm-motet for chorus is much in the style of
his earlier works, tonal and harmonically key-centered. The
sounds produced by the texture are rich, even though the
material is spare and economical (as is usual for Pinkham).
It is a fine little piece, quietly expressive, and one that
can be learned easily by an amateur choir capable of decent
pitch retention and careful vocal work." See: W170

B174. **Here Repose, O Broken Body**

    B174a. Siebert, F. Mark. "Music Reviews." Music Library
Association Notes 17:474 (June 1960)
    "Daniel Pinkham's **Here Repose, O Broken Body** is
reflective and expressive with a contrapuntal closing that
moves very nicely." See: W174

B175. **How Precious Is Thy Loving Kindness**

    B175a. Woodward, Henry. "Sacred Choral Octavos." Music
Library Association. Notes 25:609 (March 1969)
    "The fastidious are rewarded, however, by the appear-
ance of Daniel Pinkham's sixth Psalm Motet, a one-minute
setting of the verses from Psalm 36. Here we have a six-

measure opening section, five measures of contrast, and a
seven-measure reminiscence of the beginning, with altered
text and continuation. This may not be quite the best of the
six motets, but it is a piece one may be grateful for. The
accompaniment consists entirely of doubling, but with subtle
differences in sustaining tones and a re-enforced low G on
the final chord." <u>See</u>: W175

B179. In the Beginning of Creation

B179a.   Bryce, Michael E.   <u>A</u> <u>Conductor's</u> <u>Analysis</u> <u>of</u> <u>Se-</u>
<u>lected</u> <u>Works</u> <u>by</u> <u>Andrea</u> <u>Gabrieli,</u> <u>Jacob</u> <u>Handl,</u> <u>W.</u> <u>A.</u> <u>Mozart,</u>
<u>Anton</u> <u>Bruckner,</u> <u>Benjamin</u> <u>Britten,</u> <u>Daniel</u> <u>Pinkham</u> <u>and</u> <u>Vincent</u>
<u>Persichetti</u>.   M. M. thesis, Southwestern Baptist Theological
Seminary, 1982.
     Analysis of one of Pinkham's first works for electron-
ic tape, **In the Beginning of Creation** (1972).   Particular
attention is paid to questions of notation of the mixed aleatoric elements. <u>See</u>: W179

B179b.   Wierzbicki, James. "Performances Solid at Concert
of Modern Sacred Music." <u>St.</u> <u>Louis</u> <u>Globe-Democrat</u>, October
26, 1982.
     "In combination with choir and instruments, though,
the tapes seemed purposeful. . . and sometimes loaded with
specific imagery (as in the 1970 **In the Beginning of Crea-**
tion), the electronic sounds successfully complemented whatever else was going on, and the effect was appealing for as
long as it lasted." <u>See</u>: W179f

B179c.   Woessner, Bob.   "Pinkham, SNC Performers Show
Versatility." <u>Green</u> <u>Bay</u> <u>Press-Gazette</u> (Wisc.), February 20,
1971.
     In the Beginning of Creation exhibited the use of
Moog tape and a random notation arrangement which let the
choir members seemingly do what they wanted. Example: ending
a line with 'abyss,' the choir went into a hissing, sibilant
chorus which suggested everything from soaring birds to a
seething sea." <u>See</u> W179b

B181. The Kings and the Shepherds

B181a.   Slettom, Jeanyne Bezoier and D. R. Martin. "Music
on Record." <u>Minneapolis-St.</u> <u>Paul</u> <u>Magazine</u> 10:54 (December
1982)
     "The Kings and the Shepherds, an attractive carol
that's both lyrical in sound and warmly sung." **See:** D181a

B182. The Lament of David

B182a.   Finn, Robert. "Musical Smorgasbord is Tribute to
Composer." <u>Cleveland</u> <u>Plain</u> <u>Dealer</u>, March 11, 1985.

"Pinkham's interest in spicing his conservative music with modern devices was highlighted in his **Lament of David** (1973), in which the CSU Chorale was accompanied by a tape and was required to make the kind of whispering sounds made famous by the choral music of Penderecki." See: W182c

B187. Love Can Be Still

B187a. Kresh, Paul. "The Charm of the Unexpected: Four Song Cycles by Two New England Composers." Stereo Review 47:62 (April 1982)
"Translucent and delicate in the gossamer accompaniment for piano and glockenspiel woven around the vocal harmonies in Pinkham's treatments of these poems (the echoes of medieval madrigals in **Love Can Be Still** are particularly entrancing)." See: D187a

B188. The Martyrdom of Saint Stephen

B188a. Wells, William B. "Sacred Choral Octavos." Music Library Association Notes 27:574 (March 1971)
"The music ranges from the quiet tenderness of the opening and closing pages to the ferocious middle section, set in an allegro 5/8 meter. One cannot discuss this work without calling attention to the effective way in which Pinkham sets the words 'And they stoned Stephen. . . '. Beginning on an octave unison G, the voices fan out to a wildly spread minor-seventh chord for the word 'stoned' then return by sliding back to the G for the final word. The original and often independent guitar part contributes much to these successful works. It requires a skilled classical guitarist for performance." See: W188

B189. Mass of the Word of God

B189a. Wienandt, Elwyn A. "Choral Music." Music Library Association Notes 24:155 (September 1967)
"What is expected of the congregation is unreasonable. That unrehearsed and unskilled group is furnished with musical segments that are not forecast, imitated, or supported by the chorus. . . . Much of the Mass is derived from a four-note head-motive (d"-a'-e'-g') that opens most sections. Its successive descending fourths are only the first of the stumbling blocks he places before the congregation, for there are also shifting meters and veiled melodic lines made difficult by chromatic alteration. I would not carp at this kind of writing in a piece directed at trained singers or at amateurs who willingly gather to rehearse. The mode of expression is valid, even though it is aimed at the wrong people. But I find little to commend it in its present function." See: W189

B190. **The Message**

B190a. Cook, J. Tucker. "Secular Octavo Choral Music." Music Library Association Notes 30:168 (September 1973)
"Pinkham has set Seigfried Sassoon's poem "Toward Sunset This November Day," in an astringent but satisfying manner. The language is characterized by fairly continual dissonance, with both melodic and harmonic intervals resolving from relatively stronger to weaker dissonant areas. The expressive quality is enhanced through the thickening or thinning of the choral texture, as the music seems to require. The guitar is used less as actual accompaniment than a textural addition, and as such it is quite successful." See: W190

B199. **On the Dispute About Images**

B199a. Wells, William B. "Sacred Choral Octavos." Music Library Association Notes 31:689 (March 1975)
"Pinkham has supplied an imaginative setting of this text employing a highly dissonant, sober musical style. His main concern in all of this has been to allow the text to come across clearly through the use of a declamatory style. . . .The one weakness that is apparent in the work is related to the overly long prose text. Pinkham moves along phrase by phrase, reaching a nicely written climax at 'or anything in the world,' but is unable to gather the many interesting musical ideas together into one cohesive whole. Pinkham redeems himself, however, by inventing a most beautiful ending to the work, 'only let them know, let them love, let them remember'." See: W199

B211. **Sometimes the Soul**

B211a. Wells, William B. "Sacred Choral Octavos." Music Library Association Notes 27:574 (March 1971)
"The first work, **Sometimes the Soul** is a short, lyrical, mostly quiet piece that would be suitable either as an anthem or as a short work on a concert program." See: W211

B217. "This Is the Day" from **Easter Cantata**

B217a. Dumm, Robert W. "New Music by Pinkham in Premiere." Christian Science Monitor, August 17, 1960.
"A festive note was struck by Daniel Pinkham's choral fanfare on a psalm, 'This Is the Day', especially commissioned for this concert. It is short and rousingly effective and was composed in only two days. Cast in a style of angular modality, its restless rhythms, rocking from brass to choir, and its bold phrases that build sonority by wide-ranging contrary movement, give the piece a single, forceful

climax." <u>See</u>: W217a

B217b.   Titcomb,   Caldwell.   "Schmidt,   Woodworth   Share
Conducting in Summer School Chorus Performance." <u>Harvard</u>
<u>Summer</u> <u>News</u>, August 17, 1960.
       "The choral writing is rich and massive--supported by
a pungent ensemble of brass and timpani reminiscent at times
of Roy Harris. The piece is clearly in G-major, though there
are occasional passages of a polytonal character.   Performed
by the full Chorus of some 125 singers, it proved to be an
admirably rousing and ebullient curtain-raiser." <u>See</u>: W217a

B223. **Time of Times**

B223a.   Dyer,   Richard.   "For   Valentines,   an Evening of
Lovesongs." <u>Boston</u> <u>Globe</u>, February 16, 1987.
       "A welcome new friend on the program was **Time of**
Times, a cycle on poems by the late Norma Farber that Daniel
Pinkham arranged for the Quintet a decade ago,   and which the
group subsequently recorded.   Farber's poems, simple in language, strong in image, resonant in suggestion, are ideal for
musical setting. Pinkham's gently impressionistic responses
to her texts are alert, flexible, skillfully laid out for the
voices, and lovely to hear.   The opening song 'Outgoing', is
particularly beautiful--and appropriate: the central image is
of the frozen Charles River." <u>See</u>: W223a

B225. **A Tunnel in the Leaves**

B225a.   Giffin,   Glenn.   "Pinkham Works Intrigue." <u>Denver</u>
<u>Post</u>, April 9, 1979.
       "For this particular festival, the premiere of Pink-
ham's **A Tunnel in the Leaves** was given, using a large chorus,
with the composer conducting.   It uses texts by Howard
Holtzman, set for the most part in straight lines following
the poems themselves but with a vigorous choral sense that
recalls Poulenc, though with a Yankee leanness all its own."
<u>See</u>: W225b

B225b.   Giffin,   Glenn.   "Rocky Mountain Contemporary Music
Festival." <u>High</u> <u>Fidelity/Musical</u> <u>America</u> 29:MA27 (September
1979)
       "The premiere of his **A Tunnel in the Leaves**, with the
composer conducting the large choir, capped the festivity.
Using texts by Howard Holtzman, the writing is for the most
part in lyric lines following the contours of the poems themselves,   but with vigorous choral sense that marks an   expan-
sion of Pinkham's style as represented in, say the **Wedding**
Cantata.   It has integrity and a desire to communicate."
<u>See</u>: W225b

B230. **Evergreen**

B230a. Slettom, Jeanyne Bezoier and D. R. Martin.   "Music on Record." Minneapolis-St. Paul Magazine 10:54 (December 1982)
    "A male chorus sung in unison that used unusual intervals and a flowing, chant-like melody." See: D230a

B240. **Angelus ad Pastores Ait; Shepherd, Awake**

B240a. "The Cecilia Society." Boston Herald, December 5, 1959.
    "Assisted by John Corley's Boston Brass Choir, and in keeping with a service the Society has often performed, the program's high point was the advent of a strong, new composition for women's voices and brass choir by Daniel Pinkham, **Angeles ad Pastores**, a setting of the Angel's message to the shepherds in the fields, composed expressly for the Society." See: W240a

B240b. Dumm, R. W. "The National Scene." Musical Courier 161:41 (February 1960)
    "The Cecilia Society, directed by Theodore Marier, made another variant with the premiere of a Christmas Motet by Daniel Pinkham, **Angeles ad Pastores** for women's voices and brass choir. It has the clarity, the balance of sounding forces and the quiet invention that characterize Pinkham's works." See: W240a

B240c. Kelly, Kevin. "Cecilia Society Singers in Elegant Concert." Boston Globe, December 5, 1959.
    "It has been conceived with pungent economy. It is reverent, joyous and dramatic." See: W240a

B240d. Morris, Brockman. "New Motet by Pinkham Conducted by Marier." Christian Science Monitor, December 5, 1959.
    "Based on the Biblical passage commencing with 'The angel said to the shepherds: I bring you glad tidings of great joy,' Mr. Pinkham's motet comprised one short movement with a complement of brass choir and a score for women's voices. Achieving soaring moments, the extended vocal phrases were powerful and of spiritual significance." See: W240a

B245. **Company at the Creche**

B245a. Dyer, Richard. "375 Harpists Show Pluck." Boston Globe, June 25, 1977.
    "Daniel Pinkham's **Company at the Creche** is a skillful mix of infallible ingredients--Norma Farber's charming bestiary of tributes to the Christ-child and the irresistible timbres of boy-choir (the Cambridge Boys' Choir, Theodore Marier, conductor), tuned bells, and harp (Carl Swanson). The music is simple but by no means unsophisticated. The whole thing was impossible to resist." See: W245a

B245b. Kresh, Paul. "The Charm of the Unexpected: Four Song Cycles by Two New England Composers." Stereo Review 47:62 (April 1982)
   "Daniel Pinkham is a formal gardener among composers, setting out his intricate designs with economy and grace in patterned pastels, introducing amid the musical flowerbeds a daring modern accent here, a splash of vivid color there, but never really disturbing the understated tonal structure. His settings of the Farber poems, most notably of the series called **Company at the Creche**, with its adroit descriptions of such unlikely guests at the manger as storks, caterpillars, and porcupines, is exceptionally ingratiating." See: D245b

B249. **Let Us Now Praise Famous Men**

  B249a. Wells, William B. "Sacred Choral Octavos." Music Library Association Notes 27:576 (March 1971)
   "All of the pieces are short but marvelously worked out. Pinkham does not shrink from writing strong dissonance to express some idea in the text, though the voice-leadings are graceful and present few problems." See: W249

B252. **Manger Scenes**

  B252a. Dyer, Richard, "Concert Spans 29 Years of Daniel Pinkham's Works." Boston Globe, October 31, 1984.
   "In **Manger Scenes** both poems and music are sweet and tender without becoming sentimental." See: W252b

B258. **Three Lenten Poems of Richard Crashaw**

  B258a. L., K. "Glee Clubs Offer Varied Program." Boston Herald, April 2, 1964.
   "The best received of the new works on the program was also the most daring of the four, the **Three Lenten Poems of Richard Crashaw** by Daniel Pinkham. While basically modal in style, a touch of dissonance was added by way of a handbells line which was skillfully woven into the musical texture." See: W258a

B268. **Charm Me Asleep**

  B268a. Buell, Richard. "Best of Pinkham and Schuller." Boston Globe, March 1, 1979.
   "The Pinkham **Charm Me Asleep**, settings of old English texts (1977), handsomely done by Charles Robert Stephens, baritone, and Frank Wallace, guitar, gave satisfaction, too. These were admirably considerate of the words by Herrick, Breton, Greville and company, and in their slightly Britten-ish way, they were what you might call tonally oblique.

Never straightfowardly tuneful, they nonetheless knew a great deal about tunefulness; and in their reserve and thougtfulness made for a handsome sound." See: W268b

B269. The Death of the Witch of Endor

B269a. Crutchfield, Will. "Recital: Pamela Gore." New York Times, September 18, 1986.
"What came off best was the grotesquerie of Daniel Pinkham's scena, The Death of the Witch of Endor, which calls for a baleful variety of crackly, wailing sepulchral sounds." See: W269c

B269b. Dyer, Richard. "A Pinkham Premiere." Boston Globe, October 15, 1981.
"This piece is a small solo cantata on a text by Pinkham drawing on the Biblical account; it is scored for contralto, harpsichord, and percussion. Its effects are clearly intentional, but they are unsettling because the music refuses to do what you expect it to. That is, the text is full of incident, emotion and violence, and it concerns events on which the destiny of men and nations depended--the material of a full-blooded Italian cantata in the manner of Handel. . . . But instead the composer has set his text in single-syllable-per-note declamation, with occasional punc-tuating, coloristic swirls from the harpsichord and percus-sion, rather after the manner of the famous reading of the letter in Debussy's Pelleas." See: W269a

B270. Eight Poems of Gerard Manley Hopkins

B270a. Zarr, Wayne. "Solo and Ensemble Vocal Music." Music Library Association Notes 28:781 (June 1972)
"It may be best to see the poems as coming from the poet's personal thoughts about life on Earth when thinking about God and Man. At any rate, this is Pinkham's point of departure, and he is remarkably successful in capturing such personal ideas and the mysteries which arise therefrom." See: W270

B276. Heaven-Haven

B276a. Scanlan, Roger. "Spotlight on Contempoary American Composers." NATS Bulletin 33:37 (December 1976)
"An important comparison can be made in the composi-tional styles of Pinkham and Samuel Barber in a consideration of their respective settings of Heaven-Haven. While Barber's seems to emphasize the drama and fervor of the event, the Pinkham setting seems to capture the personal isolation of the decision to become a nun." See: W276

B280. **Letters from Saint Paul**

B280a. Hughes, Allen. "Marjorie H. Madey Sings at Town Hall." New York Times, April 15, 1968.
"Pinkham's settings of excerpts from the Bible are rather austere but might be quite commanding in a stronger performance." See: W280c

B280b. Schuneman, Robert. "New Choral Music." Diapason 62:16 (November 1971)
"Again, the structure and material is tightly organized, and we find the songs to have exquisite expressive possibilities, providing that a good singer is at hand for the performance." See: W280

B284. **Music, Thou Soul of Heaven**

B284a. Paton, John Glenn. "Music Reviews." Music Library Association Notes 35:996 (June 1979)
This song, composed in 1953 and revised in 1977, typifies the tonal style that Pinkham later abandoned for serialism. His sense of harmonic rhythm in a tonal framework far surpassed that of Ned Rorem, to whom this song is dedicated." See: W284

B290. **Safe in Their Alabaster Chambers**

B290a. Giffin, Glenn. "Pinkham Works Intrigue." Denver Post, April 9, 1979.
"By 1972, the composer had discovered quite a bit about electronic music, and his **Safe in Their Alabaster Chambers** for solo baritone offers an intriguing combination and highly effective music." See: W290c

B290b. Notes from the score.
"The [tape] sounds are intended to be affective. They set the mood and give occasional pitches. They are not, however, meant as accompaniment, but rather as a nonsynchronous theatrical adjunct like scenery or lighting enhancing the effect of the otherwise unaccompanied vocal line. The volume level should be set so that it does not mask the words at any time." See W290

B295. **Slow, Slow Fresh Fount**

B295a. Kulleseid, Eleanor. "Music Reviews." Music Library Association Notes 21:266 (Winter-Spring 1963-64)
"Daniel Pinkham has also fashioned a quiet and lovely song, using text from a lament by Ben Jonson. The prosody is skillfully declaimed in a well-spaced syllabic melody accompanied by the spare texture of rich chordal modulations. The inexplicable lapse into triteness in the middle section

on 'Fall grief in showers, Our beauties are not ours' is all the more lamentable for disfiguring an otherwise moving little piece." See: W295

B296. The Song of Jephtha's Daughter

B296a. Wienandt, Elwyn A. "Choral Music." Music Library Association Notes 24:155 (September 1967)
"The serial character of the piece is apparent to both eye and ear, but the manner in which the materials are used causes the music to sound triadic at many points. Conveniently, four-note segments of the series are arranged to produce seventh chords, larger groups produce more complex arrangements, but often these are related to triadic practice as well. Demands on the performers are modest, the soprano being called on to execute wide leaps a few times where text-painting is served by mild acrobatics. The piano part calls for no unusual skill, but the baritone may be forced to substitute some other pitch for a poorly placed a-flat." See: W296

B300. Three Songs from Ecclesiastes

B300a. Irgang, Jack. "American Songs of Pinkham, Rorem and Thomson True Marriage of Composer and Performer." Inquirer and Mirror (Nantucket, Mass.), July 31, 1986.
"Declamatory statements interspersed with dramatic a cappella phrases, characteristics common to each of the songs, add to the emotional intensity of the lyrics. Pinkham, as these songs reveal, can also inject a lyrical line evocative of nostalgia and wistfulness. [Vernon] Hartman approached the songs in a highly sensitive manner. Pinkham's music is tailored effectively to bring out the sentiments in the lyrics." See: W300e

B301. Transitions

B301a. Henahan, Donal. "Song: With Bassoonist." New York Times, October 2, 1979.
"Any song cycle that offers a solo bassoonist as accompanist begins with a certain amount of interest in the bank. Pianists, by tradition and mere force of composing habit, have monopolized the supporting role in vocal recitals for the better part of 200 years. There have been exceptions to this tyranny of the keyboardists, however, and Daniel Pinkham joined a comparatively short list with his **Transitions**, which had its first performance Sunday night at Carnegie Recital Hall. . . .Miss Gore, a mezzo-soprano with a pleasing voice and the ability to enunciate texts clearly, struck this listener as a little too wholesome and straightforward to get the most out of Mr. Holtzman's poems, which were concerned with evoking elegiac, nostalgic or autumnal

moods. However, she was helped little by the composer, who
merely followed along after the words, rarely making his own
comments or illuminations." <u>See</u>; W301a

B301b.   Paton, John Glenn.   "Vocal and Dramatic Music."
<u>Music</u> <u>Library</u> <u>Association</u> <u>Notes</u> 39:954 (June 1983)
    "Pinkham's rhythmic fluidity allows the restless vocal
line to follow every inflection, weigh every syllable of the
poetry. This style of text-setting, as sensitive as Hugo
Wolf's but altogether different in technique, owes some debt
to chant, perhaps some to Machaut or Stravinsky, but none at
all to traditional recitative.   Whoever suggested the poetry
of Howard Holtzman for these songs made a valuable discov-
ery. . . . Pinkham allows his music to borrow shape from the
verse forms at the same time that the complex relationships
of his contrapuntal voices reflect the impure, dusky colors
that the poet prefers." <u>See</u>: W301

B304. **Wellesley Hills Psalm Book**

B304a.   Davis, A.   "Third Candlelight Concert Provides
Delightful Evening." <u>Inquirer</u> <u>and</u> <u>Mirror</u> (Nantucket, Mass.),
July 26, 1984.
    "The earlier English poetry, going back to the Great
Bible of 1539 has a solid, 'square' vigor and rhythm.   This
quality is set admirably by Mr. Pinkham with great vitality,
and with 'prettiness'. Again the harmonies and intervals are
often unexpected and even harsh when appropriate, but always
logical and based firmly on the texts." <u>See</u>: W304b

B304b.   Pinkham, Daniel.   **The Wellesley Hills Psalm Book.**
Notes from the score.
    "In selecting these Biblical texts I avoided the 1611
King James Version in favor of these less familiar and, with
two exceptions, earlier translations. The earliest of these
are the three prose excerpts from the Great Bible of 1539.
The remaining seven texts were drawn from various Psalm
paraphrases chosen as well for their poetry as for their
metrical interest." <u>See</u>: W304

B305. **Winter Nights**

B305a.   Crutchfield, Will.   "Recital: Pamela Gore." <u>New</u>
<u>York</u> <u>Times</u>, September 18, 1986.
    "The program also included the world premiere of
another Pinkham work, **Winter Nights**, to words of Thomas
Campion, for voice, harp and oboe. On first impression they
seem well made, sensitive settings in an idiom very close to
that of Ralph Vaughan Williams." <u>See</u>: W305a

B315. **Aspects of the Apocalypse**

Bibliography

B315a.   Wierzbicki, James.   "Performances Solid at Concert
of Modern Sacred Music."   St.   Louis Globe-Democrat,   October
26, 1982.
        "Three of the pieces featured pre-recorded tapes of
sounds produced on an electronic music synthesizer, a device
with which Pinkham experimented much in the early 1970s but
has lately abandoned for more traditional media.   None was
especially daring, and the one scored exclusively for tape
was actually rather sophomoric in concept (it was a 1971
piece, ominously titled Aspects of the Apocalypse; accompanied by a showing of Pinkham's own abstract photographic
slides, it smacked too much of psychedelia to be taken
seriously)." See: W315b

Appendix I:
Chronological Listing
of Compositions

Numbers following titles refer to the **Works and Performances** section of this volume. Dates listed are those of composition.

1943   Sonata No. 1, W77

1944   Ave Regina Coelorum, W265
        Hairs of Gods Are Valuable, W274
        Pastoral XVII from Thirty Pastorals, W288
        Prelude for Flute and String Trio, W46
        Seven Epigrams, W292

1945   Duo, W32
        The Faucon, W272
        Nocturne, W285
        A Partridge in a Pear Tree, W287

1946   Beauty, W266
        Dithyramb, W316
        Narragansett Bay, W7
        Prelude for Piano, W109
        Psalm 79 (80), W289
        Sonata for Clarinet and Pianoforte, W53
        Sonatina, W54

1947   Christmas Eve, W154
        Concertino, W60
        Elegy, W160
        Four Short Pieces, W102
        Heaven-Haven, W276
        Sonata for Organ and Brasses, W76
        Songs of Innocence, W297
        Three Motets, W259

1948   A Christmas Carol, W153
        Epitaph for Janet Fairbank, W101

                    The Garden of Artemis, W3
                    Sing Agreeably of Love, W294
                    Three Lyric Scenes, W299
                    Twentieth Century, W226

1949   Elegy, W271
                    In Grato Jubilo, W14
                    Slow, Slow Fresh Fount, W295
                    Star-Tree Carol, W214

1950   Concertino in A for Small Orchestra and Obliggato
                        Pianoforte, W11
                    Suite, W98

1951   Psalm 96, W205
                    Serenade, W49

1952   Five Short Pieces, W13
                    The Lamb, W279
                    Song of Simeon, W212

1953   Four Epigrams, W273
                    In Youth Is Pleasure, W233
                    Music, Thou Soul of Heaven, W284
                    Prelude and Chaconne, W92

1954   Cantilena and Capriccio, W29
                    Concertante No. 1, W9
                    Divertimento, W12
                    Duet, W31
                    Passacaglia, W108
                    Sonata No. 2, W78

1955   Canon for Organ, W85
                    Concerto for Celesta and Harpsichord Soli, W100
                    Glory Be to God, W168
                    Hymn No. 2, W232
                    The Leaf, W183
                    Piping Anne and Husky Paul, W203
                    Prothalamion, W95
                    The Sea Ritual, W291
                    Sometimes the Soul, W211
                    Trumpet Voluntary, W55
                    Why Art Thou Cast Down? W229

1956   Beggar's Opera, W1
                    Eternal Are Thy Mercies, Lord, W161
                    Here Repose, O Broken Body, W174
                    The Hour Glass, W277
                    Revelations, W97
                    Shout for Joy, W293
                    Versicle: Call to Prayer, W227
                    Violin Concerto, W23
                    Wedding Cantata, W138
                    Ye Watchers and Ye Holy Ones, W238

1957   Christmas Cantata, W114
               Communion Service, W156
               Henry Was a Worthy King, W173
               International Geophysical Year, W306
               We Have Seen His Star, W237

1958   Concertante No. 2, W10
               Five Canzonets, W246
               Introit for Thanksgiving Day, W234
               Partita, W107
               Scherzo for Harpsichord, W110

1959   Angelus Ad Pastores Ait, W240*
               Envoi, W34
               Farewell, Vain World, W162
               Homage to Wanda Landowska, W105
               Invention No. 1, W307
               Invention No. 2, W308
               Land of White Alice, W309
               Psalm 81, W204
               Memory, Hither Come, W253
               Rondo, W47
               The Sick Rose, W255
               Scherzo, W48
               Te Deum, W257

1960   Ave Maria, W241
               Reaching for the Moon, W313
               The Reproaches, W132
               Two Motets, W302

1961   The Conversion of Saul, W115
               Easter Cantata, W119
               God Is a Spirit, W169
               Intreat Me Not to Leave Thee, W278
               A Litany, W281
               MIT Science Reporter, W311
               O Lord God, to Whom Vengeance Belongeth, W196
               Planet Earth, W312
               A Song for the Bells, W318
               Statement of Faith, W215
               Symphony No. 1, W20

1962   Catacoustical Measures, W8
               Concertante No. 3, W58
               An Emily Dickinson Mosaic, W120
               Fanfare, Aria and Echo, W36
               Festival Magnificat and Nunc Dimittis, W163
               Four Short Pieces for Manuals, W88
               I Was Glad, W178
               Pastorale on the Morning Star, W91

* copyright date; date of composition uncertain

Symphony No. 2, W21
Three Songs from Ecclesiastes, W300

1963 If Ye Love Me, W248
Requiem, W133
The Song of Jephtha's Daughter, W296
Structures, W314
Thou Hast Loved Righteousness, W218
Three Lenten Poems of Richard Crashaw, W258

1964 Concertante No. 4, W59
Eight Poems of Gerard Manley Hopkins, W270
Etude, W35
Jubilate Deo, W180
Now the Trumpet Summons Us Again, W16
Signs of the Zodiac, W19
Stabat Mater, W136

1965 Canticle of Praise, W151
Eclogue, W33
Five Voluntaries for Organ Manuals, W87
Letters from Saint Paul, W280
Listen to Me, W250
Saint Mark Passion, W134
Thy Statutes Have Been My Songs, W222

1966 Behold, How Good and How Pleasant, W148
Concertante, W30
The Lamentations of Jeremiah, W127
Let Us Now Praise Famous Men, W249
Man That Is Born of a Woman, W282
Mass of the Good Shepherd, W235
Mass of the Holy Eurcharist, W236
Mass of the Word of God, W189
Open to Me the Gates of Righteousness, W201

1967 How Precious Is Thy Loving Kindness, W175
I Have Preached Righteousness, W176
Jonah, W126
The Martyrdom of Saint Stephen, W188
Prelude, Epigram and Elegy, W26
Sacred Service, W207
Signs in the Sun, W75
Songs of Peaceful Departure, W213

1968 Magnificat, W129
The Message, W190
Mizma L'Asaph, W262
Prelude, Adagio and Chorale, W44
A Prophecy, W94
Psalm Set, W131

1969 On the Dispute About Images, W199
Pater Noster, W202
To Think of Those Absent, W224

Variations, W81

1970   Ascension Cantata, W111
        Bridal Morning, W267
        Brass Trio, W28
        Come, Love We God, W155
        Grace Is Poured Abroad, W170
        In the Beginning of Creation, W179
        Organ Concerto, W17

1971   The Call of Isaiah, W150
        Lessons, W106
        The Other Voices of the Trumpet, W69
        See That Ye Love One Another, W73
        The Seven Last Words of Christ On the Cross, W135
        The Sheepheards Song, W208
        Toccatas for the Vault of Heaven, W80

1972   Aspects of the Apocalypse, W315
        He Scatters the Snow, W38
        The Lament of David, W182
        Musette, W43
        Safe in Their Alabaster Chambers, W290
        The Temptations in the Wilderness, W216
        To Troubled Friends, W137
        When the Morning Stars Sang Together, W82

1973   Alleluia, Acclamation and Carol, W143
        Ave Verum Corpus, W146
        A Carol for New Year's Day, W152
        Daniel in the Lion's Den, W117
        Evergreen, W230
        For Evening Draws On, W62
        In My Visions of the Night, W39
        Love Came Down at Christmas, W186
        Mourn for the Eclipse of His Light, W67
        O Depth of Wealth, W195
        Pleasure It Is, W254
        The Shepherd's Symphony, W74
        Stars, I Have Seen Them Fall, W298
        Thou Hast Turned My Laments Into Dancing, W219

1974   "And the Angel Said...", W57
        Baptism Canon, W242
        Four Poems of Norma Farber, W166
        I Saw An Angel, W177
        The Kings and the Shepherds, W181
        Liturgies, W65
        The Lord Has Established His Throne, W184
        Most Glorious Lord of Life, W191
        Orbits, W25
        Seven Deadly Sins, W18
        Signs Will Appear, W209

1975   Amens, W144

Fanfares, W121
Four Elegies, W122
Going and Staying, W247
World Welter, W276
Love Can Be Still, W187
Nebulae, W68
O Beautiful! My Country, W194
On That Day, W198
Time of Times, W223
Two Poems of Howard Holtzman, W260
Witching Hour, W261

1976   Burning Bright, W149
        Garden Party, W4
        The Passion of Judas, W130

1977   Blessings, W83
        Charm Me Asleep, W268
        Company At the Creche, W245
        My Heart is Steadfast, W192

1978   Epiphanies, W86
        Gifts and Graces, W63
        Masks, W15
        Miracles, W66
        Sonata da Requiem, W52
        Take Life, W256
        A Tunnel in the Leaves, W225
        What Do You Want from Me? W139

1979   The Descent into Hell, W118
        Hezekiah, W124
        Little Bell Book, W317
        Little Brass Book, W42
        Love's Yoke, W251
        Proverbs, W96
        Serenades, W50
        Transitions, W301
        When God Arose, W140

1980   Clear Mirrors, W244
        Diversions, W61
        Manger Scenes, W252
        Man's Days Are Like the Grass, W90

1981   Before the Dust Returns, W113
        The Death of the Witch of Endor, W269
        Music in the Manger, W283
        Nativity Madrigals, W193
        On Secret Errands, W197
        Prelude and Scherzo, W45
        Three Campion Poems, W220

1982   The Dreadful Dining Car, W2
        Holland Waltzes, W104

O Wholesome Night, W286
One Shade, W200
Slumber Now, W210
Vigils, W56

1983   And Peace Attend Thee, W145
Brass Quintet, W27
For Thee Have I Waited, W165
Inaugural Marches, W40
Lauds, W128
Psalms for Trumpet and Organ, W72
Wellesley Hills Psalm Book, W304

1984   Alleluia, W239
Alleluia, W263
Before the Cock Crows, W112
A Curse, a Lament and a Vision, W116
Dallas Anthem Book, W157
The Heavens Tell out the Glory of God, W172
Introduction, Nocturne and Rondo, W41
Partita for Guitar and Organ Manuals, W70
A Proclamation, W93

1985   A Biblical Book of Beasts, W243
Goin' 60, W103
He Standing Hushed, W275
In Heaven Soaring Up, W125
The Left-Behind Beasts, W5
Symphony No. 3, W22
Versets for Small Organ, W99

1986   A Crimson Flourish, W24
De Profundis, W158
The Gate of Heaven, W167
In the Isles of the Sea, W89
The Lord My Shepherd Is, W185
A Mast for the Unicorn, W6
Winter Nights, W305
You Shall Have a Song, W141

1987   Antiphons, W264
Getting to Heaven, W123
Pastorale, W71
Sonata No. 3, W79

Appendix II:
Alphabetical Listing
of Compositions

Numbers following titles refer to the **Works and Performances** section of this volume.

Alleluia, W239
Alleluia, W263
Alleluia from Fanfares, W142
Alleluia, Acclamation and Carol, W143
Amens, W144
And Peace Attend Thee, W145
"And the Angel Said...", W57
Angelus Ad Pastores Ait, W240
Antiphons, W264
Ascension Cantata, W111
Aspects of the Apocalypse, W315
Ave Maria, W241
Ave Regina Coelorum, W265
Ave Verum Corpus, W146
Baptism Canon, W242
Be Gracious To Me, O Lord, W147
Beauty, W266
Before the Cock Crows, W112
Before the Dust Returns, W113
Beggar's Opera, W1
Behold, How Good and How Pleasant, W148
A Biblical Book of Beasts, W243
Blessings, W83
Blest Be the Ties, W84
Brass Quintet, W27
Brass Trio, W28
Bridal Morning, W267
Burning Bright, W149
The Call of Isaiah, W150
Canon for Organ, W85
Canticle of Praise, W151
Cantilena and Capriccio, W29
Carol for New Year's Day, W152

Four Elegies, W122
Four Epigrams, W273
Four Interludes, W37
Four Poems of Norma Farber, W166
Four Short Pieces, W102
Four Short Pieces for Manuals, W88
The Garden of Artemis, W3
Garden Party, W4
The Gate of Heaven, W167
Getting to Heaven, W123
Gifts and Graces, W63
Gloria, W64
Glory Be To God,a Motet for Christmas Day, W168
God Is a Spirit, W169
Goin' 60, W103
Going and Staying, W247
Grace Is Poured Abroad, W170
Hairs of Gods Are Valuable, W274
Happy Is the Man, W171
He Scatters the Snow, W38
He Standing Hushed, W275
Heaven-Haven/ World Welter, W276
The Heavens Tell Out the Glory of God, W172
Henry Was a Worthy King, W173
Here Repose, O Broken Body, W174
Hezekiah, W124
Holland Waltzes, W104
Homage to Wanda Landowska, W105
The Hour Glass, W277
How Precious Is Thy Loving Kindness, W175
Hymn No. 1, W231
Hymn No. 2, W232
I Have Preached Righteousness, W176
I Saw an Angel, W177
I Was Glad, W178
If Ye Love Me, W248
In Grato Jubilo, W14
In Heaven Soaring Up, W125
In My Visions of the Night, W39
In the Beginning of Creation, W179
In the Isles of the Sea, W89
In Youth Is Pleasure, W233
Inaugural Marches, W40
International Geophysical Year, W306
Intreat Me Not to Leave Thee, W278
Introduction, Nocturne and Rondo, W41
Introit for Thanksgiving Day, W234
Invention No. 1, W307
Invention No. 2, W308
Jonah, W126
Jubilate Deo, W180
The Kings and the Shepherds, W181
The Lamb, W279
The Lament of David, W182
The Lamentations of Jeremiah, W127

Partita, W107
Partita for Guitar and Organ Manuals, W70
A Partridge in a Pear Tree, W287
Passacaglia, W108
The Passion of Judas, W130
Pastoral XVII from Thirty Pastorals, W288
Pastorale, W71
Pastorale on the Morning Star, W91
Pater Noster, W202
Piping Anne and Husky Paul, W203
Planet Earth, W312
Pleasure It Is, W254
Prelude, Adagio and Chorale, W44
Prelude and Chaconne, W92
Prelude and Scherzo, W45
Prelude, Epigram and Elegy, W26
Prelude for Flute and String Trio, W46
Prelude for Piano, W109
A Proclamation, W93
A Prophecy, W94
Prothalamion, W95
Proverbs, W96
Psalm 79 (80), W289
Psalm 81, W204
Psalm 96, W205
Psalm: O Praise the Lord, Alleluia, W206
Psalm Set, W131
Psalms for Trumpet and Organ, W72
Reaching for the Moon, W313
The Reproaches, W132
Requiem, W133
Revelations, W97
Rondo, W47
Sacred Service, W207
Safe In Their Alabaster Chambers, W290
Saint Mark Passion, W134
Scherzo, W48
Scherzo for Harpsichord, W110
The Sea Ritual, W291
See That Ye Love One Another, W73
Serenade, W49
Serenades, W50
Seven Deadly Sins, W18
Seven Epigrams, W292
The Seven Last Words of Christ On the Cross, W135
The Sheepheards Song, W208
The Shepherd's Symphony, W74
Shout For Joy, W293
Siciliana and Sailor's Dance, W51
The Sick Rose, W255
Signs In the Sun, W75
Signs of the Zodiac, W19
Signs Will Appear, W209
Sing Agreeably of Love, W294
Slow, Slow Fresh Fount, W295

Appendix II

When God Arose, W140
When the Morning Stars Sang Together, W82
Who May Lodge In Thy Tabernacle? W228
Why Art Thou Cast Down? W229
Winter Nights, W305
Witching Hour, W261
Ye Watchers and Ye Holy Ones, W238
You Shall Have a Song, W141

Appendix III:
Poems Used as Texts

Poetic sources used by the composer as texts for vocal works. "See" references are guides to citations in the **Works and Performances** section of this volume.

Auden, W. H.

Let the Florid Music Praise W299
Look, Stranger on This Island Now W299
Sing Agreeably of Love W294, W299

Blake, William

Blossom W246
Infant Joy W297
The Lamb W279, W297
Memory, Hither Come W253
Piping Down the Valleys Wild W297
The Sick Rose W255
Spring W246

Bradstreet, Anne

The Happy Flood W194

Breton, Nicholas

A Report in a Dream W268
Say That I Should Say W268

Campion, Thomas

Author of Light W220

Appendix III

>Come, Let Us Sound With Melody W220
>De Profundis W158
>Fain Would I Wed W305
>Follow Follow W305
>It Fell on a Summer's Day W305
>My Love Hath Vowed W305
>Now the Winter Nights Enlarge W305
>Oft Have I Sighed W305
>Though You Are Young W305
>To Music Bent Is My Retiring Mind WW220
>Your Fair Looks W305

Cornish, William Randolph

>Pleasure It Is W254

Crashaw, Richard

>O Save Us Then W221
>On the Still Surviving Marks of Our Savior's Wounds W221
>Upon the Body of Our Blessed Lord, Naked and Bloody W221
>Upon the Death of a Friend W122

Darley, George

>The Sea Ritual W291

Dickinson, Emily

>The Brain is Wider Than the Sky W120
>Each Life Conveys to Some Centre W120
>Exhileration is the Breeze W120
>The Heart is the Capital of the Mind W120
>The Mind Lives on the Heart W120
>Safe in Their Alabaster Chambers W290
>There's a Certain Slant of Light W290
>These Are The Days When Birds Come Back W290
>To be Alive W120

Donne, John

>At the Round Earth's Imagin'd Corners W122
>Daybreak W246

Dryden, John

>Te Deum W257

Elizabeth I (attributed)

    Christ Was the Word W254

Farber, Norma

    After W193
    After the Storm a Star W187
    And Peace Attend Thee W145
    Bow Down Mountain W232
    A Cage of Half Light W223
    Company at the Creche (Stork, Dove, Caterpillar, Roos-
        ter, Spider, Porcupine, Lion) W245
    Da Capo W187
    Dancer, How Do You Dare? W166
    Fawn Bridge W166
    Fire, Sleet and Candlelight W261
    The Foundling W252
    Get Up! Said Mary W193
    Going and Staying W247
    Guardian Owl W193
    The Hatch W166
    How Like a Man W4
    How They Brought the Glad News by Sea W193
    In The Counting House W223
    A Lamp in the Manger W252
    Long Lullabye W223
    Love, Bone Quiet, Said W187
    Mary, Did You Falter? W283
    Moon Carol W2
    O Wholesome Night W286
    On Going W223
    The Queens Came Late, But the Queens Were There W252
    A Quiet Gospel W223
    Sing for Baby W2
    Sometimes the Soul W211
    The Star and Pulsar Discovered Waltzing W166
    A Summoning Hosanna W283
    Take Life W256
    Take Me Walking in Your Mind W187
    Tell Me About the Mother of Judas W130
    Time of Aster W223
    The Tree in the River W223
    Tree of Blame W4
    To Think of Those Absent W224
    What Did the Baby Give the Kings? W193
    What's That Music in the Manger? W283
    While Eve W4
    Why Sleepest Thou? W231
    World Welter W276

Felltman, Owen

Appendix III

Upon a Rare Voice W268

Fletcher, Phineas

A Litany W281

Freneau, Philip Morin

Take Warning, Tryants W194

Greville, Fulke, Lord Brooke

Man, Dream No More W268

Herrick, Robert

To His Dying Brother Master William Herrick W122
To Music, to Becalm His Fever W268

Hillyer, Robert

Alas, My Daughter W296
A Christmas Carol W153
Christmas Eve W154
Elegy W160, W271
Evergreen W230
Forever Year By Year W296
Hairs of Gods Are Valuable W274
I Turned To My Father W296
The Kings and the Shepherds W181
The Leaf W183
My Father Came As a Stranger W296
Nocturne W285
Pastoral XVII from 30 Pastorals W288
Piping Anne and Husky Paul W203
Seven Epigrams W292
Star Tree Carol W214
The Tidings of My Fate W296
Time Is a Long Valley W296
Twentieth Century W226
Twilight Among the Vineyards W296
What Was My Sin? W296
With Timbrels and Dancing W296

Holtzman, Howard

After-Song W197
Aubade W301

Appendix III

On the Dispute About Images W199

Raleigh, Sir Walter

The Conclusion W268

Rosetti, Christian Georgina

Love Came Down at Christmas W186

Sassoon, Siegfried

Toward Sunset This November Day W190

Shakespeare, William

Absence W268

Smart, Christopher

For Saturday W254

Strode, William

Chloris In the Snow W268
In Commendation of Music W268

Taylor, Edward

Ascended Up On High W125
The Coach for Glory W125
Thy Spinning Wheel W125

Vaughan, Henry

Silence and Stealth of Dayes W122

Watts, Isaac

Now Is The Hour of Darkness Past W143

Wever, Robert

In Youth is Pleasure W233

Wright, James

    A Breath of Air W139
    Beginning W139
    Evening W137
    Father W137
    A Fit Against the Country W137
    Milkweed W139
    My Grandmother's Ghost W139
    Saint Judas W130
    This Morning My Beloved Rose Before I Did W139
    To a Troubled Friend W137

Wylie, Elinor

    Beauty W266

Appendix IV:
Biblical References Used
as Texts

Biblical sources used by the composer as texts for vocal scores or as points of reference for instrumental compositions. The asterisk * identifies compositions without a sung text. "See" references are guides to citations in the **Bibliography** section of this volume.

OLD TESTAMENT

Genesis 1:1-3 In the Beginning of Creation W179
Genesis 2 and 3 Garden Party W4
Genesis 26:23 Blessings W83*
Genesis 32:24-29 Blessings W83*

I Samuel 28 The Death of the Witch of Endor W269

II Samuel 1:19-27 The Lament of David W182

Job 5 A Curse, a Lament and a Vision W116
Job 38:1-7 When the Morning Stars Sang Together W82*

Psalm 1 The Passion of Judas W130
Psalm 2:2 Saint Mark Passion W134
Psalm 6 Wellesley Hills Psalm Book W304
Psalm 9:1-4 Three Motets W259
Psalm 15:1-3, 5 The Passion of Judas W130
Psalm 22:1-2, 14-19 Saint Mark Passion W134
Psalm 23 Wellesley Hills Psalm Book W304
Psalm 23 The Lord My Shepherd Is W185
Psalm 25 Wellesley Hills Psalm Book W304
Psalm 25:5, 6 For Thee Have I Waited W165
Psalm 30:11, 12 Thou Hast Turned My Laments Into Dancing W219
Psalm 35:11 Saint Mark Passion W134
Psalm 36:7-9 How Precious Is Thy Loving Kindness W175
Psalm 40:9, 10 I Have Preached Righteousness W176

Psalm 42:11   Why Art Thou Cast Down? W229
Psalm 45:2, 4, 6   Grace Is Poured Abroad W170
Psalm 45:7, 17   Thou Hast Loved Righteousness W218
Psalm 47   Psalm Set W131
Psalm 47:5   Ascension Cantata W111
Psalm 51:1, 2, 5-8, 10-12   The Passion of Judas W130
Psalm 57:7-10   My Heart Is Steadfast W192
Psalm 60:1-3   Saint Mark Passion W134
Psalm 62:1, 5   Saint Mark Passion W134
Psalm 68   Wellesley Hills Psalm Book W304
Psalm 68:18, 32-34   Easter Cantata W119
Psalm 69:3, 8, 20   Saint Mark Passion W134
Psalm 76:9-10   When God Arose W140
Psalm 81   Psalm 81 W204
Psalm 83:5   Saint Mark Passion W134
Psalm 94:1, 2   O Lord God, to Whom Vengeance Belongeth W196
Psalm 96   Psalm 96 W205
Psalm 96:11-13   Three Motets W259
Psalm 97:6   The Heavens Tell Out the Glory of God W172
Psalm 100   Jubilate Deo; O Be Joyful in the Lord W180
Psalm 103:15, 16   Man's Days Are Like the Grass W90*
Psalm 103:16   Songs of Peaceful Departure W213
Psalm 103:19-22   The Lord Has Established His Throne W184
Psalm 109:2   Saint Mark Passion W134
Psalm 115:1   Three Motets W259
Psalm 116   Daniel in the Lion's Den W117
Psalm 116:1, 2, 8, 9   Jonah W126
Psalm 117   Psalm Set W131
Psalm 118:19   Open to Me the Gates of Righteousness W201
Psalm 118:24   Easter Cantata W119
Psalm 119:54   Thy Statutes Have Been My Songs W222
Psalm 121   Wellesley Hills Psalm Book W304
Psalm 122   I Was Glad W178
Psalm 130   De Profundis W158
Psalm 130   Wellesley Hills Psalm Book W304
Psalm 133:1   Behold How Good and How Pleasant W148
Psalm 134   Psalm Set W131
Psalm 134   Prelude, Adagio and Chorale W44*
Psalm 136   Wellesley Hills Psalm Book W304
Psalm 139:7-12   Jonah W126
Psalm 148   Wellesley Hills Psalm Book W304
Psalm 149   Wellesley Hills Psalm Book W304
Psalm 150   Fanfares W121

Proverbs 4:7, 9   Proverbs W96*
Proverbs 13:2   Proverbs W96*
Proverbs 16:7   Proverbs W96*
Proverbs 18:4   Proverbs W96*
Proverbs 25:23   Jonah W126

Ecclesiastes 1. 3, 9   Three Songs from Ecclesiastes W300

Song of Songs 2:10-12   Wedding Cantata W138
Song of Songs 4:16   Wedding Cantata W138

Appendix IV

Song of Songs 6:1-3 Wedding Cantata W138
Song of Songs 8:6, 7 Wedding Cantata W138

Isaiah 6:1-9 The Call of Isaiah W150
Isaiah 11:1, 2, 6 Fanfares, W121
Isaiah 13:4-6, 9, 10, 13 A Curse, a Lament and a Vision W116
Isaiah 24:15 In the Isles of the Sea W89*
Isaiah 25:9 A Curse, a Lament and a Vision W116
Isaiah 26:19 A Curse, a Lament and a Vision W116
Isaiah 27:1, 13 A Curse, a Lament and a Vision W116
Isaiah 35:9, 10 A Curse, a Lament and a Vision W116
Isaiah 40:6, 8 Songs of Peaceful Departure W213
Isaiah 53:7 Saint Mark Passion W134
Isaiah 57:1 Saint Mark Passion W134
Isaiah 60:1 Fanfares W121
Isaiah 62:10, 11 Fanfares W121

Jeremiah 9:1 Saint Mark Passion W134

Lamentations 1:1-5 The Lamentations of Jeremiah W127
Lamentations 1:16 Saint Mark Passion W134
Lamentations 4:13 Saint Mark Passion W134

Ezekiel 27:5-7, 13, 16-19, 22 Jonah W126

Daniel 6 Daniel in the Lion's Den W117

Jonah 1 and 2 Jonah W126

APOCALYPSE

Ecclesiasticus 1:11, 12 Listen to Me; Five Motets W250
Ecclesiasticus 18:9-11 Listen to Me; Five Motets W250
Ecclesiasticus 32:3-9 Listen to Me; Five Motets W250
Ecclesiasticus 39:13-14 Listen to Me; Five Motets W250
Ecclesiasticus 41:1-4 A Curse, a Lament and a Vision W116
Ecclesiasticus 43:17, 18 Listen to Me; Five Motets W250
Ecclesiasticus 43:17, 18 He Scatters the Snow W38*
Ecclesiasticus 45:1, 3, 4, 6, 7, 9 Let Us Now Praise Famous
     Men W249
Ecclesiasticus 47:3-5, 7, 8, 11, 13, 14, 16, 17 Let Us Now
     Praise Famous Men W249
Ecclesiasticus 48:1, 3, 9 Let Us Now Praise Famous Men W249

Song of Three Holy Children 29-68 Canticle of Praise W151

Bel and the Snake Daniel in the Lion's Den W117

NEW TESTAMENT

Matthew 2:2-5, 7, 8 Epiphanies W86*
Matthew 3:13-17 Epiphanies W86*

210

Matthew 16:13-19 Epiphanies W86*
Matthew 17:1-8 Epiphanies W86*
Matthew 26:14-16, 20-26 The Passion of Judas W130
Matthew 27:3-5 The Passion of Judas W130
Matthew 28:1-7 When God Arose W140
Matthew 28:5-7 Easter Cantata W119
Matthew 28:19 Baptism Canon W242

Mark 5:1-13 Miracles W66*
Mark 10:46-52 Miracles W66*
Mark 13, 14, 15 Saint Mark Passion W134
Mark 14:43-46 The Passion of Judas W130
Mark 15:33-35 The Seven Last Works of Christ on the Cross
     W135
Mark 16:14-19 Ascension Cantata W111

Luke 1:39-42 Blessings W83*
Luke 1:47-55 Magnificat W129
Luke 1:47-55 Festival Magnificat and Nunc Dimittis W163
Luke 2:29-32 Festival Magnificat and Nunc Dimittis W163
Luke 2:29-32 Song of Simeon W212
Luke 4 Temptations in the Wilderness W216
Luke 8:22-25 Miracles W66*
Luke 21:25-28 Signs in the Sun W75*
Luke 22:47, 48 The Passion of Judas W130
Luke 23:33, 34, 39-43, 46 The Seven Last Words of Christ on
     the Cross W135
Luke 24:29 For Evening Draws On W62*

John 2:1-11 Miracles W66*
John 4:24 God Is a Spirit W169
John 5:1-9 Miracles W66*
John 13:2 The Passion of Judas W130
John 14:15, 16, 18, 21 If Ye Love Me W248
John 18:1, 2 The Passion of Judas W130
John 19:25-30 The Seven Last Words of Christ on the Cross
     W135
John 20:13 Easter Cantata W119
John 14:19, 28 Two Motets W302

Acts 7:55-60 The Martyrdom of Saint Stephen W188
Acts 26:12-18 Epiphanies W86*

Romans 8:8 Letters from Saint Paul W280
Romans 8:35-39 Letters from Saint Paul W280
Romans 11:33-36 O Depth of Wealth W195

Philippians 4:4-7 Letters from Saint Paul W280

Colossians 3:1-4 When God Arose W140
Colossians 3:16 Letters from Saint Paul W280

I Thessalonians 5:1-6 Letters from Saint Paul W280

Hebrews 12:1, 2 Letters from Saint Paul W280

Appendix IV

I Peter 1:22   See That Ye Love One Another W73*

Revelations 5:9, 10   In Grato Jubilo W14
Revelations 7:11, 12   Blessings W83*
Revelations 8:13   The Other Voices of the Trumpet W69*

Index

References for each item indexed are presented in the same order as found in the text: page numbers refer to the **Biography** section, followed by references to the **Works and Performances** section ("W"), the **Discography** ("D"), and the **Bibliography**, "BG" or general references preceding the "B" references to specific works.

Index

American Guild of Organists
  Portland (Me.) Regional
  Convention W61, W61a
American Hymns Old and New
  W232
American Music Awards Series
  W28
American Music Festival (New
  York) W9e
American Recorder Society,
  Boston Chapter W31
American Songs for A Capella
  Choir D173a, D183a, D203b
An Analysis of the Solo Organ
  Works of Daniel Pinkham
  BG19
An Analysis with Historical
  Background of Selected Com-
  positions of American Organ
  Music B82a
"And All the Bells Rang Out
  the Good News" W99
And Peace Attend Thee W145
And the Angel Said . . ."
  W57
"And the Angel Said Unto
  Them" W119
Anderson, Carol W74a
Anderson, William B114a
Andover, Mass. see Phillips
  Academy
Angelucci, Rhadames D154a
Angelus ad Pastores Ait W240,
  B240
Annis, Robert W15b
Antiphons W264
Apgar, Laurence W318
Appelwhite, Herff W119
Arlen, Walter, B134a
Aronson, Phyllis W66c
"As It Was Foretold" W99
"Ascended Up on High" W125,
  B125a
Ascension Cantata W111, BG40,
  B111
Aschaffenburg, Walter W100e
Aschbrenner, Charles W104a
Aspects of Compositional
  Styles of Three Selected
  Twentieth-Century American
  Composers of Choral Music:
  Alan Hovhaness, Ron Nelson,
  and Daniel Pinkham BG7
Aspects of the Apocalypse
  W315, B315

"At the Round Earth's Imag-
  in'd Corners" W122
Atkinson, Jim W36b
"Aubade" W301
Auburn, N. Y. St. Mary's Ro-
  man Catholic Church D91a
Auden, W. H. W294, W299
Aurora, N. Y. see Wells Col-
  lege
Austin, Betty Lou W133a,
  W133b
"Author of Light" W220
Ave Maria W241
Ave Regina Coelorum; Antiphon
  in Honor of the Blessed
  Virgin W265
Ave Verum Corpus W146
Avery, Scott BG1
"Awake, O North Wind and
  Come Thou South" W138
Baldwin Wallace College Con-
  servatory W98b, W133c,
  W136b
Ball State University BG1
Ballard, Catherine W221a,
  W259a
Ballinger, J. Stanley W42
Baptism Canon W242
Barber, Samuel p.5, B276a
Barker, John W. B21a
Barnes, O. Keith W90
Barryman, Warren W98b
Barth, Joseph W201
Bartok, Bela B100d
Battisti, Frank W50b
Baum, Carol W56, W56a, W56d,
  W61a, W61b, W123a, W125a,
  W264b, B56a, B123a, D56c
Bay Village (Ohio) Church
  W112, W112a
"Be Alert, Be Wakeful" W157
"Be Gracious to Me, O God"
  W147
Beauty W266
Before the Cock Crows W112
Before the Dust Returns W113
"Before the Ending of the
  Day" W302
Beggar's Opera W1, B1
"Beginning" W139
Behold, How Good and Pleas-
  ant W148, B148
Belland, Douglas D. W247,
  W261
Belt, Byron B121a

214

217

Index

Colgate University Chorus
W262a
College Park, Md. University
Methodist Church D68a
Collins, John F. W151
Collins, Leo W258a
Colorado State University
W8d, W19b, W117e, W143b,
W179e, W225, W225b, W258c,
W300d
Columbia University W9b,
W95c, W100a, W114f, BG43
Columbia University. St.
Paul's Chapel W95c, W114f
Columbus, Ohio. First Con-
gregational Church W116a
Columbus, Ohio. Ohio State
University see Ohio State
University
Combs, Stephen W117g
"Come, Let Us Sound With
Melody" W220
Come, Love We God W155, D155
Communion Service W156
Company at the Creche W245,
BG8, B245, D245
Concertante W30
Concertante No. 1 W9, B9, D9
Concertante No. 2 W10, BG11,
B10
Concertante No. 3 W58, B58
Concertante No. 4 W59, B59
Concertino W60
Concertino in A for Small
Orchestra and Obbligato
Piano W11, B11
Concerto for Celesta and
Harpsichord W100, BG32
B100, D100
"The Conclusion" W268
A Conductor's Analysis of
"Magnificat a 7" from the
1610 Vespers by Claudio
Monteverdi, Missa Brevis
St. Joannis De Deo by Franz
Joseph Haydn, and Stabat
Mater by Daniel Pinkham
B136a
A Conductor's Analysis of Se-
lected Works by Andrea
Gabrieli, Jacob Handl, W.
A. Mozart, Anton Bruckner,
Benjamin Britten, Daniel
Pinkham and Vincent Persi-
chetti B179a

A Conductor's Analysis of Sel-
lected Works by Giovanni
Pierluigi da Palestrina,
Orlando de Lasso, William
Byrd, Giovanni Gabrieli,
Dietrich Buxthude, and
Daniel Pinkham B127b
Conductor's Analysis of Se-
lected Works by Roland de
Lasseu, Johann Herman
Schein, George Frederick
Handel, Ralph Vaughan Wil-
liams and Daniel Pinkham
B117b
Conrad, Richard W122a, W122b,
W133a, W133b, W134a, W187b,
W264a, W275, W280, D187a
Contemporary Music Festival
(New York) W29c, W133
The Conversion of Saul W115
Conway, Joan W104a
Cook, J. Tucker B190a
Cook, Terry W117f, W140a
Cooke, Francis Judd B10a
Cooksey, Stephen W81a
Coonamessett Music Festival
W23a
Coons, Anne W134b
Copes, Ronald W67a
Copes, V. Earle W67a
Copland, Aaron p.4, p.9, W32,
B151e
Corley, John B240a
Cornish, William Randolph
W254
Corzine, Michael Loyd BG6
Cottle, Andrew W117g
Couture, Michael B22a
Cowell, Henry p.6, W100
Cox, Dennis B140a
Cox, Dennis Keith BG7
Craighead, David W75b
Craighead, Marian W75b
Crashaw, Richard W122, W221
Creditor, Bruce W38a
A Crimson Flourish W24
Crist-Janer, Albert W232
Cronkite, Walter W313
Crow, Todd B81a
Crowell, Allen W130a
Crozier, Catherine W84
Crumb, Rupert BG8
Crutchfield, Will B269a,
B305a
Cuenod, Hugues W233

218

Finney, John W100g, W133k
"Fire, Sleet and Candlelight"
W261
Firth, Everett W58c
Fisk, Charles B. p.7, W59,
W93, W94, B59a
Fiske, Judy Mayberry BG19
"A Fit Against the Country"
W137
Fitch, Conover W12b
Fitts, Dudley B19d, D19a
Five Canzonets W246
Five Short Pieces W13, B13
**Five Voluntaries for Organ
Manuals** W87, BG19, BG29,
D87
Flagstaff, Arizona see Nor-
thern Arizona University
Flanagan, William p.5, p.7,
BG20, B9e, B21d, B107a
Flanders, Peter W114f
Fleming, Jean W97a
Fletcher, Phineas W281
Florida Vocal Association
W177
"A Flourish for a Festive
Occasion" W42
Flowers, Vladimir W72
Folk Song W160
"Follow Follow" W305
For Evening Draws On W62,
BG4, B62, D62
"For Saturday" W254
For Thee I Have Waited W165,
B165
Ford Foundation p.7
Forest City, Iowa see Waldorf
College
"Forever Year by Year" W296
Foss, Lukas W14, W14a
Foster, J. Michael W117g
"The Foundling" W252
Four Elegies W122, B122
Four Epigrams W273
"Four Interludes" W37
Four Poems of Norma Farber
W166
Four Short Pieces W102
Four Short Pieces for Manuals
W88, BG19
Frankenstein, Alfred B9f,
B19e, B100d, B107b
Frankfurt, Germany W29a
Franklin, John W130b
Frederick, Lisa W250a

Frederick, Md. see Hood
College
French, Isabel W288, W292
Freneau, Philip Morin W194
Freundlich, Ralph W302a
Frisbie, Judith B5b
Fromm, Herbert W14
Fromm Fellowship Players
W136a
Fromm Music Foundation W136
Ft. Collins, Colo. see
Colorado State University
Ft. Worth, Texas. All Saints
Episcopal Church D173a
Ft. Worth, Texas, Texas
Christian University see
Texas Christian University
Fuller, Albert W107
Fuller, David W107, B107c
Fuller, R. Buckminster W314
Gabrieli, Andrea B179a
Gabrieli, Giovanni B114d,
B114k, B127b
Galloway, Michael W69c
Gamble, Edward W58b
Gammons, Edward W114d
The Garden of Artemis W3, B3,
D3
Garden Party p.9, W4, B4
Gardner, Jerry W68
Garrabrant, Mark W64b
Garretson, Robert W143b,
W179e
Gaskill, Ellwood p.7
The Gate of Heaven W167
Gauss, Christy W33b
Gauthier, Eva see Eva Gau-
thier Song Society
Gay, John W1
General Electric Co. W309
George, Collins B120a
Germanic Museum see Harvard
University
"Get Up! Said Mary" W193
Getting to Heaven W123, B123
Giffin, Glenn BG21, B117c,
B225a, B225b, B290a
Gifts and Graces W63
Gilow, Darrell W135a
"Gloria" from **Christmas Can-
tata** W64
"Gloria in Excelsis Deo" W114
**Glory Be to God; Motet for
Christmas Day** W168, B168,
D168

City
Kansas State University
W163a, W174c, W183b, W187,
W230a, W230b
Kashanski, Richard W30a
Kay, Ulysses p.7
Keaney, Helen W30, W30a,
W30b, W106, W106a, W107b
Keen, Neil W33a
Kellow, Suzanne W250b
Kelly, Kevin B114h, B240c
Kennedy, John F. W16
Kennedy Center see Washing-
ton, D. C. Kennedy Center
Kerner, Leighton B59a
Kibler, Keith W4a
Kienzle, Kathy D230a, D245a
Killmer, Richard D154a
Kind, Silvia W107
King, Gordon D173a, D183a,
D203d
King Chorale D173a, D183a,
D203d
The Kings and the Shepherds
W181, B181, D181
King's Chapel see Boston,
Mass. King's Chapel
Kirk, Theron BG28
Kjelson, Lee B121d
Knapp, Barbara W125a
Knickerbocker Chamber Players
W9e
Koehring, David W64b
Kolb, Bruce, W125a
Koussevitzky, Serge W14, W14a
Kratzensteen, Marilou B121e,
B122a
Kresh, Paul B187a, B245b
Kring, Walter Donald W199
Kroeger, Karl B19f, B20a
Krusenstjerna, Mary B66a
Kuemmich, Ramona W272b, W294c
Kulleseid, Eleanor B295a
Kurz, Neal W245c
Kutik, Ronald W69a
Kyrcz, Diane W94b
"Laetentur Coeli" W259
Lagerquist, John W33a, W74a
The Lamb W279, W297
Lament for April 15 and
Other Modern Madrigals
D160a, D203a
The Lament of David W182,
B182
The Lamentations of Jeremiah

BG41, B127
LaManna, Peter W121, W121b
"A Lamp in the Manger" W252
Land of White Alice W309
Landowska, Wanda p.5, W54
Lang, B. J. p.7
Langejans, Calvin W193
Lannom, Allen C. W257a
Lansing (Mich.) Symphony
Orchestra W21a, B21e
LaRosa, Joseph W114c
Laspisa, Joseph W36a
Laster, James W250c
Lauds W128
Laurent, Georges W46
Lawrence, Arthur W107c,
W130c, W138g, W160c,
W173b, W183c
Layman's Guide to Modern Art
W310
The Leaf W183, D183
Leatherman, Brian W117e
Lee, Eric W163b
Lee, Patricia W138b
The Left Behind Beasts W5, B5
Legon, Ernest W. W130
Lehl, Allan W216a
Leinsdorf, Erich W136, B8b
Lenox Brass Quintet W40c,
W123a, B123a
Leone, Luciano W74b
Lepak, Alexander W58e, W65a
Lepore, Richard W58e
Lesley College W40
Lesser, Laurence W40
Lessons W106
"Let All His Saints Rejoice"
W304
"Let God Arise" W304
"Let God Arise, Let His
Enemies Be Scattered" W72
"Let the Florid Music Praise"
W299
"Let the Heavens Rejoice"
W259
"Let the Word of Christ Dwell
in You Richly" W280
"Let Us Be Patient and Watch"
W99
Let Us Now Praise Famous Men
W249, B249
Letters from Saint Paul W280,
B280
Levitz, Lisa W113a
Levy, Jane W158b

227

About the Authors

KEE DeBOER is Social Sciences Group Leader at the California State University, Long Beach.

JOHN B. AHOUSE is University Archivist and Special Collections Librarian at California State University, Long Beach.